ISBN 978-0-9897754-0-3   Paperback
ISBN 978-0-9897754-1-0   e-version

From A Raven's Perch
A Bird's Eye View of Cold War Reconnaissance

Dedication

This book is dedicated to the memory of Lieutenant Colonel Robb Hoover. Robb was a Raven (Electronic Warfare Officer) in the 55th Strategic Reconnaissance Wing. He was a contemporary of mine during my time in the 55th · We served together at each of the locations described in the book, Forbes AFB (Air Force Base), Yokota AFB, Kadena AFB and Offutt AFB. Following retirement he was very active in the 55th Wing Association and in compiling historical records of the units that were engaged in Cold War Reconnaissance.

In early September of 2012, my wife and I attended a 55th Association reunion in Colorado Springs. I asked Robb to review this book and offer his informed critique. He graciously consented. I received two e-mails from Robb in that regard;

Subject: Re: From a Raven's Perch
Date: Oct 19, 2012   9:52 AM
Jack,
I wanted to get back to you about your story. Unfortunately I was taken ill after the reunion and did not have a chance to read it at first. So I'm looking forward to reading your story in the next few days. I'll report back to you shortly.   Robb

Subject: Re: From a Raven's Perch
Date: Oct 22, 2012   10:12 AM
Jack
I'm through the first 120 pages and am very impressed. You have a flair for writing and being able to explain material that could be difficult to understand for the uninitiated. I know that I learned a lot from your memoirs, and I think that when you are ready to publish you should have a copy sent to the 55th historian John McQueney. Your work is a very valuable reference document. Two questions I wanted to follow up on at this point.
1-The Tell Two landing crash at Incilik. I had never heard that the aircraft had been involved in a dust-up with the Russians. I have had the same question posed to me (this summer) by someone who referenced Alwyn Lloyd's

book. I was thinking of calling Barrie Hammond and asking him about it. Have you talked to Barrie?

(By the way, I knew Al Lloyd and have a copy of his book on SAC, but not on the B-47. I see by the Social Security Death Index there is an Alwyn Lloyd listed as born in 1940, died in 2007. Al came to one of the SAC Reunions several years ago and I seated him at the same table with Hank Dubuy. I'm wondering if Al got confused between Hank's story of the MIG encounter in 1965 with the Tell Two accident. Al was not in good health at the time of that reunion)

2-Your reference to the AOB (Air Order of Battle)

I think you meant the EOB (Electronic Order of Battle). The EOB contained the radar listings by site and status. It was published in several volumes including Volume 1 of the USSR. SAC published Volume 1. And then there was the EPL (ELINT/Electronic Parameters list). The EPL contained all the parameters on foreign radars...ground, sea and airborne. The AOB was another document/data base published by the country/area that listed airbases and aircraft loading, but I don't recall that it listed the specific types/parameters of air borne radars.

I'm so glad that you asked me to read your story. It has been an honor and a delight, and I'll have more comments to come.

   Regards   *Robb*

Robb passed away on October 29th of 2012. He will be sorely missed by all of us that were privileged to know him and work with him.

Contents

<u>Preface</u>

The preface of a book can serve a variety of purposes for an author. Most works are not completed in isolation. So the preface is often the place where the author acknowledges or credits those who assisted in its preparation. This assistance can take the form of research assistance, editing, proof reading etc. The preface can also set the scene - so the reader is aware of the situation, environment, etc. - from the start instead of forcing the reader to figure things out as the narrative unfolds. Another frequent use is to explain the author's motivation or perspective. Unfortunately, the preface is also often the part of the book that many readers, occasionally including myself, skip. The reasons vary but included I'm sure is either they find it boring or they just want to get to the meat of the book as quickly as possible.

I have elected to limit my primary focus; in the preface; to the final two reasons mentioned above, motivation and perspective. The first motivation for me is that I have always had a desire to write. I have been an avid reader my entire life. Books have been among my prized possessions. I find a book to be a treasure that enables the reader to get into the minds of people with different perspectives and experiences from our own. The author may come from distant places and times. This door to their minds has been preserved in their writings and can still be opened long after they themselves have passed from this earth. I have always strongly favored non-fiction or historical fiction in what I selected to read. History has been my passion.

Most of us enjoy an attentive audience when we are in a story telling mood or even just telling a joke. It seems to me a natural extension of that same feeling to want to express one's thoughts and stories in writing. It can potentially expand your audience and may touch people you have never met.

I have always enjoyed writing. To date my writing has been confined to memos, letters and correspondence as part of my jobs or as college term papers. The objective of job related writing had generally been to be brief, concise and often limited to a single page.

Preface

The subject was normally dictated by the demands of the job. It did require me to focus my thoughts and frequently to edit and rewrite the drafts until they met that objective. Doing a detailed outline to organize my thoughts was seldom required. College term papers were a little more involved but seldom required a long term effort and a major commitment of time. Writing a book is a major step above anything that I have done before. So why would a person, namely myself, with no prior major writing experience, spend the time and toil it takes to properly complete such a project when the prospects that anyone else, outside of a few close friends or relatives, would be interested in reading it. Is it simply an ego trip or an attempt to aggrandize events that are really quite ordinary? While it may have a flavor of both of these motives, I hope the reader finds that my motives are more genuine and practical.

The desire to write a book has to this point in my life been only an aspiration. Raising a family and working in a demanding career didn't afford me the time necessary. Now that I am retired I have that time. Several years ago I took a community college class on creative writing. One of the first things that the instructor emphasized is that an aspiring writer should start by writing about a subject with which they are very familiar. This normally means something from their own life experiences. Therein lies another advantage to being retired. When you are retired most of the major events in one's life have already occurred. This gives you a larger reservoir of experiences to draw on. In my lifetime my active duty time in the military was the most eventful and provided me with the best material to write about. Therefore I've chosen to start my writing efforts about this period in my life. The period covered is from September of 1961 through March of 1970. I have endeavored to relate my perception of the events as accurately as I can. It is important to note, however, that I am relating the events primarily from memory some 40 years after the fact. I have, however, included a number of dates, names and locations which would have been difficult if I only had my memory to rely on. Fortunately, I have always been a pack rat and a voracious note taker (never a formal diary but close to that). While I was on active duty I put every written set of orders I received during those nine years in a binder. When I left active duty that binder went into a storage box and stayed there. It remained in my storage areas thru my numerous moves. In the years since I left active duty I have lived in ten different cities and sixteen different residences. This should have given me ample opportunity and incentive to rid myself of stuff that remained in storage boxes. Fortunately, I never did that so I still have them as a reference for this book. I also kept a detailed flight log. Standard flight logs have places to track flight time, departures, destinations and type of aircraft. I added the names of other crew members and notes concerning flight activities, types of missions and any unusual happening that occurred. This flight log suffered the same fate as the binder with my orders so I also have it to rely on. I spent time reviewing these sources as I considered writing this book. This helped me to revive old memories and sort events that would otherwise become somewhat entwined over time to a more accurate chronology.

The desire to write, would not alone, however, fully explain my motivation. There are two additional motivations that prompted me to undertake this effort. The first, and perhaps the most important to me, is related to the greatly increased mobility of contemporary American society as compared to the 1940s and 1950s when I was growing up. During my parents and grandparents time families often lived as extended families or the generations lived in the same proximate area. Morsels of family history were often passed from generation to generation by word of mouth. I had an early interest in history which fostered a curiosity concerning my own families' history. I listened attentively whenever the story telling began. I inherited this interest in history from my mother. She was a high school English and History teacher during the early years of her career. She is the source of much of what I learned of my heritage. I took a great deal of pride in being a part of the family. In the locale which I grew up most families knew who their relatives were and spent regular time with them. Most of the people you knew worked in similar types of jobs. Neighbors and family had much in common.

Preface

In my family, the men had predominately been farmers and the women had been either housewives or school teachers and often both. My family had lived in the same area for several generations. I was part of the fourth generation to live in the area. Sons followed fathers in their life's work. My generation was the first to leave the substantially rural setting and seek lives and careers in other, often far away, places and in diverse occupations. This seems to be a somewhat typical pattern in many families today. Our careers take us to widely separated locations.

Children, once they become adults, tend to live hundreds of miles away from their parents and see them only on rare special occasions. Grandchildren often barely know their grandparents and the communication between the generations is typically quite limited. This is true of my own family particularly in regard to the extended family. My sons have had minimal contact with any relatives outside of the nuclear family. My grandsons have had even less.

In modern American society the interaction between parents and their children has been significantly reduced. The factors that contribute to this are many. Most modern families have both parents working. The television, video games and computers increasingly occupy the attention of young people. Families used to all gather at the dinner table for the evening meal, a daily opportunity for generational interaction. Contemporary teens lead busy lives. They are involved in numerous activities which often extend into the evening hours. Parents often have widely different work schedules. The daily gathering for the evening meal has been greatly reduced. If my family history, even bits and pieces, are to be passed along, it would likely have to be written down. I want my sons and grandsons to know who they are and from whence they came. They may not have an interest now, but hopefully as they reach my age they will.

The second reason is a little more subtle. Nearly every major historical event has a series of lesser events and players that led up to or contributed to it. Major historical changes do not occur in vacuums. The history books detail the roles of the major players and depict events as dynamic breaks when the reality may have been more like a boiling pot that suddenly boiled over. The history books also treat events and people in a rather dry manner. Missing are the nuances and humanity that had to be a part of these events. This was illustrated to me while visiting my aging mother several years ago. She had been a high school teacher and also became the school librarian the last ten years or so before she retired. I had been browsing through her book cases. She had bookcases in several places in the house. I discovered a book written by a man named Christian Ahlness. The book was rough bound, hand typed and written in less than perfect English. There were numerous pen and ink corrections on the pages throughout the book. I asked her about the source and background of the book. She informed me that Christian Ahlness, the author, had lived in the small Minnesota town, Hanska, where she was raised. The book was his autobiography.

Christian Ahlness had been a highly respected man in town. My mother had been a good friend to his granddaughter. As a small girl she had often played in his yard. She said she remembered him as a stern old man of whom she was slightly fearful and she had avoided him when possible. Christian Ahlness was born in Norway in the 1860s. He immigrated to the United States during the 1880s. The book was written for and distributed on a very limited basis to a few of his friends and relatives.

My mother received a copy from her childhood friend after Mr. Ahlness, her friend's grandfather, had passed away. My mother has since passed the book to me. It is one of my prize possessions. It captures the fears, hopes and trials of his life as an immigrant in nuanced detail putting a human face on events of the time. A perspective that could not be found in the history books covering the period.

I was particularly interested in the period following his arrival in this country until he had found his place in it and become established. Histories of the period describe in general terms the hardships that the arriving immigrants to this country encountered making this transition. This book made it quite clear that the history books simply did not do justice to the realities. A couple of examples from his book clearly illustrate this point. Mr. Ahlness left Norway as a man in his early 20s. He was able to gain passage on a ship bound for the St. Lawrence Seaway with the help of a friend. The voyage was difficult. When they finally arrived they were transported by train to Chicago and dropped there. There they stood in the train station in a strange land with no place to go and unable to speak the language. No guides, no one to greet them, they were left to fend for themselves. It was two weeks before they found some one who spoke their language.

Immigrants to this country came and continue to come to this day for a better life. Most who came in the late 1800s came from rural areas in their native land. Available land in the countries of their birth was generally scarce. What was available went to the oldest son. The stories that circulated concerning America told of opportunity and abundant land to farm. This was a powerful lure for younger sons to seek their fortunes far from home. This is precisely what Mr. Ahlness did. Most of the immigrants, however, did not immediately realize their dreams of finding a piece of land to settle on. They had to find jobs. Their lack of skills and limited grasp of the language made them easy prey for unscrupulous operators. A situation that is not unfamiliar to many of today's immigrants. The work was generally hard, the pay low and uncertain. Stories of short, delayed or non-existent pay checks were common place.

One of the early jobs Mr. Ahlness had obtained was in a saw mill on the shores of a large lake in Wisconsin. The workers were transported to the remote location and housed in large barracks style quarters. The area was heavily forested with a single rough, dirt road in and out. Meals were served in a large mess hall. The work was hard, the hours long, the food bland and often in short supply. The area was damp and illnesses common. Within a few months one of the workers came down with a strange sickness and died. Several others became sick with similar symptoms. There was not a single medically trained person available. The manager's reaction was to panic and leave the camp together with all of the foremen. The owner then sealed the area off. Guards with guns were placed on the roads blocking every way out. The workers were left there to fend for themselves or starve. It wasn't long before anarchy reined in the camp. Workers were assaulting each other. Panic was setting in. Mr. Ahlness tried to keep to himself. He describes an incident which illustrates the anarchy and despair that prevailed. One day a starving man from the group saw a deer swimming in the lake. The man swam out and tried to kill the deer with a knife. His efforts were ineffective. He wrestled with the deer in the deep water. His only reward for his efforts was to drown. His body washed ashore and was left there. Mr. Ahlness finally managed to escape the area by fashioning a makeshift raft and floating across the large lake. He had to evade guards on the far side of the lake and walked to a farm house. Fortunately, the family that owned the first farm house he encountered was Norwegian and took him in.

Mr. Ahlness was a minor player in the history of the massive immigration and settlement this country experienced in the last 30 years of the 19th century. The stories that he and others could tell are important to fully appreciate the events they witnessed. Where individual accounts were recorded it was often in the form of the diaries they kept. Most of these have been lost with the passage of time. Rarely were they recorded in book form. Had many more of these immigrants written down their experiences as Mr. Ahlness did in his book, this period, which is rather dry reading in the history books, would become for us a living drama. Individual stories of minor players add immeasurably to our historical picture. It is difficult for historians to capture the essence of events. My point here is that to truly capture the historical perspective of events or periods in history one needs some personal accounts. These are valuable whether written by one of the prime players or a minor one. Mr. Ahlness' autobiography made this clear to me. Hopefully mine, obviously as a minor player, will add to the record available to future generations, particularly those in my own family.

Secondly, in addition to explaining my motivation, I want the reader to understand my perspective in writing this book. It will explain why I have chosen "From a Raven's Perch" as the title of the book. The reference to the raven is natural. My story is about my active duty time in the military. My job during these years was as an Electronic Warfare Officer (EWO). The job of an Electronic Warfare Officer is as part of a flight crew.   Their function is to employ electronics in defense of the aircraft or to gather electronic information that will aid other crews in defending their aircraft. In Air Force lingo, Electronic Warfare Officers were known as Ravens or Crows. In fact our professional association is called the "The Old Crows Association". The explanation for this moniker is explained in more detail in chapter 4 of the book. The aircraft manuals, which covered the configuration of the aircraft positions where we worked, referred to them as Raven One, Raven Two or Raven Three. So the events and individuals described herein are from the perspective of a "Raven", namely myself.

As I have explained above I had an abiding interest in history dating from my teen years. At that time my primary interest was in the history of the settlement of the old west. I read everything on the subject I could get my hands on. The likes of Wyatt Earp, Buffalo Bill and Wild Bill Hickok appeared frequently. Most of the material, however, was highly romanticized. That is to say, as a historical document, it did not represent a completely accurate portrayal of the life styles of the vast majority of pioneers who settled the western part of the United States during the latter half of the 19th century. The tales made good stories but often lacked complete historical accuracy. There was a great deal of poetic license. This was not a major concern for me at the time. I have become more interested in historical accuracy over the intervening years. The majority of non-fiction writing often suffers, when measured against the standard of historical accuracy, some of the same problem. They may not be romanticized but are written from the perspective of the author. A reader can often find other writers that have a different perspective on the same subject. Their perspectives may even conflict.   Any one whose interest is to determine the true facts, which is the true burden of the historian, must study all of the perspectives and resolve the conflicts. Most of us when we read a book are not concerned with that burden. This is true of my narrative contained in this book. It is written from my own perspective. I describe the events and persons as I see them. This is, of course, no guarantee that they are historically accurate or factual. I have tried to relate them as accurately as I can as well as to resist the urge to overly romanticize them. I do, however, want to retain the reader's interest and attention so I try to describe them as a good story. This book is a description of events and persons as I viewed them much like a Raven sitting on a perch observing what is going on around him, thus the title, "From a Raven's Perch. A Bird's Eye View of Cold War Reconnaissance."

I have also included descriptions, often brief, about the individuals I worked with, played with or encountered during my travels. I include some hint about their appearance, personality and abilities. The military, if it does nothing else, mixes people from all parts of the country and from a wide variety of backgrounds. The military services tend to absorb those differences. Years of military service develops a common core of experience which tends to bond military people together. This mix of differences and commonality makes for some interesting individuals and occurrences. It develops a tolerance for each other that is often lacking in the larger society. Military training attempts to remake personalities and egos. It does not erase the differences they bought with them when they joined but strengthens the common bond that was developed. This is critical when they are exposed to the stresses of military actions.

Finally, every writer, when they undertake the effort, must have a target audience in mind. Textbooks aimed at graduate students assume a level of pre-knowledge. If the author digressed into detailed basic explanations of the concepts involved, concepts that the students had mastered in earlier classes or life experiences, the book would be to them long winded, repetitious and the author runs the risk of losing their attention. Conversely, if the book that is written for an audience of graduate level students were used as text for middle school students they would not be able to grasp any of the concepts. The writer could not try to address both groups. Any attempt to bridge that gap and satisfy both groups would render the effort irrelevant to both groups. So the author must select a target audience and keep them in mind while writing the book. My target audience for this book reflects the reasons I've stated above for undertaking this effort. These primarily include my family and friends.   The majority of those in this group have only a limited understanding of military life generally and the Air Force of the 1960s specifically. I have used a level of detail and background in my explanations that my contemporaries in the Air Force of the time might find laborious and unnecessary. Most of my target audience would also find detailed technical explanations troublesome and perhaps confusing. I have, therefore, included the majority of technical elaborations in the appendixes. This would allow those interested in the technical aspects to pursue them and not burden those not interested

I do want to acknowledge those individuals who assisted me in the preparation and editing of this narrative. As I explain earlier, this narrative is directed at an audience of people who are uninitiated (as Robb indicated) in matters of military reconnaissance and the mode of operations of the United States Air Force of the decade of the 1960s, both of which are the focus of this book. In my own experiences, I have occasionally sat through a lecture or a briefing and left somewhat confused. The briefer may have used a number of unfamiliar acronyms or provided limited details on an unfamiliar concept. I wanted to ensure that my target audience fully understood the information I relate. To this end, I asked several friends and relatives to read the draft with an eye to their clarity of understanding. In terms of the level of understanding, I saw three distinct groups of people;

1-My target audience, those completely unfamiliar with the subject.

2-Those with some military background in areas other than reconnaissance.

3-My contemporaries of the period who were intimately familiar with the subject.

I wanted feedback from individuals in each of these groups. I owe a debt to the several people who agreed to review the draft and provide their comments. I asked the following to perform this task;

my brother Jim and his wife. Jim had served in the Navy and had some military background. His wife, Geneva, a school teacher, had no military background other than having a husband and son who served. I also asked my son, Jason, to review it. He had served six years in the Army. A family friend, Valerie Ogami, also reviewed it. She, also, had a husband and son who had served but had no direct experience. Finally, I asked Robb Hoover, a contemporary of mine in the Air Force. I received some feedback from each of them. I greatly appreciate their help.

I further asked Valerie Ogami, who is a school teacher, to review it with an eye to its grammar and construction. She provided me with a detailed review.

I am indebted to her for her assistance.

John (Jack) Mitchel Perrizo, Lt. Colonel, USAFR Retired
Tacoma, Washington   December 2012

Chapter 1   Joining the Air Force

Early Years

I grew up on a farm near the southern Minnesota village of Delavan. During my teen years, the 1950s, Delavan was a thriving farm village of about 300 people which boasted two grocery stores, a community bank, one café, a drug store, a barber shop, two farm implement stores, a grain elevator, a welding shop, two churches and three drinking establishments. The commercial establishments supported the town and the surrounding farms for a radius of approximately 5 to 7 miles. The farms in the area were still family owned and run. Most farms consisted of about 160 acres. The main crops raised were corn and soybeans. Most farms also had several types of livestock. Farms were often worked by father and son(s). When the father became too old to actively work the farm, the son(s) would take over. When the father passed away, the farm would be passed to one of the sons. Occasionally the father would retire and buy a small house in the village. Most of the families had lived in the area for at least three generations.

Delavan is located about 12 miles north of the Iowa, Minnesota border and centered along the boundary between the two states. Many of the farm communities in southern Minnesota were and still are ethnically homogeneous. There are still belts of Norwegian, Swedish and German settlement. Frequently, the old language rivaled English in the stores and churches of these communities. Old world celebrations were practiced and traditional foods were in abundance. Delavan, however, was in an area of mixed ethnicity. In addition to a mixture of the nationalities mentioned above there was a large contingent of French-Canadians. My father's family was of French-Canadian descent. My mother's family was of Norwegian and German descent. French-Canadian families of that period were quite large. Frequently they numbered between 7 and 10 children. The Perrizo families, including my own, were no exception.

I attended school in the Delavan Consolidated schools thru the 12th grade. My senior class was one of the larger that had graduated from Delavan High School. We had 28 in the class. All but a very few young men in the area finished high school. Following high school the majority then either went into farming, normally with their father, or into the military. A few members of my graduating class went on to college. I had graduated from high school in June of 1959. My academic record in high school was not very good. Scholarships to college were few in those days and I did not qualify for any. The males on the Perrizo side of the family had traditionally attended St. John's University in Collegeville, Minnesota. I was to follow in their footsteps. I applied there and to my surprise was accepted. I started my college education there in September of the same year. I fully intended to spend the next four years pursuing a college degree.

A college education was not common among the farming families in the area. Those that did have college training were normally involved in teaching. Both sides of my family had individuals with some college education. My mother, grandmother and several aunts had been teachers. Three of my uncles had gone to college and two had become military officers. So I was encouraged, particularly by my mother, to follow that course. The family did not have the resources to help with my college expenses. My parents were separated and my mother's income was the sole support for me and my siblings. My mother's teaching salary was stretched thin supporting my sister and five brothers.

My father had a serious drinking problem and so during my mid teen years much of the farm work had fallen to me as the oldest. During my last year of high school, however, my father had rented the farm land to a neighbor. So I was relieved of the responsibility for our farm. I worked at a variety of jobs, particularly during the summer. I worked as a farm hand for neighbors, for the local canning factories and mowed lawns. I had saved enough money to start college.

St. John's is a small all-boys Catholic liberal arts college. It is located about 12 miles west of the city of St. Cloud, Minnesota. The college is run by the Benedictine order. It is a secluded campus located between two large lakes, the Watab and the Sagatagan. The closest town, Waite Park, is 3 miles away. Most of the students were not permitted to have cars on campus. That privilege was reserved for second semester Juniors on the academic honor roll and Seniors.

2

Joining the Air Force

To help with expenses I had a part time job in the university dinning hall. In addition, I was able to obtain a small student loan during my second year. Student loans were not as prevalent at that time as they became a couple of decades later. This allowed me to pay my college expenses for the first two years. However, by the end of the second year I had run out of money. My sister Mary was a year behind me in school and was attending St. Benedicts College in Waite Park, Minnesota. St. Benedicts was the all-girls school associated with St. Johns. My brother Bill had just finished high school and was bound for St. Johns in September of 1961. They had both been valedictorians in high school and had some scholarship support.

My sources of summer income had also disappeared. When I started college my family was still living in Delavan. At the start of my second year at St. Johns, my mother had transferred to a teaching job at Central High School in Norwood-Young America which is located just west of Minneapolis. When the family moved to Norwood-Young America I, of course, also spent my summers there. My source of summer jobs, that had been plentiful in Delavan, had dried up. I could find no jobs in the Norwood area and jobs in nearby Minneapolis were few for a farm boy. It was obvious I would not be able to continue my college education, so I decided to look into entering the military.

Interest in the Military

There were few aircraft or pilots in the farming area of my youth. A farmer by the name of Jesse Pool lived in a town nearby. He owned a Piper Cub, the only aircraft in the area. Periodically, the local fox population would become numerous enough that they would begin to raid local chicken coops. This prompted local farmers to get together to hunt them. The piper cub would be used to drive the foxes, once they were located, toward the hunters. This was the only prior exposure to airplanes that I had. I had, however, developed a strong interest in aviation by the end of my second year in college. This interest was largely a borrowed one. One of my cousins, Jim Hassing, lived in Minneapolis and had an interest in being a pilot. His

3

high school counselor had encouraged his interest and provided him with information and guidance. Guidance counselors in rural high schools, like the one I was attending, were non-existent. So with my college career at an impasse, I set out to find out about military flying programs.

St. Johns did not have guidance counselors, but did have a career reading room where brochures were available for the students. I recalled reading about a Navy pilot training program called Navy Cadets (NAVCADS). It was an in-service, commissioning, and flying training program. By the end of my second college year, I had determined that this is what I would pursue. On June 8, 1961 I went to the Federal Building in Minneapolis in search of the Navy recruiting office to inquire about the program. Unfortunately, there was no Navy recruiter working in the building, so I wandered into the Air Force recruiter's office. I told him of my desires and asked for directions to the Navy recruiter. He advised me that the Air Force had a similar program called Aviation Cadets (AVCADS) and offered to discuss it with me. I sat down and listened. He advised me there was a screening test, but it required completion of at least two years of college before I could take the test. I told him that I had just completed two years. So I took the screening test. It took about an hour to complete. The recruiter returned a few minutes later and he seemed very excited. He said my score was the highest he had ever seen. He said that he wanted to send me for further testing. I asked him if it would cost me any money or if I would incur any obligations. He said no to both so I agreed. What did I have to lose. I didn't have the money to continue my education and didn't have a job. He made several telephone calls and then cut a set of orders to send me to Offutt AFB in Omaha. In addition, he gave me a bus ticket from Minneapolis to Omaha to use two days later.

Air Force Testing

I went home and informed my mother about what had taken place. I was afraid she might oppose entering the military, but she encouraged me to continue. I packed a bag and took the bus trip to Omaha. I was 20 years old and though Delavan had only been 12 miles from the Iowa border, this was only the second time that I had been outside the state of Minnesota. The first had been a Boy Scout trip to Philmont Scout camp in New Mexico at the age of 12.

The bus departed Minneapolis early in the morning of June 10th. The trip to Omaha was about 300 miles and took all day. An older lady sat beside me on the bus. She was a teacher from Minneapolis going to see her grandson in Omaha. She informed me that Offutt AFB was the former Fort Crook of the Indian wars period. I had been an avid reader about the old west during high school and she was a high school history teacher. We had a lengthy and interesting discussion during the ride. In the seat behind us was a young lady with a strong southern accent and a foul mouth. She talked constantly. We were happy when she left the bus in Northern Iowa.

The recruiter had advised me that there was a small Air Force receiving office located in the Omaha bus terminal. It proved to be a little difficult to find. There were no signs. A baggage clerk finally directed me to the office. When I finally found it, there were two young men in civilian clothes and a young airman in uniform waiting there. The two young men were there for the same reason I was. The airman called the base. A short time later an Air Force vehicle took the four of us to Offutt Air Force base. When we arrived at the base, we were ushered into the housing office and each of us was given a folder which described our itinerary for the next three days. We were assigned to individual rooms in the Bachelor Officers Quarters (BOQ) located just off the parade field. I put my luggage in my room. The first event on the schedule in our folder was not until the following morning.

It was still light out and I had time on my hands, so I left my bag in the room and went for a walk around the base. The barracks were close to the flight line and I immediately spotted a large multi-engine propeller driven airplane making landings every few minutes. I went over to the retaining fence and stood there watching the airplane do what I later learned were touch and goes. I was pretty enthralled. I stayed there until they finished. About an hour had passed and since it was getting dark I went back to my BOQ room.

The next day I joined the other young men who were there for the tests. The testing lasted the next two days. The first day was devoted to a series of written tests on a variety of subjects. They were called the "Air Force Officer Qualification Tests" (AFOQT). The subjects included pictures designed to test spatial perception, grammar, aeronautical knowledge, math problems and general information questions. The second day was devoted to comprehensive physical and psychological tests. I still remember one of the questions the psychiatrist asked me. He wanted to know how I would respond to the following situation. I had stated that my mother was the world's greatest mother and someone took exception to my statement. This man became angry and said his mother was the greatest. He insisted that I retract my statement. My reply to the psychiatrist was that this guy is a nut case and I would avoid him in the future. This was not the answer the psychiatrist was looking for. He was trying to equate the situation to defending one's country. Apparently I answered the other questions to his satisfaction because I passed that phase.

The third day we received the results of the tests and a lecture on Air Force careers. The results of the tests were not in the form of scores, but in levels of qualification. There were three levels of qualification. The first level was the Officer qualification. This meant that we were mentally, physically and psychologically qualified to enter one of the Air Forces' Officer training programs. The other two levels were based primarily on additional physical criteria. The Navigator level was the less stringent of the two with the Pilot level the most stringent. The Pilot level focused heavily on the eye tests. The Pilot level also had a maximum sitting height requirement. My notes tell me that there were 61 applicants taking the tests. Fifty qualified thru the Officer level, 25 thru the Navigator level and only 4 thru the Pilot level. I had, fortunately, been one of those qualified through the Pilot level.

I returned home on the bus. The day after I returned, June 15th, the Air Force recruiter in the downtown Federal Building called me and advised me that I should go to the Air Force recruiting office in St. Louis Park, Minnesota; a suburb on the west side of Minneapolis. It was much closer to Norwood. I would, if I chose, continue my processing there. I was to contact a Staff Sergeant Weber at that office. I still had some interest in the Navy program but my focus was now on the Air Force one. I considered it a day or so and decided to continue. I was now intent on getting into the Pilot Aviation Cadet Training Program.

Applying to Cadet Program

On June 18, 1961 I went to see Sergeant Weber at the St. Louis Park recruiting office. He had a copy of the test results from Offutt and seemed quite excited about them. It seems that the recruiters, at that time, got a lot more points if they recruited an officer candidate. I told him since I had qualified to the Pilot level, I wanted to go into the Aviation Cadet Pilot Training Program. The Aviation Cadet program had separate schools for pilots and navigators. I was not interested in the navigator school. He seemed a little pessimistic about this. He told me that the wait to get into the Aviation Cadet Pilot training was running about 18 months. The wait for the Aviation Cadet Navigator training was, however, much shorter, probably 6 months or less. He must have sensed that I was about to walk out, because he quickly started to go into details about the two programs. He told me that candidates for pilot training schools came from several sources, not just the Aviation Cadet program. Pilot training was one of the most sought after and competitive programs in the Air Force. The Air Force had established quotas for various source groups. Previously rated flying personnel, specifically navigators, was one of these source groups. The quota for this group was seldom filled. I asked him why this would be the case. He said he wasn't sure but that the feeling was that navigators were already rated and had just endured a lengthy and demanding school. They did not want to immediately go into another lengthy and demanding training program. He convinced me that this was a practicable way for me to get into pilot training. I would then have two ratings which would help with promotions later in my career. I was naively persuaded and submitted the application for Aviation Cadet Navigator training.

I was in a situation where I lacked the money to return to college in the fall and would likely have to wait six months before I could expect a call from the Air Force. I needed to find a job. I found an employment agency in the Minneapolis telephone book and went to see them. Employment agencies in those days were few and focused primarily on full time work. I, of course, was not interested in a full time job. My intention was to go into the Air Force (Aviation Cadets) when they called. The counselor told me she would do some research for a summer job. I was to return a couple of days later. When I returned, she told me that she had a summer job at a place called Camp Manikiki. The job was as a camp counselor. Camp Manikiki was located near Waconia, Minnesota which was about half way between Minneapolis and Norwood-Young America where my family lived. It seemed convenient. I would be living at the camp. Camp Manikiki was the summer camp owned by the Pillsbury Settlement house, a community service facility. The Pillsbury Settlement house was located in a troubled inner-city part of Minneapolis. It was just off Washington Avenue along the Minnesota River. Washington Avenue was well known for its' population of drunks and derelicts. The area was home to the poor and disadvantaged families of the city. The Settlement house was a gift from the Pillsbury Milling Company as a community center. It was used to give inner city youngsters activities to keep them on a positive track. The activities included a two week summer encampment at Camp Manikiki.

The camp was on the shores of a large lake of the same name as the adjacent town of Waconia. There were extensive wooded areas around the lake. The camp was located in these wooded areas. The camp had a headquarters house where the director and his wife stayed. It also had a recreation center which was used for activities during inclement weather and for meetings. There were several cabins where the children and the counselors would stay. Each counselor would be assigned a group of 8 to 10 youngsters of the same age for a two week period. The counselor would spend literally day and night with your assigned group of children. At the conclusion of the two weeks you would be assigned a new group of children. Your job was to get them to all of the scheduled activities including meals, monitor their activities and sleep in the same cabin with them at night. In other words, you stayed with them throughout their stay at

8

Camp Manikiki. The children would sleep in bunk beds in the main section of the cabin. There was a single door with access to the cabin. The counselor had a bed in an ante room near the door. This way the kids would have to go past the counselor's bed to get out of the cabin. The arrangement kept them from wondering off at night as some were want to do.

On July 31, 1961 I received notification that my Aviation Cadet application had been received and processed. I was being placed on the candidate list. On August 23, 1961, I received a set of Air Force orders appointing me as an Aviation Cadet and assigning me to class 63-03 at James Connally Air Force Base near Waco, Texas. The effective date was to be September 24, 1961. This would work out well. My term at Camp Manikiki was scheduled to conclude the last week of August.

On Sept 20st I reported to the Federal Building in Minneapolis for In Processing. Initially I was sent to a room for a written test. There were about 50 other people taking the test. It turned out to be a literacy test. I was the first to finish the test. It took me about half an hour. The airman in charge directed me to a room where his desk was located and instructed me to wait for the others to finish. Another half an hour passed and no one else had yet finished. At this point another young airman walked into the room and whispered something to the airman in charge of the testing. They both came over to me and asked me to follow them. I was advised that a mistake had been made. The literacy test was to be given to new enlisted recruits only. I guess it was assumed that my having completed two years of college meant that I could read and write. I was taken into a separate room and waited for about another half an hour. Then one of the Airmen returned and escorted me to another large room. I re-joined the group who had just completed the literacy test and we all received physicals. This physical was much shorter than the one I had undergone at Offutt. On the following day, September 21, 1961, I returned to the Federal Building and was sworn into the Air Force. The airman who handled the ceremony told me that since I never smiled he felt I would make a good officer.

9

Entering the Air Force

The recruiter made my travel arrangements to Waco, Texas. I was to fly on an American Airlines flight 3 days later. The irony of the situation was that I was committed to starting a career in flying and this flight would be the first time I had been even close to an airplane. On the morning of September 24, 1961, I boarded an American Airlines flight from Minneapolis to Dallas, Texas. I had to change aircraft in Dallas. The remainder of the trip would be on a DC3 aircraft to Waco, Texas where James Connally AFB was located. The ride from Minneapolis to Dallas was smooth and enjoyable. The ride from Dallas to Waco, however, was very bumpy and uncomfortable. It was a typical early fall Texas day, building thunderstorms and a lot of turbulence. I got a little queezy and wondered if I had made the right decision. Did I really want a career in flying. It was too late to change my mind.

When I arrived at the Waco airport I went to the Air Force Reception area. There were three other prospective cadets there at that time. We waited for transportation to the base. An Air Force van took us to the base and dropped us off at the cadet barracks. Our orders had instructed us to arrive prior to 1300 hours (1 O'clock) on the 24th. We arrived at about 1430 (2:30 PM). We soon learned that this time lapse was not acceptable. I tried to explain the reason for our late arrival. It had been beyond our control. Several young men with very short hair and in Air Force uniforms started yelling at us. I had just begun my explanation when one of them started to yell at me to stop. He immediately backed me against the wall. My first lesson as a new cadet was that there is no such thing as an excuse for a cadet. They screamed at us to stand at attention and royally chewed us out for being late. This was my welcome to cadet school.

Chapter 2   The Aviation Cadet Program

The Cadet Corps

The Navigator Aviation Cadet program was approximately 11 months in length. Training included academics, military training and flight training. Those cadets who successfully completed the program were commissioned as Air Force Second Lieutenants and received the wings of a rated navigator. The academics included military as well as flight subjects. They were taught by commissioned Air Force officers. The military program was similar to that which is typical at the service academies (Army, Navy and Air Force Academies) and is described in more detail later. Military training was both classroom and practical. Commissioned officers conducted the academic part and upper class cadets with Commissioned officer oversight conducted the practical part. The flight training was conducted in the T-29 flying classroom by Commissioned officers who were also rated navigators.

The cadet corps consisted of a Cadet Wing sub-divided into four cadet squadrons. These squadrons were designated by the letters "A" thru "D". A new class of cadets would enter the cadet wing about every two to three weeks. The new class would be assigned to one of the four squadrons. Each squadron took its turn. This meant that each squadron would receive a new class of cadets about every ten weeks. Thus, each squadron consisted of four classes spaced about ten weeks apart.

Most of a cadet's activities were confined within the individual squadron environment. Each cadet was assigned to a squadron when they entered the program and remained in that squadron until they graduated or were "Washed Back". Being "Washed Back" meant your training was held up and you were assigned to a later class often in another cadet squadron. There were several reasons for washing a cadet back. The primary reasons were the result of medical problems, emergency leave or training deficiencies. The latter was the most common cause.

Each squadron lived in a separate two story barracks. The barracks were divided into separate rooms. During the first half of a cadet's time in the program (The two junior classes) we would be assigned

11

three cadets to a room and occupy the upper floor of the barracks. During the latter half (the two senior classes) this was reduced to two Cadets to a room and we occupied the lower floor of the barracks.

Cadet Ranks

Military discipline in all of the military services is based on a specific rank structure. Thus rank structure is part of the cadet training environment. The cadet rank structure had four general levels, FIRST CLASS through FOURTH CLASS. FIRST CLASS cadets were the highest rank and FOURTH CLASS cadets were the lowest. As cadets successfully progressed through the program they advanced through each of the four general ranks. As each cadet squadron received a new class, the existing classes were advanced in rank with the new class assuming the lowest rank. Thus about 2 ½ months were spent at each of these ranks. In addition, there were two short transition ranks. The first was an orientation period called the GREEN TUX. The new entering class began their cadet life as GREEN TUX. The other was a graduation preparation period called the DOUBLE GOLD. DOUBLE GOLD cadets were not actively involved in most cadet activities. Each of these transition ranks lasted for two weeks.

FIRST CLASS cadets directed the activities of the squadron and served in its command positions. When a squadron's senior class (FIRST CLASSMEN) were promoted to the DOUBLE GOLD rank they relinquished command of the squadron to the newly promoted FIRST CLASS cadets (from SECOND CLASSMEN). This included promoting selected members to cadet officer rank. The cadet officer ranks mirrored Air Force's officer rank structure (i.e. Cadet Captain through Cadet Lt. Colonel). The acting cadet squadron commander was a Cadet Lt. Colonel. The other ranks would be staff or subordinate commanders. These ranks were rotated at intervals during the two and a half months cadets spent at the FIRST CLASS rank.

The cadet wing also had a command structure. This rotated between the squadrons. The final two weeks prior to promotion to DOUBLE GOLD selected members of that squadron's FIRST CLASS cadets also hold Wing officer rank. The acting cadet wing

12

commander held the rank of Cadet Colonel. Other wing level staff ranks were Cadet Lt. Colonels.

New Cadets

The new class of cadets would enter ranked as GREEN TUX. The GREEN TUX was an orientation period for them. They would spend the entire two weeks wearing only their green flight suits without any rank insignia. During their time as GREEN TUX they were intensely trained in the life of a cadet by the THIRD CLASS cadets in their squadron. When the orientation period was completed, they would be promoted in a ceremony to the FOURTH CLASS rank. This was an important day for the squadron. Each of the classes within the squadron would also be promoted to the next higher rank during the ceremony. The FOURTH CLASS cadets would become THIRD CLASS cadets etc. and FIRST CLASS cadets would become DOUBLE GOLD.

Cadet Uniforms

Cadets had five different types of uniforms. These uniforms were the same as those worn by all Air Force personnel except for the cadet rank insignia. Distinctive rank insignia was worn on all uniforms. There were two types of dress uniforms which included a tie and shoulder epaulets. The rank insignia for the two dress uniforms were a set of boards worn over the shoulder epaulets. The boards were black boards with narrow colored stripes. The color of the stripes depicted the rank. Two long rank colored stripes ran along the board and a short stripe ran across the wider part of the board. FOURTH CLASS cadets had green stripes, THIRD CLASS cadets wore red stripes, SECOND CLASS cadets wore blue stripes and FIRST CLASS cadets wore gold stripes. If a cadet also held squadron or wing rank, the standard Air Force insignia was also placed on the boards. There were two types of work uniforms as well as an olive drab flight suit that did not include a tie. The rank insignia for these three uniforms was a colored neck scarf. The neck scarves were the same color as the stripes on the boards. A GREEN TUX cadet's only uniform was the olive drab flight suit with no rank insignia.

13

DOUBLE GOLD cadets wore white boards with gold stripes.

Cadet Duties

The activities of the cadet corps was run by the upper class (FIRST CLASS and SECOND CLASS) cadets with commissioned Air Force officers overseeing the process. Each of the four squadrons had a group of cadets in each of the four general class ranks. About every ten weeks a new class of cadets arrived in the squadron and became GREEN TUX cadets. The squadron's THIRD CLASS cadets were responsible for the intensive orientation training the GREEN TUX cadets receive in the two weeks they spend at that rank. This includes such things as teaching them to march in formation, how to shine their shoes, how their rooms are to be arranged, the cadet knowledge system and the demerit system. GREEN TUX cadets could not receive demerits.

Prior to the arrival of a new GREEN TUX group, the squadron's FOURTH CLASS cadets were responsible for the maintenance of the hallways, stairs and the general areas of the barracks. This now becomes part of the GREEN TUX cadet's duties. The GREEN TUX cadets are given a Standby Inspection (described later) in the uniform of the day on the final day. This is the first time they can be given demerits. They are then marched to a squadron ceremony at which time each rank group within the squadron is promoted beginning with the highest ranks and moving down to the GREEN TUX. The GREEN TUX are given their FOURTH CLASS boards of rank. The FOURTH CLASS cadets are responsible for maintenance of their person's, rooms and the squadron's general areas. They are frequently inspected and bear the wrath of the higher three rank classes. There focus is learning to follow orders. The THIRD CLASS cadets have much the same duties as the FOURTH CLASS cadets, except they are not responsible for the maintenance of the general areas and now have fewer cadets that rank higher and a few that rank lower. During the final two weeks they devote their entire attention to the new GREEN TUX cadets.

The SECOND CLASS cadets conducted most of the daily inspections of the lower class cadets within the squadron. They also served as squadron Non-Commissioned Officer (NCO) rank positions within the squadron. These NCOs acted as squad leaders when squadron level activities are being conducted. The FIRST CLASS cadets were the ones that ran the squadron. They held all the formal (weekly Standby) inspections. They held the command positions and oversee the SECOND CLASS cadets. Double Gold cadets had few duties other than to prepare for graduation.

Cadet Movements

Movements by cadets outside and beyond the barracks area were strictly controlled. The majority of the movements out of the squadron area were done in marching formation. This includes going to and from class, the chow hall or the Base Exchange. Some of these formations included the entire squadron, such as marching to the parade field (for squadron or wing reviews) or reveille (morning wake up roll call). Most marching formations, however, involved much smaller groups. For example, the academic classes that the squadron's FOURTH CLASS cadets must attend were different in time and location from those that the THIRD CLASS cadets attend. They must there fore go in separate formations. In fact the majority of formations were restricted to cadets within a squadron of the same rank class. This had the advantage of allowing the lower class (FOURTH CLASS) cadets the chance to experience giving marching commands and controlling a smaller formation with simpler marching commands. Thus, they could learn before they would have to control the larger formations using more complex marching commands. The marching commands used by the FOURTH CLASS were sufficient to move the formation to the required locations.

Marching formations had the right of way on the base. Each formation would use Road Guards to stop traffic at intersections. As the formation approached an intersection the formation leader would yell "ROAD GUARDS OUT". Two designated Road Guards would run ahead and stop crossing traffic for the formation. When the formation had passed the intersection, the Formation leader would give the command "ROAD GUARDS IN". The Road Guards would return to their position in the formation.

Demerit and Honor Systems

The activities of most cadets (particularly the lower classes) were closely prescribed and monitored between 5 AM and 5 PM on week days. A cadet's life was filled with discipline. Disciple involved proper appearance and conduct. The demerit system was the formal system of enforcing the necessary standards of discipline. Demerits could be dispensed for a wide variety of infractions from minor to major transgressions. Each cadet was given a list of the infractions and the demerit value of each and became intimately familiar with it. The list assigned a set number of demerits to each type of infraction ranging from 1 demerit to 72 demerits. The majority of the demerits were earned by the lower two classes since the upper two classes were normally the ones passing out the demerits. GREEN TUX cadets could not get demerits. It was a grace period.

The way the system worked was as follows;

1. Each cadet was required to carry on his person a supply of demerit slips. The 3 by 5 slips were to have his name and squadron on them.

2. Any cadet of superior rank, who noted an infraction by a lower ranked cadet, would inform the offender of the infraction and ask for a demerit slip. The offender would provide the requested slip. The requesting cadet would fill in the infraction on the slip and forward it to the offending cadet's squadron orderly (administration) room. Not having a demerit slip when asked was an infraction that yielded 10 demerits.

3. The number of demerits each cadet accumulated would be tallied on a weekly basis. Cadets were permitted a maximum number of allowable demerits per week based on their rank.

FOURTH CLASS cadets were permitted up 6 demerits per week.

THIRD CLASS cadets were permitted up to 4 demerits per week.

SECOND CLASS cadets were permitted up to 3 demerits per week.

FIRST CLASS cadets were permitted up to 2 demerits per week.

As might be imagined, the lower two classes seemed to exceed their limits more often.

4.   Any number of demerits in excess of the allowable limit resulted in <u>Ramp Tours</u>.   Each excess demerit resulted in one <u>Ramp Tour</u>. <u>Ramp Tours</u> had to be marched off. Each one required one hour of marching on the Tour Ramp.

5. The Tour Ramp was a specified assembly area on the cadet grounds.   <u>Ramp Tours</u> could only be marched off on Saturday and Sunday staring at 1 PM. Four <u>Ramp Tours</u> (4 hours of marching) could be completed on Saturday and 2 <u>Ramp Tours</u> on Sunday. Each day of <u>Ramp Tours</u> began with an <u>Open Ranks</u> (described later) inspection. This was an additional opportunity to receive demerits. The ranking cadets on the tour ramp conducted the inspections and "called cadence" during the marching.

6. All cadets who had outstanding <u>Ramp Tours</u> were also on Restriction. This meant that whenever a cadet's earned privileges (discussed later) allowing them more individual freedom of movement, those on Restriction would relinquish these privileges until they were no longer on restriction. The privileges were normally confined to evenings and week ends. These privileges were primarily earned with increases in a cadet's rank. Restriction meant you were confined to barracks during these times.

Cadets were also required to assimilate a range of information know as <u>Cadet Knowledge</u>. This included such crucial information as "How many ears does a snake have?" or "Does a mosquito bite with its nose or tail?" Cadets were required to memorize the answers to these and other questions known as <u>Cadet Knowledge</u>. They must respond quickly to queries by upper classman. This system was enforced by the use of <u>Honor Slips</u>. These <u>Honor Slips</u> were similar to demerit slips and handled in much the same way. They did not count as demerits. Too many honor slips would result in a meeting with the squadron staff.

Cadet Living

A cadet's day began at 5 AM each morning including the week ends. They were awakened by the sound of a bugle playing REVEILLE. They dressed as quickly as they could in their fatigues and formed up in squadron formation in front of the squadron

17

barracks building. The squad leaders would check to see that all members of the squad were present. The squads would then be ordered to REPORT in turn. When the roll call was finished the formations would be dismissed. The cadets then returned to their rooms to prepare for the day.

Preparation, of course, included shaving; cleaning up and getting dressed in the uniform of the day. The rooms needed to be cleaned and the items in the dresser properly folded and arranged. By 6 AM the cadets and their rooms had to be ready for inspection. The GREEN TUX cadets would then have a STANDBY inspection (described later) each morning. The FOURTH CLASS cadets would have a STANDBY inspection for the first several weeks. Unscheduled STANDBY inspections were not uncommon especially for the lower two classes. At 9 PM each night the squadron duty officer would yell "Lights Out" and TAPS would be played. All cadets without regard to rank were required to be in bed with the lights out. From 5 AM to 5 PM each day there were ongoing cadet activities. Regular duty hours were from 8 AM to 5 PM on week days. Each squadron had a commissioned officer who had an office in the squadron building. He was in this office periodically during regular duty hours. During non-regular duty hours the squadron assigned a cadet as the squadron duty officer. There was a desk at the entrance to the barracks which served as the cadet duty officer's duty location. The cadet duty officer was normally drawn from the lower two classes. The duties were simple. They monitored who entered and left the squadron barracks and called the building to attention when ever a commissioned officer or cadet officer entered or left the building. Everyone in the building was expected to come to attention until the officer gave the "AT EASE" command. The duty officer would call out "AT EASE" and the cadets could resume their activities.

At 5 PM the structured part of the cadet's day ended. They would assemble in formation and march to the chow hall for the evening meal. Upon returning from the chow hall the remaining time would be devoted to study, preparing for inspections and related activities. Upper classmen could enter lower classmen's rooms during this time

18

but it was normally not to conduct inspections or test for cadet knowledge. The GREEN TUX, of course, were the exception, they were under fire from Reveille to TAPS.

Cadets were also required to follow very strict procedures in many of their daily activities. A good example is at the chow hall. Cadets were required to eat at attention. This was rigidly enforced for the under classmen (particularly for FOURTH CLASS but also THIRD CLASS) cadets. They could only divert their eyes to put food on their fork or spoon. Then the eyes must return straight ahead. Movement of the fork to the mouth may not be watched. In addition, upper class cadets may be walking around the table asking cadet knowledge questions of the under classmen. When asked a question the under classman must chew twice and then swallow (Chew Chew Swallow), then answer the question. Cadets learned to take small sized bites so this could be done.

Inspections were a primary source of demerits. Inspections could be individual and informal or formal. The informal might be any time a higher ranking cadet decided to inspect a lower ranking one. They could stop him and inspect his uniform, ask him questions or interrogate him on cadet knowledge. Formal inspections were of two types, Open Ranks or Standby. The Open Ranks inspection was done in formation in uniform. The inspecting officer (an upper classman) moved form one cadet to the next, inspected their uniform and asked cadet knowledge questions. Each session of the Tour Ramp started with an Open Ranks inspection. Standby inspections were conducted in the cadet's room in the barracks. Cadets would stand by their bed in the appointed uniform. The inspecting officials would inspect the uniform, the shoes, the room, the dresser drawers and the bed. Shoes had to be shined to a mirror finish. The items of clothing in the dressers had to folded in a specified manner and placed in a prescribed position in the drawer. White gloves were often used to locate any unauthorized dust on the floor. Each cadet would have a laundry bag tied to the base of their bed. This was the only area the inspectors could not open to inspect unless it appeared particularly bulky or odd shaped. We learned to use the laundry bag as our panic place for unauthorized, questionable or unclean items.

19

Each cadet spent a significant amount of time preparing for some type of inspection. Standby inspections were conducted every Saturday morning for all except FIRST CLASS and DOUBLE GOLD cadets. They were conducted by the FIRST CLASS cadets in the squadron. Standby inspections could be done with minimum notice at any time if the need was felt. FOURTH CLASS cadets received a limited standby inspection each week day morning conducted by the SECOND CLASS cadets in the squadron. Evenings for underclass cadets were normally spent studying, cleaning their rooms and shining shoes. When a Standby inspection was expected the floors were cleaned by hand. The recommended method was to run the hand along the floor to remove the dirt and dust. Beds had to be made with military corners and tight enough a quarter would bounce when dropped on the bed.

Freedom of movement, other than in formation, was considered a privilege. Movement privileges for most cadets were only available outside of normal (5 AM to 5 PM on week days) work hours. Privileges increased as a cadet advanced in rank. DOUBLE GOLD cadets had unrestricted movement privileges within the cadet areas from Reveille to Taps. Cadet wing and squadron officers had relatively free movement. FIRST CLASS cadets were given fairly free movement when not engaged in scheduled activities. FOURTH CLASS cadets had little unrestricted movement and GREEN TUX cadets had none.

Individual movement privileges were of two general types, Base and Off Base. Base privileges allowed freedom of individual movement within the cadet area or approved base areas such as going to the BX or to the snack bar after 5 PM. The snack bar was a burger type place similar to McDonald's. (McDonald's, however, was still an unknown.) Trips were frequent. We always seemed to be hungry. Cadets on restriction could not go to the snack bar. Often those cadets not on restriction would get things for the cadets on restriction. THIRD CLASS cadets and above, not on restriction, had Base privileges after 5 PM week days and on week ends.

Open Base privileges allowed the cadet to leave the cadet or approved base areas. You could even leave the base and go to town.

Open Base   privileges were restricted to SECOND CLASS cadets and above and normally only on week ends (Exception-DOUBLE GOLD cadets also had OPEN BASE privileges after 5 PM each day). Open Base privileges were given to SECOND CLASS cadets one week end each month and FIRST CLASS cadets every week end

Upper class cadets frequently had GI parties for their underclassman. A GI party for FOURTH CLASS or GREEN TUX cadets typically started with cadence controlled marching up and down the barracks halls. Frequently upper classman would each march a small group of underclassman. Under classman were instructed to dig their heels in which would leave black marks on the floor. It was also an excellent opportunity to teach disciple standards. One of the favored methods of harassment was to yell "Halt Rabbit". If the underclassman stopped, he was asked "Mister, are you a rabbit?" If the answer was "Sir no sir" he was then asked why he had stopped. If, however, the answer was "Sir yes sir" he was informed he didn't have long ears so he couldn't be a rabbit. If he had not stopped he was royally berated for not responding to a superior. It was a no win situation. When an ample supply of black heel marks covered the floor the GI party could begin. It meant cleaning up all those black marks. The GREEN TUX cadets regularly enjoyed GI parties, FOURTH CLASS less often, particularly after the first two weeks.

As the cadets approached the Day and Night Celestial phases of their academic and flight training, they were issued a hand held sextant (Model A-2). A sextant is an instrument to measure the angular elevation of a celestial body (like a star or the moon) above the horizon. This is an important part of determining position by celestial references. This phase would normally occur during the early to mid part of the SECOND CLASS stage. It was normal during these periods to see cadets behind the barracks with sextant in hand pointing it at the sun, moon or stars. This would often go on until just before Taps. It was considered inappropriate to bother them while engaged in this activity. The sextants were returned after the Night Celestial phase was completed.

21

Flight Training

Flight training was conducted in the T-29 aircraft. The T-29 is a two engine, prop driven aircraft manufactured by Convair (Similar to a Convair 404). It has a crew area for the pilots and the navigator in a compartment in the nose of the aircraft. The area behind the cockpit was the navigation training area used by the cadets and their instructors. The area just behind the cockpit had Radar scopes used for the Radar phase. Behind the Radar positions were about 10 desk positions used by students during the other phases of training. A flight would routinely have students in different training phases on the same flight.

Aerial navigation, as taught by the Air Force, is based on a technique known as <u>Dead Reckoning</u>. This means that the navigator starts from a known position (or departure point) and calculates the expected position of the aircraft at a selected time in the future. The aircraft's heading and airspeed are used to calculate a projected (<u>Dead Reckoned</u>) position for a specific future time. At the selected time the navigator determines the exact (<u>Fix</u>) aircraft position using one of the fixing techniques. The <u>Dead Reckoned</u> position is compared to the actual (<u>Fix</u>) position. This allows the navigator to calculate the actual effect of the wind. A new projected (<u>Dead Reckoned</u>) position is then calculated and the wind from the previous leg applied. This allows the navigator to make projections on the time (Expected Time of Arrival or ETA) over future positions.

Once a navigator masters the <u>Dead Reckoning</u> technique, the remainder of the navigation process is how the fixed position is determined. There are several techniques that are used. Each phase in the Aviation Cadet Navigator training program is devoted to one of these fixing techniques. Each of the techniques augments the <u>Dead Reckoning</u> process and each phase of the training program is titled as such. (Example-The Radar training phase is entitled "Dead Reckoning Aided by Radar"). The academic training for each phase was conducted by one of the instructors who would be flying with us. Then we would get several flights to practice the technique. Finally, we received a check flight using the technique. The current phase must be successfully passed before proceeding to the next one. The names of the phases are listed below;

    1-Dead Reckoning aided by Double Drift and Groundspeed by Timing

    2-Dead Reckoning aided by Map Reading

    3-Dead Reckoning aided by Pressure Patterns

    4-Dead Reckoning aided by Day Celestial

    5-Dead Reckoning aided by Night Celestial

    6-Dead Reckoning aided by Grid Navigation

    7-Dead Reckoning aided by Loran

    8-Dead Reckoning aided by Radar

A more detailed explanation of each phase is provided in Appendix 1.

Chapter 3   My Cadet Experience

Cadet Corp Moved to James Connally AFB

The Air Force's Navigator Aviation Cadet training program had been based at Harlingen AFB in Harlingen, Texas. Harlingen is located close to the Texas/Mexican border a short distance inland from the Gulf of Mexico. Harlingen had been the home of the Navigator Aviation Cadet Corps for several years. The Air Force had a second navigator flight training program for individuals who were already commissioned officers. It was based at James Connally AFB. James Connally is near the city of Waco, located in south central Texas. The two programs used similar resources including the same type of aircraft, the T-29. The curriculums were similar. In the summer of 1961 the Air Force decided to co-locate the two programs at James Connally. This meant that the Aviation Cadet program at Harlingen would have to move. The transfer, however, was not as simple as moving everything from one location to another. The method of transition the Air Force chose was to gradually phase out the program in the original location (Harlingen) while gradually phasing it in at the new location (James Connally). This meant that the last four classes of cadets arriving at Harlingen from May thru July of 1961 would complete training there. There would be no classes following them to become their underclassmen. Conversely, the first four classes of cadets arriving at James Connally from mid-August until mid-October would be the first to arrive at the new location. They would never have a class of cadets above them as an upper class. They would always be the senior class in their respective squadrons.

The Air Force, typically, uses a numbering system too identify its different training classes. The first two numbers are the final two digits of the year in which the class graduates. The classes are then sequentially numbered through the year. Governmental agencies used the fiscal year rather than the calendar year which the rest of the country used. A fiscal year, at that time, began on July 1st and ended on June 30 th. As a result the fiscal year was 6 months ahead of the calendar year. The number was added to the base where the training took place. So a typical response you would get to the question "What class were you in?' would be "Harlingen 61-04" or "Webb 63-09". The Aviation Cadet Training program was approximately 11 months in length. This meant that the first class to graduate in fiscal year 1963 would have to start training in mid-August of 1961 (About month and a half into fiscal year 1962). The last class at Harlingen would be the final class to graduate in fiscal year 1962. James Connally's first class arrived in mid-August of 1961. They were designated class 63-01. They were assigned to "A" squadron.

The preceding chapter described the cadet corps and the cadet training environment as it would function with a full complement of cadets, that is, four separate squadrons with a class of cadets at each of the four major class ranks. A class of Double Gold cadets would graduate as new Second Lieutenants about every two to three weeks as a new class of Green Tux cadets would replace them. The size of corps remained relatively stable. This was in fact the way the cadet corps had functioned at Harlingen AFB and would function again at James Connally once the transition was completed. That transition, however, would take about 8 to 9 months to complete.

The training environment described in the preceding chapter was a time tested system that the Air Force valued. A system they wanted to continue in the James Connally program. An attempt to approximate the environment with some form of upper class would have to be made. The lessons of discipline, grooming, espirite de corps and military culture that were so valued in the leadership of military organizations had to absorbed while they were lower classmen so they could in turn pass them on to the classes that followed. The cadet corps at James Connally would have to be built from scratch. The Air Force did have a plan. They assigned eight newly commissioned Second Lieutenants, fresh from cadet life at Harlingen, to the James Connally cadet corps to act as the upper class for the early arriving classes. Initially, these young Second Lieutenants would live, eat, discipline and monitor the cadets from REVEILLE to TAPS. They led the marching formations, taught the discipline and grooming techniques and molded the group into cadets. They dispensed the demerits and ran the Tour Ramp.

The base had set aside four adjacent two story barracks type buildings to be used as cadet housing. The barracks were being converted from the open bay type that were typical for enlisted personnel of time to individual rooms large enough to accommodate two or three cadets.

The first cadet class (Class 63-01) arrived at James Connally AFB in late August of 1961. They spent their two weeks as GREEN TUX cadets. Class 63-01 was assigned to "A" squadron. Class 63-02 arrived in early September. On the 24th of September a new class of cadets arrived. This was the class I had been assigned to, class 63-03. The corps now had two classes of cadets at the Fourth Class rank, a class of Green Tux cadets and the eight young lieutenants. The first class, Class 63-01, was now considered seasoned enough to train the new class of cadets (my class) during their Green Tux phase. So we felt the wrath of the cadets with less attention from the young lieutenants. It was mid-October when class 63-04 arrived. My class was now Fourth Classmen. The focus of both of the upper classes (63-01 and 63-02) was now on the new group of Green Tux. Both classes were considered seasoned enough to train the new class.

At this point the eight officers from Harlingen were divided into four groups. Two of them were assigned to oversee each of the squadrons. The senior cadet class in each squadron was given expanded responsibilities. We were considered competent enough to march ourselves but there was always one of the officers with us where ever we went observing the movement of the group.

A new class of cadet trainees would arrive every two to three weeks. In mid-November we were ready for the first real underclassmen, the cadets who would be assigned to class 63-05. As the senior class in our squadrons for the remainder of the program we would occupy rooms on the ground floor. The rooms on the ground floor were somewhat larger than those on the second floor. There were now three cadets to a room. The only people who could issue demerits were upper classmen and the Harlingen officers.

In the next three months a second group of new cadets would be added to each squadron. The senior class in each squadron had assumed responsibility for training the under classmen in their respective squadrons. The officers from Harlingen remained part of the program but their role was less direct. The cadet corps reached full strength in late May of 1962. The Harlingen lieutenants left the corps in the early spring of that year. The transition had been successfully completed.

My Green Tux Training

As I explained at the end of chapter one, I had arrived late at the cadet area. I received immediate intense attention due to my late arrival and unsuccessful attempt to explain that I was not at fault. I was informed there was no such thing as an excuse. Two cadets in uniform with green boards spent about 10 minutes telling me how worthless I was and how miserable my life was going to be. I learned that the appropriate response should have been "Sir no excuse sir". They then escorted me to my room telling me along the way that I was to march, not walk. I was instructed to drop the small bag I was carrying in my room and was escorted to the street in front of the building where a large group of young men were standing in three lines. They had been waiting for our arrival. I joined the formation with the other three young cadets that had arrived with me. The group was still clad in civilian clothes. We were assembled in formation and a roll call was taken. We were told that the proper response was "Sir here Sir". Then we were instructed on the fundamentals of marching. The formation was surrounded by yelling cadets. A short while later, they apparently thought we were ready to give it a try so we started to march. Our instructors were obviously not happy with the result because the yelling continued. We were marched to the barber shop and were shaved bald. This was not as traumatic to me as it might be to some. I had a crew cut which was common for the time and my hair was already pretty short. This was only the first stop. Next we were marched to supply to receive our clothing issue. The clothes were packed into a large blue bag that we learned was called a B4 bag. We were then marched back to our rooms with the bags over our shoulders.

They left us alone for about 15 minutes. The cadet barracks described above was being renovated. The renovation was not complete so we were assigned BOQ rooms which were smaller than the ones in the barracks. Temporarily we were assigned only two cadets per room. My roommate was one Ralph Heffer from New York state. He had arrived about 10 o'clock in the morning so he had received a lot more instruction than I had. Soon two cadets in uniform re-entered the room and began to instruct us on how to fold our clothes, where to place them in the drawers, how to clean our room and the many skills that were required. This lasted about an hour or so at which point we were instructed to dress in our flight suits and marching boots for a little close order drill. To our surprise, this close order drill was not done outside but in the hallway just outside of our rooms. "dig in your heels" they yelled. The marching lasted for about a half an hour. The hallway had a linoleum floor which was now loaded with black heel marks. Finally, one of the cadets, who seemed to be in charge, shouted "Who wants to go to a party?" No one answered so he picked out one of us moving in close to him. "Mister, are you a party animal?" The answer he got was "sure sometimes". The cadet in charge got right up in the man's face. He was nose to nose with him and yelled "Its sir yes sir, do you understand?'. He got the answer he was looking for. He continued "We're going to have a special kind of party we call a GI party." He turned back to the same man and asked "Mister, do you know what a GI party is?" The man answered "No". Back into the man's face he went shouting "Its sir no sir, do you understand?'. Then he turned and shouted to the rest of us "Does anyone know what a GI party is?'. We had learned the lesson. We all shouted back in a robust voice "Sir no Sir". This bought a smile to his face. We learned that a GI party means cleaning up the black marks that seem to appear, periodically and magically, on the floor of the hall way. The GI party lasted another hour. We got down on our knees and scrubbed until the black marks were gone. The cadet who had been yelling instructions had us stand at attention while they inspected our handy work. It was not good enough. We started scrubbing a second time. The third time, however, was the one that proved to be a charm, we passed. We were ordered to fall out on to the street and form up.

We formed into three separate lines similar to our earlier

formation but the lines were all a different length. The yelling started again. The next formation was to the chow hall for dinner. I think most of us expected this would be a break in the harassment. We were wrong. We learned the <u>Chew, chew swallow</u> lesson. I recall not getting much food eaten. When we returned to the rooms we received instruction in cadet knowledge, those gems that every leader of men can not do without. "Is a rabbit's tail made of cotton?", " Can a walrus touch his toes?". "Can a flying squirrel do a loop?". Unfortunately, there were no correct answers to these questions. Whatever you answered it would be wrong or it would be followed by a further question or you would be asked to explain your answer. It was a game but could be a stressful game. It was possible for the harassed to play the game too and occasionally we did. I remember one of the members of our class being asked "Mr. are you a penguin?" The normal answer was "Sir no sir". The questioner would then say "Are you sure? You look like a penguin". This was a common question because we spent so much time at attention with our backs straight like a penguin. In this instance, the answer came back "Sir yes sir". The next question was "Mister, what kind of sound does a penguin make?'. His answer was "Sir bleep bleep sir". The questioner started to laugh but caught himself. These activities continued until after 8 PM. TAPS, which signified the end of the day and lights out, was at 9 PM. I was happy to see the end of my first day of cadet life.

We would be awakened each morning by a bugle sounding reveille. This happened precisely at 5 AM. Lights out and Taps always sounded at 9 PM each evening. The hours between were filled with instruction by our upper classmen from class 63-01. Not a single minute was wasted. Someone always seemed to be yelling. The flight suit was our sole attire during this period. During the first week the marching instructions and cadence were done by a member of the upper class. During the second week each member of our class took a turn at giving marching instructions under the watchful eye of an upper classman. There were no academic classes during the Green Tux phase. Training focused on cadet routines, cadet culture, personal grooming and marching. Every move we made was scrutinized and corrected on the spot. Occasionally we would be given an hour to prepare for an inspection. We would rush back to our rooms and get everything in order. Items in the dresser drawers had to be properly arranged. The clothing had to be properly folded. The floors had to be devoid of dust such that they could pass a white glove inspection. The beds had to be made with military corners and tight enough that a quarter could be bounced on the bed spread. Our laundry bag was tied to end of the bed. The laundry bag was the one area that was not subject to inspection. It was to hold your dirty clothes that would go into the laundry once a week. We called it our panic bag. Any item that did not meet standards at the last minute would go into the laundry bag. The only inspection of it was that it had to have a normal shape and did not seem to be overstuffed. This could result in the bag being emptied to see if you had some contraband (unauthorized materials).

By the end of the two week period we had to be ready to conduct ourselves in a manner expected of all cadets. The Green Tux phase ended with a <u>Standby Inspection</u> at bedside. We awoke that morning as Green Tux, were marched to morning chow then returned to our rooms and given an hour to prepare for the inspection. We were instructed to wear our starched 505s for the inspection. This was the uniform of Fourth Class cadets. During this inspection we were considered to have been promoted to the Fourth Class rank. The importance of that was that now we could be assessed demerits. Ralph and I had readied ourselves for the inspection. We were standing beside our beds at parade rest. It was then that I noticed a small length of web belt on the top of my dresser. The 505 uniform used a military web belt. When we were issued this belt everyone got one of the same length. It was far too long for most of us. It had to be cut to the proper length. Sometimes it took a second cut to get it right. I had done that the night before. This was a small piece of the excess. I could hear the inspectors coming down the hall. There was no time to put it in my laundry bag. I panicked. I ran into the bathroom and tried to flush it down the toilet. Dumb, but I was in a panic. It clogged the toilet and water ran all over the floor. I ran back to my bedside just in time. Two upperclassmen entered the room. We called the room to attention and the inspection began. It went fine until one of them went into the bathroom and saw all the water on the floor. They asked who had done this. I confessed that it was me. I received the biggest demerit infraction possible for this, seventy two demerits, a terrible start. As a Fourth Classmen I was allowed 6 demerits per week. I had already exceeded it by 66. This, of course, meant that I had earned 66 Ramp tours to march off at the rate of 6 per week. I would be on restriction for at least 11 weeks. I was sure that my cadet career was at an end.

Life in C Squadron

The Harlingen officers who had lived with the cadets until class 63-04 was promoted to Fourth Class rank remained in the BOQ when we moved to the cadet barracks. The two officers assigned to "C" squadron were Second Lieutenant Steelquist and Second Lieutenant Bailey. They had an office on the ground floor of the barracks which they used during the day. Lt. Steelquist was a slight, slender man that stood only about 5 feet 6 or 5 feet 7 inches in height. He had bright red hair with a very light freckled complexion. There always seemed to be a sneaky smile on his face with the side of his mouth slightly curled. We felt that he really enjoyed handing out demerits. Lt. Bailey was just the opposite. He was of average height with an athletic build. He only handed out demerits when it was clearly warranted. As you might have guessed, we liked Lt. Bailey and disliked Lt. Steelquist. During our private moments when we were sure of not being overheard we would mimic Lt. Steelquist. "Hello, my name is Lt. Steelhead. I'll have a demerit slip for good measure".

Each of the first four classes (63-01 through 63-04) looked forward to their first Green Tux class. They would finally have someone within their squadron lower in rank. They would be promoted to the Third Class rank at the end of the two weeks of Green Tux training. Class 63-01 reached this landmark when class 63-05 arrived in early November. Class 63-03, my class, had to wait until early December. The cadet corps did not have cadet wing

31

officers until class 63-01 reached the Second Class rank. This occurred in mid February. They would then hold these positions until they reached the Double Gold rank. At that point the Wing leadership would be passed to class 63-02. Until that time the Harlingen Lieutenants would fill these roles. Cadet squadron and wing officers had an active role only when the activity involved the entire squadron or the entire corps (Wing). Since the majority of the cadet formations were much smaller units their role was somewhat limited. The two regular occasions when they did have a role was the morning assembly formation and the week end reviews on the parade grounds.

Morning assembly was a required formation for all cadets seven days a week. It was a routine and normally uneventful formation. That is, it almost never resulted in any demerits. Once the roll call was complete the Cadet Wing Commander would dismiss the squadron commanders who in turn would dismiss us. We then headed back to the barracks to clean up and prepare for the first activity of the day. When Lt. Steelquist was the acting squadron commander instead of dismissing us he would occasionally say "C squadron parade rest". When the other three squadrons had re-entered their barracks he would call us to attention and would walk slowly through the formation to see if he could spot any violation that could warrant a demerit. This was well within the squadron commander's prerogative but was seldom done, except of course, by Lt. Steelquist.

The first activity of each day was to form up to march to the chow hall for breakfast. This would happen precisely at 6 AM. We had the rest of the hour after morning assembly to shave, shower, brush our teeth and get dressed. The barracks had a large common bathroom area rather than the semi-private one we had had in the BOQ. The sinks and showers were community type facilities. Each floor was similarly equipped. With a single class in the squadron there was enough room at the sinks so most of us could shave at the same time. This would become more of a problem as the squadron built in strength. A starched pair of 505s was normally the uniform of the day. On the mornings that we were scheduled to fly our uniform for the day would be the flight suit. We marched to chow in individual formations of a single class rank within a squadron because from the

32

chow hall we would go directly to class. Each class rank within a squadron was at a different point in their academics so they would each be bound for a different class room.

The barracks buildings we lived in had a front door and a rear door. There was a large desk near the front door. The desk was not used during the day from reveille until the formations returned from the evening meal which was about 6 PM. From 6 PM until Taps the desk was manned by a FOURTH CLASSMAN from the squadron who acted as the duty officer. The job was evenly rotated amongst the FOURTH CLASSMEN. The evening was normally the quiet part of the day except during the two week period when the squadron had a new class of Green Tux cadets. It was an unwritten rule that upper classmen would not enter an underclassmen's room from 7 PM until Taps on Sunday evening though Thursday evening so the time could be devoted to study, shining shoes and cleaning the rooms. The duty officer would also use the time to study. The major responsibility of the duty officer was to call the building to attention whenever a commissioned officer entered the building. This would alert us to the fact that they were in the building. It was considered bad form for an officer to sneak in the back door. The entering officer could, however, try to say "At ease" before the duty officer could yell "Barracks Ten Hut". This would stop the duty officer from alerting us. Lt. Steelquist did this frequently. Lt. Bailey never did. The duty officers started the practice of calling the barracks to attention when they saw him approaching the front door before he could open it. This was obviously somewhat frustrating to Lt. Steelquist. He continued, however, to surprise us in the evenings by popping unannounced into a room even during the quiet period after 7 PM. On a couple of occasions when he appeared in this manner we asked the duty officer if he had come through the front door. The answer both times was "No". He was obviously now sneaking in the back door. Lt. Bailey never entered the barracks in the evenings.

Self Initiated Elimination (SIE) and Washing Back

The pace of cadet life was demanding and stressful. Some handled it better than others. We had to balance our scarce free time between

33

study, shinning our shoes and preparing our rooms for inspection. There didn't seem to be enough time to do all of them properly. We all, however, had volunteered for this program. Therefore, we had the option of dropping out (un-volunteering) if it got to be too much for us. This was known as SIEing (Self-Initiated Elimination). A few in my class took this route during the first couple of months.

Continuation in the program required each of us to successfully pass each phase before we could proceed to the next one. A phase normally entailed classroom academics, a written test, several airborne practice flights and an airborne flight check. Those that were not successful would have to repeat that phase. This meant you fell behind your class and reassignment to a later class was required. We called this <u>Washing Back</u>. Failure to pass a phase was the most common reason for <u>Washing Back</u> but there were others such as temporary medical problems, emergency leave, etc.. A cadet being <u>Washed Back</u> would join the class that was just starting the phase they had failed to complete for any of the above reasons. A cadet could also request to be <u>Washed Back</u>. The reasons for the request were reviewed by the commissioned officers overseeing the program before it would be granted.

Cadet Life

Assignment of roommates was rotated at intervals. When we first moved from our temporary quarters in the BOQ to the cadet barracks I was assigned to a room with two other cadets. Marty Hayduk was from West Virginia and Bruce Wilson was from Georgia. Marty was a tall raw boned fellow with a slight accent. He was quiet and seemed at times lost in thought. I feared he would SIE which he did about two months into the program. Bruce was an African American, the only one in our class. He was an affable person with good military bearing and adept at marching and drilling. He became the class <u>Guide On</u>. The <u>Guide On</u> is the position in the left front of the formation and the first to initiate the command given by the formation leader. Marty was replaced by Ron Canada from New Jersey. Ron was a loud, outgoing individual. Often in the morning, before the first formation, Ron would put his head into the hallway and shout out the <u>Word For</u>

34

the Day. A typical pronouncement, "The word for the day is …" "Contrary to popular belief peter pan is not a wash basin in a whore house."

Our first squadron underclass, 63-07, arrived just after Thanksgiving. The training of a new class is normally done by the squadron's Third Classmen who will be promoted to Second Classmen at the end of the two weeks of training. We were still Fourth Classmen but were permitted to train our new class of Green Tux cadets. I was assigned as a group of three upperclassmen to train the new cadets in marching. I was amazed at how disorganized they were. I'm sure we looked the same when we first arrived but it didn't seem that disorganized at the time.

My first several months as a cadet were very restricted. I had acquired 66 Ramp Tours as a result of my first inspection. This meant that I had a minimum of 11 weeks in Restricted status barring any demerit total in excess of 6 on a weekly basis. Fortunately, I only exceeded 6 demerits twice during the remainder of my time as a Fourth Classman. I felt this is what kept me from being eliminated from the program.

We turned Third Classmen in early December. My classmates now had some freedom of movement after 5PM daily but I was still on Restriction and confined to the barracks. I finally got off of restriction in mid-January.

Personal Fitness Testing

Physical conditioning is an integral part of the training programs in each of the military services. Military duty can be and often is physically demanding. It requires the soldier to be in good physical condition. Everyone must be prepared. We had several scheduled physical training periods each week. Normally, the sessions involved a single cadet class. The majority of these sessions were in the late afternoon. Cadets would return to their barracks from the classroom in formation. We would dress in shorts, T-shirts and tennis shoes and form up in standard formation outside the barracks. The class was then marched to the parade field in double time (a jogging pace). The sessions involved an hour or so of vigorous exercise.

Each cadet was required to pass a physical fitness test in order to graduate. The test was called the PFT (Physical Fitness Test). There were minimum standards in each of four separate exercises; SIT UPS, PULL UPS, PUSH UPS and a timed 300 yard shuttle run. We would have to meet or exceed the minimum in each of the exercises. Initially, only a few of us were able to meet the minimums. Our numbers were recorded during each session. Each of us was expected to continue an exercise as long as we were able. I don't remember the exact minimums but you had to be in good shape to meet them. Each of the tests except the shuttle run also had a maximum. When you reached the maximum you could stop the exercise. I had been an active runner and had been on the varsity wrestling teams in both high school and college so I was able to pass the PFT early in the program. I was able to reach the maximum in the sit ups and the push ups. The maximum for sit ups was 112 and the maximum for pushups was 50.

Dropped Back to Class 63-06

I was progressing through the program without much problem, aside from the early period when I was on restriction for excessive demerits. In February of 1962 I received a letter from my family that caused me some concern and would impact my cadet training. My parents had been separated since the start of my freshman year in college. The breaking point apparently came when my mother accepted a teaching position at Central High School in Norwood-Young America. Norwood was some 120 miles from the families' farm. She moved the family to a house in Norwood. It was at this point my parents were legally separated. This occurred in 1960 while I was still attending St. John's University. My father had gone to live with the family of one of his sisters. My parents were divorced in 1961. The family, including myself had adjusted to the situation.

The February letter informed me of a confrontation between my parents. My brother Bill had had to intervene. I couldn't get the incident out of my mind and had trouble sleeping at night. I was dead tired during the day. The pace of the cadet program required me to be fully alert and rested. I had difficulty concentrating. Shortly before I

36

received the letter we had started the Night Celestial academic phase in the training program. This had been my favorite phase and I was getting pretty good with the sextant prior to the arrival of that letter. I subsequently flunked the written exam for that phase. My situation required a decision by the one of the officers managing the cadet program. I was required to meet with a First Lieutenant Gillquist, the officer now responsible for "C" squadron. Since my progress in the prior phases had been good with no indication of problems he tried to determine why I now had a problem. I had successfully passed both the academic and flight test for the DAY CELESTIAL phase with flying colors. The Day Celestial phase was considered the more difficult of the two. I advised him of my family situation. The discussion lasted about half an hour. He said he understood the reasons for my concern but advised me that I had to make a decision. If I felt that I could not keep up I would have to drop out of the program through the SIE process. If I wanted to stay I would get one more chance and if I was not successful I would be eliminated. I told him I wanted to stay in the program. His decision was to place me back into class 63-06. They were just starting the Night Celestial phase. I accepted his decision and moved into the "B" squadron barracks and joined class 63-06. The experience had served to refocus me and I successfully passed the remaining phases.

Trip to Bermuda

In late May my new class began the DEAD RECOKONING AIDED BY LORAN phase. We would learn to use Loran A to fix the aircraft's position. It was used by aircraft as well as ships. Loran A used transmitted radio signals. Transmitting sites were located up and down both U.S. coasts at intervals. Transmitting sights were paired and special charts were used. Loran A navigational usage was limited to coastal waters only. It could not be used over land nor used in areas beyond a couple of hundred miles off shore. The signals could be reliably received only over the oceans. A more detailed explanation of Loran A can be found in Appendix A. Loran A has since been replaced by Loran C. Loran C transmitting sights are located inland and are usable anywhere in the world. As Loran C

37

sights became available <u>Loran A</u> sights were decommissioned. This transition occurred a couple of decades after my cadet training. The Loran A phase curriculum included four over water flights. The first flight was from James Connally AFB over the Gulf of Mexico to Homestead AFB near Miami, Florida. We would stay over night at Homestead. The next day we flew from Homestead to Kindley AFB in Bermuda. We remained in Bermuda for two days and then reversed course. The flights from Homestead to Kindley and return were flown over the infamous <u>Bermuda Triangle</u>. We were new enough at this business that we had not yet heard the ample lore (fact or fiction) associated with this stretch of ocean so there was no apprehension by myself or any of my class mates. The first three flights were practice flights for us. The final flight from Homestead to James Connally was the check flight.

The trip to Bermuda would be our first taste of temporary duty (TDY). In addition, the trip would also be our first encounter with the <u>Air Defense Interior Zone</u> or ADIZ. The ADIZ is an arbitrary line a given distance off the United States coast lines that surrounds the country. There are no landmarks to mark it but it appears on all aviation charts. The concept is based on the need for our military to identify all aircraft approaching our coasts to determine if they were friendly or hostile in nature. Setting the ADIZ line off shore would allow for time to identify the aircraft and respond to it in sufficient time to ward off any hostile intent if necessary. All aircraft that expected to cross the ADIZ were required to file a flight plan with The Federal Aviation Administration (FAA) depicting their route and expected timing. They were required to adhere to the route on their flight plan. Oceanic flights into the United States are normally quite long because the vast majority of departure points are hundreds of miles away. Also, oceanic navigation is more demanding. Many of methods used over land are not available over water and those that are tend to be less precise. This was truer in the 1960s than it is today (The modern navigational systems [GPS, Loran C and VLF] have significantly changed this situation). Celestial navigation tended to be the primary method. Day Celestial, as described in the appendix, may yield only a course line or speed line, not sufficient to determine the actual (Fix) position. As the coast came within the range of the airborne radar the actual position could finally be accurately determined. It was not uncommon for the navigator to discover that the flight was several miles off course and several minutes ahead or behind schedule. The flight would turn to intercept their planned point to cross the ADIZ and update the timing by radio with Air Traffic Control. The flight would have appeared on the FAA's ground radar well beyond the ADIZ. If the flight did not cross the ADIZ at the planned point or did not communicate with the FAA, an Air Force fighter aircraft would be launched to identify it. Our instructors had tried to impress on us the importance of precise navigation whenever we planned to cross an ADIZ. They told us that if we missed our point and a fighter aircraft had to be launched the navigator would be required to pay for the gas burned by the fighter. This would be a sizable bill. We were not sure whether this was true or just designed to scare us. In point of fact on all of our training flights a rated navigator was part of the front end crew and doing the actual navigation of the aircraft. Neither the students nor our instructors were actually guiding the aircraft. The two days spent in Bermuda were considered days off. We spent them on the beach enjoying ourselves and watching the girls. The bathing suits of the 1960s, that the girls wore, were normally one piece rather than the bikinis that are common today.

The final phase was devoted to <u>Dead Reckoning Aided by Radar</u>. Radars transmit a short signal (a pulse) that radiates in a beam in the direction that the antenna is pointed. The pulse strikes objects in its path. The part of the pulse striking an object is reflected off of it in many directions. A portion of this energy is reflected directly back toward the radar antenna. The amount of time it takes for the signal to travel to the object and return allows the system to calculate the distance that the object is from the radar site. The process of transmitting a signal and listening for a return is called a radar cycle. The antenna then moves a degree or so after each radar cycle. When it has rotated a full 360 degrees a full picture of the surrounding objects can be displayed on a screen. This 360 degree display is compared to a chart (map) and similar features matched. The position of the aircraft is determined by the distances from these features on the chart. The size, composition and shape (flat objects reflect better than round ones) of each object determine how much radar energy is reflected and how prominent these objects appear on the radar display. Metal is a good reflector, wood is not. Cities show prominently on the display. One of the interesting things we discovered was that some cities show up better than others. An example was the city of Ft. Smith, Arkansas. It did not show up well because of the high degree of wood used in the construction of the buildings.

Receiving Assignments

A few weeks prior to our scheduled graduation we were gathered as a class to receive our next duty assignments. The procedures were precisely laid out and we would be allowed to participate in the process. The process would proceed as follows;

1-A composite score based on compilation of our scores in each phase of training; military training, academic and flying was developed.

2-A rank order list was compiled of the members of the class based on that composite score.

3-A list of assignments equal to the size of the class was given to each one of us.

4-We were allowed to select our assignment from the list based on our position on the rank order list. The person at the top picked first. That assignment was then removed from the list. The second choose from the remaining and so on until all of us had assignments.

The assignment list included slots in operational flying units and advanced navigator schools. Assignment to an operational unit meant we would join an aircrew as a navigator. There were two advanced schools; Navigator-Bombardier and Electronic Warfare. Both of the schools were located at Mather AFB in Sacramento, California. Most of us favored being assigned to an operational unit. We had just finished a lengthy school and didn't want to go immediately to another. My position on the list was about a third of the way down the list. The operational assignments were all gone by the time it was my turn to select.   I would have to choose between one of the two advanced schools.   I knew that I did not like the   idea of being a bombardier. I knew very little about electronic warfare. I decided to try the unknown. I selected the Electronic Warfare advanced school.

James Connally class 63-06 graduated on September 21, 1962. It was traditional for a newly commissioned officer to give a silver dollar to the first enlisted man that saluted him. There was normally a group of enlisted men near by following the graduation ceremony.

Traveling Home on Leave

Cadets were not allowed to have cars on the base at James Connally AFB.   The first thing that most cadets did when they graduated was to buy a new car. The salesmen at the local dealerships were expecting us and were ready to make a deal. I spent the final week looking for a car. I finally bought a new Ford Falcon. The Falcon was the bottom of Ford's line and the cheapest car they sold. It had a small engine and was a stick shift. This fit my budget. The day following my graduation from cadet school I picked up my new car, loaded my few possessions and started for my mother's house in Minnesota for a week of leave. I drove from Waco, Texas to Kansas City, Missouri on the first day. I was able to use parts of the new interstate highway system and the Kansas Turnpike on this part of the journey. I departed Kansas City at about 8 AM the following morning. The intensive construction of the interstate highway system, that had begun under the Eisenhower administration was, however, not yet complete. This was generally true north of Kansas City. Many of the major roads still ran through the cities and small towns along its route. I had just crossed the Missouri state border into Iowa when I entered the small town of Lamoni, Iowa. The highway ran down the town's main street which was only a few blocks long. In the middle of the road was a mobile school stop sign. I stopped quickly and proceeded. Before I got through the intersection a man in blue jeans and a plaid shirt ran out in front of me and indicated for me to stop. He directed me to the side of the road. He flashed a badge and identified himself as the town constable. He advised me I had just run a stop sign. It was 10:30 in the morning. I asked him why they still had a mobile school stop sign out when all of the kids should have already been in school. He told me this town protected its children. This was obviously a speed trap to raise revenue for the town. In the 1960s the use of speed traps was not yet common knowledge, at least not to me. The fact that I had Texas license plates on my car probably made me an obvious target. He wrote out a traffic ticket. I felt like commenting that the town must be gathering revenue to buy him a police car so he would not have to make his traffic stops on foot but I held my tongue.

The next step became even more bizarre. He pointed to a parked car on a side street and told me to follow him over to it. There was a man in the car dressed in clothes that one would use if they were going hunting. He wore a cap with fur lined ear flaps. The man in the car told me to get in on the passenger side. He informed me he was the justice of the peace and this was his court. I started to laugh. He got a stern look on his face and lectured me that I needed to take the situation more seriously. I was fined $10 and allowed to go on my way. I arrived at my mother's house in Norwood, Minnesota that evening.

Chapter 4   Electronic Warfare School

Traveling to Mather

My leave was a chance to interact with my family again and was a welcome diversion. On October 10, 1962 I finished my leave and began the trip to Mather AFB in California. I traveled due west thru South Dakota and Montana. Then I turned southwest across Nevada, thru the Donner Pass to central California. Mather is located on the Southeast edge of the city of Sacramento in the middle of California's central valley. The trip to Mather AFB from Norwood, Minnesota took me three full days.

Advanced Navigation Training

In the fall of 1962 James Connally Air Force Base (AFB) was the sole site for Air Force Basic Navigator training. Many of the graduates from the basic course were assigned directly to Air Force units in the Military Transport Command, the Tactical Air Command and the Air Defense command. The Strategic Air Command (SAC), however, required advanced training for its navigators. Mather AFB was the training base which specialized in advanced training for Air Force Navigators. There were two major advanced navigator training programs based at Mather, the Navigator-Bombardier school and the Electronic Warfare Officer School.

The Navigator-Bombardier school taught advanced radar navigation techniques as well as radar bombing techniques. The length of the course was approximately 10 months. The majority of its graduates became navigators and/or bombardiers on crews flying the B-47, B-52 or the B-58 aircraft in SAC. SAC's bomber crews maintained a 24 hour a day 7 days a week vigil in readiness for an order by the national command authority to conduct retaliatory nuclear bombing raids. This formal process was known as Alert Duty. Crews on alert duty were housed in special facilities which enabled them to become airborne in less than 15 minutes from the time they were alerted (notified). They were alerted by the sound of a klaxon. This was an essential element of the nuclear deterrent concept of the cold war period.   The Navigator-Bombardier program facilities included academic classrooms, flight simulators and airborne flight training. The T-29 aircraft was used for flight training.

The second school was the Electronic Warfare Officer (EWO) training program. It was approximately 11 months in length. The Basic Navigator training was a pre-requisite for this course as well. The training focused on two general areas, each having its application to SAC crews. The first area was called Active Electronic Counter Measures (ECM). Active ECM meant disrupting, disabling or confusing enemy electronics capabilities. Their radars were the primary target but communications frequencies were also targeted. In short Electronic Warfare Officer's task was to jam the enemies' radar and communications systems so as to deny them effective use of them during a war time situation. This was an important feature in SAC missions because it would increase the chances of their aircraft reaching their assigned targets. The second area was called Passive Electronic Counter measures (ECM). Passive ECM meant monitoring and recording enemy radar systems to map their electronic capabilities (airborne reconnaissance). The battle plans for the SAC alert bombing crews were formulated from databases of enemy capabilities. These databases were constantly verified and updated by the reconnaissance crews. The majority of the graduates from the EWO training course were assigned to crews engaged in Active ECM. They staffed the same types of crews as described for graduates of the Navigator-Bombardier program. A small number of the graduates were assigned to the reconnaissance crews based at Forbes AFB in Kansas. The unit specialized in Passive ECM (reconnaissance).

The EWO program included academic courses, simulator lab exercises and flight training. The instructional program was divided into three phases. The first phase was devoted to classroom study of electronic principles. The next two phases, Active ECM and Passive ECM, included classroom academic training, simulator training in the lab and flight training. The C-54 aircraft was used for the flight training. The equipment configuration in the simulator labs and on board the aircraft for the Active ECM phase was the same as the

44

EWO position on the B-52 aircraft used. The equipment configuration for the Passive ECM phase was similar to that used by the EWOs on the B-47s at Forbes.

Mather Air Force Base (AFB)

Most Air Force bases have some housing to accommodate assigned personnel. A common procedure is used at the majority of bases. Those personnel with families are placed on a priority list when they first arrive. Placement on the priority list is based on rank and the number of family members. Many new arrivals must find their own housing in a community near the base until their number on the priority list comes up to fill a vacancy. They are provided an allowance to help cover the added expense. Housing for officers with families are typically 3 or 4 bedroom houses. Non-commissioned Officers (NCO) with families may also be assigned a house or town house style quarters. Visiting officers on temporary assignment and single officers are housed in the Bachelor Officers Quarters (BOQ). The BOQ quarters consist of a single room and a bath. The bath is shared by two adjacent rooms. Each pair of rooms would have a bath room between them with access from either room.

Student Bachelor Officer housing at Mather, however, was different. Single students were quartered in standard three bedroom houses. Three students were assigned to each house. The houses were separated from the main family housing area. The houses did not include garages so the cars were parked on the street. Each house had a full kitchen. Students could and often did do their own cooking. They were expected to perform routine maintenance on the house which included cutting the grass. Most of us hired teenage Air Force dependents to do this. This relieved us of the need to buy a lawn mower. The student housing area was located across the base on the opposite side of the runways form the main part of the base. There was a back entrance adjacent to the student housing area so we could leave without driving around the runway complex. Access to the student housing area was unrestricted. Non-military could drive in without passing any security. Security was not as big an issue on training bases as it is today. Bases with residence operational units had greater security procedures. Social activities in the student housing area were restricted during the week from Sunday evening through Friday afternoon. On the weekends there was often a party in one of the houses.

My house mates were 2nd Lt. Willie Weeks and 2nd Lt. Larry Furth. They were students in the Navigator-Bombardier program and in the same class. They had arrived about two months before me. Both had been in the cadet corps at Harlingen. Willie was from Pekin, Illinois near Peoria. He was a talkative, high energy extrovert. He had a real gift of gab and was popular among the students as well as the girls who were part of most weekend social gatherings in the housing area. Larry was less outgoing but socially active and tended to spend a lot of time following Willie around. He was from New Jersey. Their circle of friends were mostly other students in the Navigator–Bombardier program. I often attended the parties with them but tended to socialize more with several of the students in neighboring houses.

The nearest neighbor was an officer by the name of Albert Parsons who lived in the house next door. He was also in the Electronic Warfare program several classes ahead of me. I believe he also had graduated from the Harlingen Aviation Cadet program. His nickname was "Alby". He had a light complexion and had very reddish hair. Several of his friends from his class called him "Apple". Alby, like myself, would subsequently be assigned to the 55th SRW at Forbes Air Force Base following graduation. He would be killed in an aircraft accident at Incirlik Air Force Base in Adana, Turkey in 1965. I will address that in more detail in a following chapter. Alby married a girl from Minnesota a short time before his graduation. I had a couple of long conversations with her about our home area before they were transferred to Forbes.

The Zurch Bird

First Lt. Don Williams lived across the street from me in student housing and was a close friend. Don had completed Basic Navigation training at James Connally as part the same class as myself, class 63-06. I in the cadet part and he in the commissioned officer part of the program. His assignment after James Connally had been to the Navigator-Bombardier program at Mather. He hailed from Tulsa, Oklahoma. Don had a very wry sense of humor. I never saw him in a bad mood. He had a joke for every situation. I marveled at his ability to recall a joke once he had heard it and then later retell it flawlessly. The Navigator-Bombardier training program was shorter than the Electronic Warfare Officer program so his graduation was a couple of months prior to my own. Following his graduation during the summer of 1963 Don was assigned to Glasgow Air Force Base in Glasgow, Montana as a bombardier on the B-52D aircraft. I would cross paths with Don again several years later in Okinawa.

One day Don asked me if I had ever heard of the Zurch bird. I, of course, had not. He explained that the Zurch bird was a large bird with an extremely long neck similar to a crane. It had a large wingspan, often more than 6 feet. The bird, however, had one problem. One of its wings was only half the size of the other. This meant it could not fly in a straight line. If it wanted to fly from point "A" to point "B" it had to start by offsetting at an angle. When the bird flew longer distances, due its anatomy, it would fly in ever smaller concentric circles. This would obviously continue until it flew up its own asshole. Just prior to entering its own anus it would shriek a loud surprised screech, "ZUURCH", hence its name, the Zurch bird.

He explained that subordinates often feel that their superiors or peers are out of touch with reality similar to an ostrich with its head in the sand. We referred to this as having their head up and locked. I'm sure you can see the analogy. So from that point forward whenever we saw or heard something where we felt someone was out of touch (had their head up and locked) we would look at one another and yell "ZUURCH". If the situation didn't permit us to speak it we would mouth the word "ZUURCH". No one else seemed to understand what we were talking about.

Military Electronics Usage

The use of electronics in warfare expanded rapidly after World War II. The British use of Radar was only one of the early applications. Radios had been used for communications on the battlefield starting not long after its invention by Marconi and DeForest. Monitoring of enemy communications probably started soon thereafter. As the number and capabilities of electronic devices advanced the militaries' use of and the sophistication of its' electronic devices also advanced. By the early 1960s electronic devices were being used in warfare by most nations. The United States Air Force was a front runner in use of electronic systems to monitor and track an enemies' military activity and capabilities as well as to disable, disrupt or confuse an enemies' ability to do the same. It resembled an electronic cat and mouse game.

The United States Air Forces' Strategic Air Command (SAC) become a major player in the use of Electronics in warfare. It had added positions known as Electronic Warfare specialists to many of its Air crews and equipped its combat aircraft with some of the latest technology. Originally, Electronic Warfare Specialist positions were filled by a mixture of enlisted personnel and commissioned officers. The Air Force decided in the early 1960s that all of these specialists should be officers. To implement this policy change all of the enlisted specialists were sent to commissioning schools and became officers. The position name for all of these specialists was now Electronic Warfare Officer (EWO). The new technologies required sophisticated training of specialists to efficiently apply the techniques in the use of increasingly complex equipment. The early Air Force school for certification for EWOs was on Kessler AFB which is located near Biloxi, Mississippi. It remained there until 1961 and was then moved to Mather AFB in California.

Ravens

The use of electronics on the battle field is a relatively recent phenomenon in the history of warfare and is confined to the last century. The earliest use was for communications. Radios were used to communicate between commanders and their units, between units in the field and as propaganda devices to affect the moral of the enemies' troops. It was followed somewhat later by Radar. Radar could be used to track enemy vehicles and aircraft. The active use of Radar in warfare began during the Second World War. The British used Radar to track incoming German aircraft during the battle of Britain. It was a highly classified activity and as a result considered somewhat spooky for the era. In the decade following WWII the use of Radar and electronics in warfare developed rapidly. By the early 1950s most countries had developed Radar nets to monitor aircraft operating near and within their borders. As the use of Radar expanded, the military establishments of most countries began to develop specialists in this area of expertise. The activity, however, remained under a cloak of secrecy and was shrouded in mystery. Those that specialized in electronic applications were seen as secretive and a bit mysterious. The raven has often been portrayed in literature as mysterious. The name "Raven" began to be applied to those working in this mysterious activity. It began as a nickname. By the late 1950s, however, the aircraft manuals had begun to identify the positions engaged in airborne electronic applications as Ravens (i.e. Raven One, Raven Two, etc). The term Raven now applies to Electronic Warfare Officers.

Electronic Warfare School

The art of airborne electronic warfare, as noted earlier; had developed into two distinct areas, Active Electronic Counter Measures (jamming) and Passive Electronic Counter Measures (reconnaissance). The curriculum at Mather began with several weeks of an intensive study of electronic principles. I had taken courses in Physics at St. John's which gave me a good base knowledge of many of the principles. I was familiar with conductors, capacitors, inductors and circuits. The first couple of weeks were easy. It would get harder (multi-vibrators, phased arrays and tuned circuits). I seemed to have an affinity for it, so I did well and enjoyed this phase. We eventually learned how to, in theory, build a radar system from individual components.

The second phase of the program was devoted to Active ECM systems. The equipment configuration that was used in the labs was the same as the EWO position on the B-52 aircraft. We were taught how to operate each piece of equipment. Once we were familiar with the equipment we learned how to monitor for potential threats and to counter those threats with the electronic systems available to us in the lab. We also learned to use a device know as Chaff. Chaff is strips of highly reflective material that can be dispensed into the air. These strips would appear on the enemy radar scopes as additional aircraft or more precisely as false targets. In the labs, this of course, could only be simulated. We had to pass several graded labs to complete this phase and advance to the next. Flight training mirrored the lab exercises. The actual jamming done on flights was limited and selective. The flights were conducted in the U.S. and the Air Force did not want us to disrupt our own systems.

Active ECM had become an increasingly important aspect of air warfare. During the Viet Nam conflict the Air Force instituted a new mission entitled the Wild Weasel program. The Wild Weasel program used fighter aircraft with an extra seat for an EWO. These were specially configured aircraft whose job was to use active electronic countermeasures in defense of an accompanying strike force and target and destroy enemy Surface-To-Air Missile (SAM) systems. Today, most offensive aircraft operations involve some form of Active ECM.

The next phase of training was devoted to Passive ECM. The equipment in the labs included receivers, pulse analyzers and recording equipment. SAC's reconnaissance crews recorded electronic intercepts of interest so they could be analyzed in detail later in the labs. Electronic intelligence gathering supports both tactical and strategic goals. The Strategic Air Command's (SAC) reconnaissance crews were tasked with gathering electronic intelligence primarily for strategic planning purposes. Knowing the enemy's capabilities is the objective of the intelligence forces of every country. It allows them to make accurate assessments in their decisions to use or not use military force. Inadequate intelligence on the battlefield often leads to overreaction. The Strategic Air Command maintained several data bases that were an assessment of enemy electronic capabilities. The primary job of the SAC EWO, involved in reconnaissance, is to maintain (update and verify) the accuracy of those data bases. They are used to plan mission profiles. In SAC it was used to plan mission profiles for the alert forces to enhance their ability to reach their targets and complete their mission.

C-54 use in the Berlin Airlift

Each of phases of training following the basic electronics phase included lab exercises as well as flight training. The aircraft used was the aging C-54. The group of aircraft used in our training had served several roles in the preceding years. One of those roles had been during the Berlin Airlift in 1948. Our aircraft had several holes in the hull of the aircraft. I remember seeing pencils of sunlight shinning through these holes. As the aircraft turned the end of the pencil of light would track along the interior of the aircraft. Coal had been one of the major commodities transported to Berlin during the airlift. This was clear to us. I remember slapping the interior side of the aircraft and raising a cloud of fine coal dust.

Receiving Our Assignments

My Electronic Warfare class was scheduled to graduate in early September of 1963. The next Permanent Change of Station (PCS) duty assignment for members of the class would be to a Strategic Air Command (SAC) operational unit as a member of a flight crew. The assignment process was completed in early August. A block (a list equal to the number of graduates) of duty assignments was allotted to the class. The same method of distributing assignments that had been used at James Connally was used again. We would take turns selecting from the list. The selection sequence was based on the final class standing (academics and flight training). The man at the top of the list was given first choice, then the second in line a choice of the remaining assignments and so on until all the assignments were gone and each of us had one. A Major from the school met with the class as a group and the selection of assignments was completed. I again ranked about a third of the way down the list.

The assignment list included 5 slots to B58 aircraft. This was the Air Force's lone supersonic bomber. Most of us considered these to be the best assignments on the list. The B58s were based at Bunker Hill AFB in Indiana. It was the newest bomber in the SAC inventory and the most sophisticated. The Raven rode in a seat surrounded by an ejection capsule which would slam shut during the ejection sequence. The capsule would protect them from the wind blast if they had to eject at supersonic speeds. There were two assignments to the reconnaissance wing at Forbes AFB (the 55th SRW) in Topeka. They flew the B-47 aircraft. The remaining slots were to bomb wings flying B-52 aircraft. As expected, all of the B58 slots were taken before it got to me. I would have to decide between a bomb wing (active ECM) or reconnaissance (passive ECM) slot. I knew that the bomber wings all stood alert duty. Alert crews would be confined to the alert area for several days, 24 hours a day. They had to be ready to respond at a moments notice. We had also heard rumors that General Curtis LeMay had been very tough on his bomb wings and his successor, General Powers, was continuing that posture. None of this appealed to me. So, when it came to my turn, I selected one of the two slots to the 55th at Forbes AFB. Again, I knew nothing about the unit or its mission. I had, as before, been forced to select (at least in my mind) the lesser of two poor choices. On August 13, 1963, 1st Lt. Roger Busch and I received orders assigning us to the 21st Strategic Aerospace Division at Forbes AFB effective October 1, 1963.

Chapter 5   Air Force Survival School

Survival School

Each of the Air Force's specialty fields has a training track that personnel assigned to that specialty must complete before they are considered to be fully qualified and are placed in an operational unit. The courses vary considerably in length. The courses for flying specialties, Pilot, Navigator, Boom Operator, Load Master, etc are some of the longest and most intense. There are also a number of courses that are not tied to any particular specialty. They addressed specific needs of a particular theatre of operation, an operational situation, an individual command's specific requirements or in response to crisis situations that the Air Force must respond to. The Basic Survival Course is a one of these courses that all combat ready flying personnel must complete as a one time requirement. Combat ready crews are those whose mission might involve combat with an enemy. Flying personnel normally complete the course after their initial specialty courses and prior to their first assignment to an operational unit.

The need for survival training was recognized by the military leadership after the Korean conflict. There had not been a formal course to that point in time that was designed to prepare our military personnel to cope with the survival situations that they might face. This was particularly true for those who faced the prospect of captivity as Prisoners Of War (POWs). Military personnel had traditionally been briefed that they were required to provide their captors with their name, rank and serial number and nothing further. This was formalized with the ratification of the Geneva Convention accords. The majority of the countries of the world were signatory to those accords. The concerns of our military hierarchy in this area increased dramatically following the Korean conflict, as a result of the poor performance of U. S. military personnel as Prisoners Of War (POWs). Flying personnel generally operated over enemy territory and were therefore a vulnerable group. Much of the curriculum for the school was developed with flying personnel in mind.

The Basic Survival Course was attended by Air Force personnel in a variety of work specialties but the curriculum was geared to address

53

the needs of flight crew members. Airplanes do not always safety reach their planned destination. This is a fact that is quite significant for military flights. The nature of military flying deems that much of it is done over inhospitable, unfriendly or even hostile territory. Fortunately it is infrequent but airplanes do crash land and crew members are forced to bail out of airplanes. When it occurs it may happen over land or water. Even when it occurs over friendly territory the locale may be inhospitable. Basic survival skills may mean the difference between life and death. When it occurs over hostile territory evasion skills are needed. When crew members are captured escape and evasion skills are needed. Each of these skill sets was the subject of a separate phase in the Air Force's Basic Survival school curriculum.

The Basic Survival Training course in September of 1963 was held at Stead Air Force Base (AFB). Stead AFB is located near Reno, Nevada. The course was three weeks in length. Graduates of both of the courses at Mather AFB accomplished this training as a Temporary Duty (TDY) assignment while en-route to their first operational assignment. As the classes at Mather approached their graduation date rumors would circulate among the students concerning some of the more stressful aspects of the survival training course. These rumors often originated with acquaintances from earlier classes that had recently completed the course. The subject was widely discussed. It didn't occur to us that the stories may have been embellished. I think it is fair to say that most of us looked toward our upcoming time at Stead with some sense of foreboding. We could be certain that the instructors would be using techniques to test our resolve and our ability to cope.

I drove up to Stead from Sacramento on September 17th. The training was to start the following day. Stead AFB was much higher in elevation than Mather had been. It was in the foothills of the Sierra Nevada mountain range. The curriculum included academic as well as practical training exercises. The survival course curriculum was designed to prepare Air Force flight crews to cope with the most likely survival situations they might face. The first week was devoted to academics. That was the easy part of the course. The academics

54

covered techniques and principles that we would practice during the practical phases.

Survival Kits

Survival kits were a regular part of the equipment on all combat ready Air Force aircraft. The contents of the kit, over time, had been standardized. The same kit was used for both over land and over water flights. The kit was in the form of a seat pack. The pack was approximately 20 inches square and about 18 inches deep. Aircraft with ejection seats normally had a well that was part of the seat into which the kit could be fitted. The crew member then sat on top of the kit. In other aircraft the kits was stacked in an aisle readily accessible if needed. The kit had two webbed straps attached, one on either side. At the end of each strap was a clip type receptacle. The crewmember's parachute harness had two heavy metal rings which were clipped into the kit's receptacles. A dingy for over water use was part of the kit. It could be activated by pulling a lanyard. Pulling the lanyard would inflate the dingy. The dingy was just large enough to accommodate a single person in the sitting position. Pulling the lanyard was delayed until the crewmember had left the aircraft and the parachute had opened. A full day of the academics was devoted to the contents of the survival kit and the intended usage of the equipment.

The kit contained most of the typical items you might find in a boy scout's camping kit such as canteen, fire starter, water purification tablets, etc. There were also food items. The food items included Pemmican bars, dried fruit bars and water pouches. Pemmican is a dried meat product. It is highly concentrated and difficult to eat in its raw form. It is intended to be mixed with water and heated to make a meat stew. The kit also contained bilingual conversation books in several languages, coins from several countries that could be used to pay for goods or help. Finally it had a collapsible 22 caliber rifle with ammunition for hunting game.

Prisoner of War Training

Military personnel are expected to adhere to specific standards of conduct. These standards are drilled into them during training from the time they enter military service and continuing throughout their active service career. The standards are dependent on the situation in which they are operating. Historically, military personnel who became Prisoners Of War (POW) were expected to resist efforts by an enemy interrogator to extract meaningful military information from them. The United States military POW code of conduct permitted the prisoner to provide only their name, rank and military service number to their captors and nothing more. This code seemed to work reasonably well in the wars our soldiers had fought in up to the time of the Korean War. The Korean War POWs faced a different kind of environment. The techniques used by the Chinese interrogators went well beyond anything that had been used before. Their techniques attempted to break the POW down mentally and render them compliant and easy to manipulate. In several cases they even attempted to get the POW to admit to heinous war crimes. These confessions would then be used for purposes of propaganda. The techniques become popularized in the press of the era as Brain Washing. The techniques focused more on mental torture rather than physical torture. The record of our Korean War POWs to adhere to their expected code of conduct had been very poor. In fact, at the end of the conflict 23 of our servicemen, who had been POWs, refused to be repatriated. They elected to stay in North Korea rather than return home. The press dubbed them Turncoats. One of the 23 was from the small town of Alden, Minnesota which was close to where I grew up. The problem was considered severe enough to prompt the military leadership to take an in depth look at the state of preparedness. It had become apparent to our leadership that almost everyone had their breaking point. If the proper techniques were applied the vast majority of POWs could be forced to their breaking point.

The Geneva Convention had established rules that applied to the treatment of POWs. The majority of countries were signatory to that convention. Several of the techniques used by the Chinese interrogators violated these rules. The techniques were also forbidden by the United States Uniform Code of Military Justice (UCMJ). Our leadership recognized that in spite of the fact that these techniques were illegal our servicemen may still be faced with their use. Our servicemen needed some new coping skills. This thinking had resulted in a dramatic and relatively recent change in the course curriculum regarding POW behavior. The academic portion of the course spent a full day on these new coping skills. The starting point of this concept was to recognize that we, as prisoners, would likely not be able to adhere to the name, rank and serial number rules indefinitely. This was only a starting point of our resistance. As a POW's resolve weakened we were taught how to feed the enemy with bits of seemingly creditable information that was in fact erroneous. It gave the POW options beyond pure stiff backed resistance until it was no longer possible. This might also shift the value of the POW toward being an information source rather than one who was confessing to a heinous crime to be used for propaganda. We would get the opportunity to practice these skills in the practical exercises that were expected during week three of the course.

Practical Exercises

The second week was the start of the practical exercises. This part of the training was broken up into four separate phases. The first of these phases was devoted to surviving in inhospitable territory. The downed airmen's survival kit provided some help but surviving often meant being able to live off the land for food, water and shelter. The phase was four days long and conducted in the field in a wilderness type area. We remained in the field for the full time and camped out at night without the benefit of tents. Most of us were clad in a summer flight suit and flight jacket. We would stay in these clothes for the duration of this phase and the one that followed it which covered a period of five and a half days. The location where both of these phases would normally have been conducted was in a public wilderness area. Deer hunting season was in progress when we were scheduled to begin and the area was open to hunters. To prevent us from becoming a target for reckless hunters the training was moved to a nearby game preserve which was at a still higher elevation. The nights in early October at that elevation were quite cold. During the first 4 days we were broken into small groups of 7 or 8 and guided by an instructor. He taught us techniques to survive in the wilderness. Our food supply was rations in the standard survival kit and what we could scavenge in the wild. We learned how to set snares to trap game, select edible wild plants and use the rations in the standard Air Force survival kit. My group set snares, but were unsuccessful in catching anything. The survival kit contained Pemmican meat bars, dried fruit bars and water pouches. Pemmican could be eaten raw and cold, but it was highly concentrated, so it was advisable to drink lots of water with it. Cold Pemmican was difficult to eat unless you were very hungry. Later in the next phase I became hungry enough to try pemmican straight. Our guide had us make a broth with it as a hot meal. During the days we normally stayed on the move. We followed our guide. Most of us felt that our guide was part mountain goat. He seemed to be able walk forever at a rapid pace and up any grade no matter how steep. He was also not very tolerant when we had trouble keeping up.

At the end of the four days we started the next phase. This was devoted to evasion skills. Our hypothetical situation had changed from being down in inhospitable territory to down in hostile territory. We were divided into teams of two people and given a map of the game preserve. The task was to travel in pairs over land to a designated point about 15 miles away. We started this phase at the point where the previous phase had ended. Our guide left us and we were on our own with only the map and our training to rely on. Since the situation called for evading in hostile territory we would also have to deal with hostile personnel (the school's instructors) that were out looking for us. They would have vehicles. If we were caught they would punch a card we had been provided with and let us go. Two punches on your card and you had failed the phase and must redo it with the next class.

My partner was an airmen first class (3 stripes) named Roger. He was with the Green Berets. The Green Berets, at that time, were a Special Forces group. The Special Forces command was a small command within the Air Force that used unconventional techniques. They operated in small groups, often behind enemy lines. Their mode of operation was to gather intelligence, engage in hit and run tactics or go behind enemy lines to make a surgical kill on a specified target. They also acted as advisors to foreign military units. Roger had already completed two temporary duty (TDY) tours in South Viet Nam attached to one of their units as an advisor. As advisors they would be attached to a South Vietnamese unit. They would be the only non-Vietnamese in the unit and a prized target for the enemy, the Viet Cong. I should remind the reader at this point that the Tonkin Gulf incident, the incident that led to the American involvement in South Viet Nam, did not occur until August of 1964. American combat units did not enter the conflict until February of 1965. This was October of 1963. The war in Viet Nam was being fought solely by South Vietnamese troops. The advisors were providing unofficial assistance.

The Green Berets were required to be in exceptionally good physical condition. Roger certainly was. I had been on the college wrestling team and was a regular runner so I also was in very good physical condition. The terrain in this area was very hilly. Roger and I studied the map. Roger advised that it was best to stay to the higher terrain. The bad guys would likely stay near their vehicles which would be confined to the valleys. We also thought it best to go to the edge of the preserve and trek along the outer edge. This would lengthen our route by several miles and greatly increase the number of hills to climb and descend. We reasoned that most people would use the shortest and easiest route which went through the valley area. This is also where you might expect the majority of the enemy to be. On our route the chances of encountering any enemy personnel would be small. We could also travel faster without the need to maintain constant concealment to avoid detection. Since we were both in good shape the added distance was not considered to be a problem.

The trek began at about 3PM in the afternoon. We reached the edge of the preserve in about four hours. We paused to rest and realized that we were both quite hungry. The amount of food we had eaten during the previous 4 days was minimal. Our snares hadn't yielded a thing and berries were not very filling. We had been taught to be careful in the use of fires to cook in hostile territory. It can quickly give your position away to an enemy that is searching for you. So we tried to eat the Pemmican raw. It was difficult to swallow and made you very thirsty. We had a good supply of water in the canteens and there were numerous sources along the way to refill them. We walked until the sun was setting. We decided to bed down in the open and went to sleep. It was a cold and fretful night.

Bright and early the next morning we continued our trek. We had not seen a single one of our class mates and really didn't expect to. About noon of the second day we reached the top of a fairly steep hill. From our vantage point we saw a camp site about a half a mile ahead. There were several people in the camp. We concealed ourselves in bushes and watched them for a while. The map indicated that they were outside of the game preserve. There were about 5 men in the camp. All of them had on hunter's garb. To the best of our knowledge the enemy (instructors) would not have been dressed in hunter's clothes. So we crept in closer. We could see that two of them were drinking a beer. It was clear they were not our instructors acting as enemy. We walked into the camp. They looked a bit surprised to see us in our dingy green flight suits. We had not changed clothes nor groomed ourselves for 5 days so we must have been quite a sight. We soon struck up a good conversation with them. They were in fact hunters. They offered us something to eat (hot dogs) and a beer. We accepted the food but not the beer. It would have made the remainder of the trek a lot more difficult.

Roger and I reached the destination point about 5 PM that evening. The busses were not scheduled to pick us up until noon the next day. Nobody else was around. We had been the first to arrive. Dead tired and with nothing to do but to wait we lay down and went to sleep. We were awakened by a rain storm and realized that it was getting dark. So we moved under the cover of a downed tree and went back to sleep. The next pair to arrive was at day break the next morning. We had beaten all the other pairs by about 12 hours.

The busses arrived at noon to take us back to the base. Two of the pairs had not yet reported in so two of the instructors remained at the spot in a van to wait for them. We returned to the base, a shower and blissful sleep. We later learned that one of the missing pairs arrived several hours later but the final pair never did arrive. They were located by an Air Force rescue helicopter two days later some 10 miles outside of the game preserve.

The third practical phase was a mock prison camp. On Monday of the third week we reported to the classroom, as instructed, dressed in our fatigues. They briefed us on the rules of the game for the prison camp. The camp would be out of doors with no cover surrounded by a high fence. We would be divided into groups of 5 or 6. At night the entire camp would be lit by overhead spot lights. Each group would be seated together but separated by 10 yards or so from the other groups. We would be prohibited by the guards from any communication between the groups. The camp would last through Tuesday night (about a day and a half). We were expected to attempt escapes. To provide some incentive for escaping the lead instructor explained the final rule. Anyone who successfully escaped without physically confronting the guards and was able to move undetected to a lighted flag pole about a hundred yards away would be excused from further participation in the camp. The classroom instruction dealt with several techniques that we might use. One that was discussed was to create a diversion to cover an escape attempt by others.

At about noon we were loaded into busses and driven to the entrance of an obstacle course. The course was covered in vegetation growth to a height of about 12 inches. It also had numerous trip wires that would set off flares. We would have to avoid them. The task was to navigate through the course staying under the cover of the vegetation. Several instructors were stationed around the perimeter of the course to try to detect our position. If we were detected they would direct us back to the start of the course to try again.

The obstacle course was intended to simulate our having been downed in enemy territory and attempting to hide from (evade) an enemy that was aware of our presence and looking for us. We had to move through the course on our bellies. You had to use your elbows to move along the ground in the manner of a snake. If you raised your head up so that instructors along the edge of the course could see you they took you back to the starting point. It took me about two hours to get through the course. As we exited the obstacle course enemy guards were there to capture us. We were taken to an open area and instructed to sit and wait for the rest to finish. It was late afternoon before the last of our class completed the course. We were marched as a large group to the camp which was about a half mile away, instructed to break up into the pre-arranged groups of 5 or 6 and each group was led to their assigned area inside the camp fence.

The guards periodically wandered between the groups to ensure that there was no communication between them. They chastised us even if we spoke within our own group. We were forced to whisper and try to conceal our efforts to communicate. One of the other groups decided to lie down and pass the time by sleeping. The guards made it clear this was not allowed. We were to sit up. It became quite cold after the sun went down. The temperature had been in the high 40s during the day and was now much lower. We were expected to just sit there in clothing not suited for the conditions. Occasionally one of the guards would roust a group and have them do push-ups or sit-ups. We actually welcomed this because it let us warm up.

My group did develop an escape plan. The retaining fence was only woven wire and did not appear to be too tight. We felt it was loose enough to lift it and roll under it. The plan was for two of our group to get into an argument and start wrestling with each other. We decided to wait until the guards got tired of wandering around and gathered by the entrance gate for conversation, coffee etc. On queue one member of our group jumped up and started to yell at another of the group. This attracted the immediate attention of the guards. Several of them came running over. The two guys began to wrestle each other. This was our queue to move toward the fence. The fence was about 15 yards from our area. We managed to roll to the fence before the guards had physically separated the wrestling pair. We found that we could indeed raise the fence enough to roll under. Once under the fence we continued to roll as fast as we could until we were out of the camp's overhead lights and into the dark. We stood up and started to walk as rapidly as we could without making a lot of noise. After proceeding about a hundred yards we stopped to get our bearings. We couldn't see the flag pole. We felt that it must be on the opposite side of the camp obscured by the camp's lights. So we set a course perpendicular to a line running through the camp. It was hard to move in the pitch dark over rough terrain without making noise. Progress was very slow. After a short while we did indeed see the flag pole on the opposite side of the camp. We set a course for the flag. We had passed abreast of the camp and made it about half way to the flag when a flashlight came on near us. We stopped dead in our tracks. The flashlight was obviously searching. We just stood there hoping we could wait it out. Unfortunately, it eventually moved over us and we were detected. Suddenly several flashlights came on and they were all focused on us. We had been re-captured.

POW Interrogations

The prison camp ended on Tuesday afternoon. The final phase was devoted to prisoner of war interrogations. It covered two and a half days of the third week. A significant part of the academic training had been devoted to this subject. As noted earlier, the rules for American soldiers who became POWs during the Korean conflict was to give your name, rank and serial number and nothing more. This had not worked well. The Chinese interrogators had used methods that proved far more effective than any our troops had previously had to face. They had minimized physical abuse and relied heavily on psychological methods and sleep deprivation. The methods were popularized in the press as <u>Brain Washing</u>. Our training recognized the effectiveness of the Chinese methods. The conclusion was that, given enough time, these methods could eventually break almost anyone. The American military establishment recognized the need for a different approach. We were taught to resist as much as possible. When this became too difficult, provide some false or misleading information that the enemy would accept. During the practical phase we were expected to try these techniques.

This phase began at sun down on Tuesday night. We had returned that afternoon from the prison camp phase and were not given time to rest or clean up. We were transported directly to the classroom. None of us had been allowed any sleep the previous night. In the classroom each of us was given an individual mission profile and a situation that had led us to be captured. We were given an hour or so to develop how we might provide some misinformation during the interrogations. When the bus arrived at the POW camp, each of us was given a helmet bag. The helmet bag was a bag about 12 inches square that a crew member's crash helmet would be kept in when not in use. A guard placed mine over my head and then I was led to a cell. I realized that I would have to rely mainly on hearing from this point on. As soon as I was sure the cell door was closed I removed the helmet bag to survey the scene. It was very dark in the cell but I could tell that it was about 3 feet square. There was no window. There was an empty coffee can on the floor. This was to be used to urinate in. The cells were tall enough to stand up in but not wide enough to lie down. We were instructed to always stand with the bag over our heads. The guards would come by and periodically knock on the door. When they knocked on our door we were required to respond "here". They could tell by listening to our response whether we were standing or sitting. Sitting was forbidden. I soon discovered that one could sit down with your back against the wall, extend your feet in front of you with the knees bent and sleep. It was very cold. I was shivering at times. I must have been exhausted because I was still able to sleep. The cells were obviously in a row. When the guards made the rounds and knocked on the doors, you could hear them work their way down the line. My cell must have been well down the line so I had ample warning they were coming. I would stand up and respond. When they were gone I would sit back down. This worked well until one time the knocks didn't wake me up. I didn't respond. The door came open. The urine can I had used a couple of hours earlier was thrown over me. I was lead out of my cell to an area for special treatment. It was a maze of small boxes. I was forced into one of the boxes by two guards. The box was not large enough to sit up in. You had to assume the fetal position. My legs were forced up to where my knees were against my chest. I had to bow my head forward to touch my knees. My toes still stuck out slightly. They closed the door forcing my toes up. It was a good thing that I was not claustrophobic. I later learned that they would leave us there for a maximum of 20 minutes. They kept a chart tracking the time we were in these boxes. The circulation in your legs would be restricted and

64

they would become numb. When the door was opened again I fell out and slumped toward the ground. My legs wouldn't support my weight. Two guards caught me. After about a minute or so when some circulation had returned to my legs, I was able to stand and walk. They returned me to my cell. The checking rounds continued all night. I was very cold in the cell. I had discovered that the small box was much warmer. So, when the door closed, I sat down and went to sleep. I was caught sleeping twice more that night and received the same special treatment. I had found it warmer to undergo the special treatment in the small box than to stay in my cell.

The next morning the interrogations began. I was subjected to several interrogation sessions on each of the next two days. I don't remember which specific techniques were used during each session but I do remember some of the techniques that were used. Let me describe a few of them. Each session began with my being led by a guard from my cell, helmet bag still over my head, to a building and guided through a door. I could hear them slide a chair up behind me and I was told to sit down. One of the guards would then remove the helmet bag. I was immediately blinded by several high intensity spot lights focused on me. The questioning normally began with two interrogators screaming questions. One would start directly in front of me while the second walked around behind me. Both moved throughout the session occasionally walking behind me as the questioning continued. One of them would suddenly move in close and would be nose to nose then move away near the lights. It was impossible to focus on either one of them. I would be squinting badly and only be able to make out the outline when they moved away into the lights. I attempted to follow the training by starting with only my name, rank and serial number the first session and providing some misinformation during later sessions. They would get angry and order me to drop down and do 15 pushups. This procedure was repeated for several cycles. I was able to do the pushups in rapid succession. Our warm up sessions during my college wrestling practices had required us to do 75 pushups so the 15 at a time proved to be relatively easy for me. I could sense a little frustration in their voices. After a few of these cycles the guard behind me would put the helmet bag back over my head, wait several minutes then remove the helmet bag. My eyes would have to continually adjust. During one of the sessions the two guards left me alone for a while and a third guard entered. His tone would be soft and consolatory. He offered me a cigarette. He tried to convince me that the treatment would improve greatly if I would be more cooperative. Our academic training had referred to this as the good guy/bad guy technique.

The course obviously was designed to expose us to the effects of disorientation and sleep deprivation. We were kept continuously in the dark – with the helmet bag over our heads – except when we were surrounded by high intensity spot lights. This had the effect of losing track of the time of day and having some difficulty focusing on things that were going on around us. Another technique that I recall was to place the helmet bag back over my head. I was then instructed to stand up, raise my arms above my head and hold them there for extended periods of time. All but one of the techniques used were stressful to me but were tolerable. The one that I found difficult to cope with was the water treatment. For this technique, I was placed on a table and strapped down so I could not move my arms or legs. A thin cloth was placed over my face so I could not see what they were doing. One of them held my head so I could not move it from side to side. They then poured several pitchers of water over the cloth and onto my face. It gave me the sensation of drowning. I tried to hold my breath until they had finished a pitcher but they would stop and start so this did not work very well. I still got a lot of water up my nose and started coughing. They would pause between the pitchers so I wouldn't know when the next one was coming. This particular technique was described to us during the critique of the course as one which was prohibited by the Geneva Accords but had been used by the Chinese interrogators on U.S. Korean War prisoners. It has received wide attention at the time of writing of this book as one now being used by U.S. interrogators. The press has called the technique Water Boarding. Fortunately, this technique was only used on me during one session.

One of the important purposes of our experiences during these practical exercises, particularly during the prisoner interrogations, was to demonstrate to each of us that we had a far greater capacity to tolerate and cope than we realized. I found this to be true. While it was obviously impossible to fully duplicate these survival situations we had at least been exposed to them and would be better prepared if we had to face them in the future.

The final day, a Friday, was reserved for graduation. The ceremony was finished by noon which gave me time to return to Mather AFB where my belongings remained. I had a couple of days to clear the house on the base and prepare to travel to my assignment at Forbes AFB, some 1800 miles away. I spent a lot of this time sleeping. I had one unfinished piece of business to complete before I left the Sacramento area.

Buying a Comet Caliente

About a month before I completed my training at Mather I decided to look for a new car. Many of my class mates had a similar idea. The Ford Falcon that I had purchased a year earlier was still in good condition but many of my class mates had bought fancier cars. I had seen a number of their convertibles and wanted one myself. So I made the rounds of the dealerships and settled on a light blue Mercury Comet. It was a convertible. The model name was the Caliente. The list price was $3500, a good deal more expensive than the $1200 I had paid for the Falcon. It was a larger and definitely fancier car. The salesman was a recently retired Air Force Sergeant. I was hesitant on the price. The salesman was aware that I had been reassigned and would be leaving the state within a few days. He indicated that there was a way to avoid the sales tax. He suggested that I take delivery across the border in Nevada. I would not have to pay the sales tax. I was skeptical as to how this could be accomplished. He said that I would drive the Falcon and he would drive the Caliente into Nevada. We would get the title transfers notarized there and the transaction would be complete and I could continue toward Kansas from there. He would return to Sacramento with the Falcon. He also raised the offer for my Falcon. This was enough to convince me. I consented to buy the car.

The next afternoon, a Saturday, the salesman and I left Sacramento for the Nevada border. We stopped in a small town by the name of Stateline, Nevada. He had to work that day so we got a late start and it was dark by the time we arrived in Stateline. He said the only notary available at that time of the day would be a justice of the peace. The salesman explained to me that in Nevada towns they worked later hours. He had obviously done this before. It took us about a half an hour to locate a Justice of the Peace to notarize our documents. When we entered the building it became clear why the justices kept late hours. There was a line of people. They were in pairs standing side by side. Each pair had one young woman and one young man. In front of us was an obvious Saturday night marriage mill. The salesman and I took our place in the line, I, a crew cut young man and he, a short, bald, middle aged man. As each couple reached the front of the line the couple behind them would move to the side and act as their witnesses (best man and bridesmaid I guess). Following a short ceremony they would both sign the documents and the witnesses would move to the front of the line and be married. When the couple immediately in front of us had their turn we acted as their witnesses. The salesman was on the bridesmaid side. Then it was our turn. The justice of the peace gave us a dirty look and said "Now, just what do you guys have in mind". We were quick to let him know we only wanted a car title transfer notarized. He notarized our documents and we were quickly on our way

Travel To Forbes

It was evening when I took possession of my new car. I immediately left for Kansas. The route I took was through nearby Reno to Las Vegas. I then used Route 66 which I picked up an hour or so southeast of Las Vegas. I would follow Route 66 as far as Oklahoma City. Then I would turn north to Wichita and finally use the Kansas Turnpike to Topeka. The Interstate highway system, which was started during the Eisenhower administration, was not yet complete. Route 66 was still one of the major east/west routes. Route 66 would become famous as the subject of a popular sit-com of the era. When the interstate system was completed major portions of Route 66 fell into disuse. I arrived in Las Vegas during the early morning hours of the following day. I was stopped at a stop light when I saw a well dressed man hitchhiking. I asked him where he was going. He said New York City. I advised him that I was going thru Oklahoma City and offered to take him that far. He got in the car. This is something I would definitely not do today. I did not see it as risky at that time. He was well dressed and well groomed. His story, if true, was an unusual one. He said that he had been the manager of a small radio station in San Francisco. He had gone through a divorce. California law was apparently quite strict in awarding joint assets entirely to the wife. He said she got everything. He was headed to New York to work for a radio station there. It was a fascinating story. I'm not sure how true it was but he was obviously an educated man and was very courteous. I dropped him off in Oklahoma City and continued to Topeka. It had taken me two days to drive nearly 2000 miles. I checked into the Bachelor Officers Quarters (BOQ) at Forbes AFB and went to bed.

Chapter 6   The 55ᵗʰ Strategic Reconnaissance Wing

Intelligence Gathering

My arrival at Forbes Air Force Base (AFB) marked my entry into our nations' intelligence gathering community. Most of the countries of the world engage in some form of gathering intelligence and do so for a wide variety of reasons. Many of our large corporate enterprises do as well. The activity takes several forms, some of which are seen as legitimate while others are clandestine in nature and are often seen as illegitimate. The latter is frequently referred to as spying or espionage, at least by those that are the subject of this clandestine scrutiny. Spying has been an ongoing activity by one group on another since antiquity. It is used during periods of peace and periods of warfare. The need for the intelligence that it provides is intensified during periods of warfare and serves both tactical and strategic objectives. Tactically to know what the enemy is doing on the battle field, strategically to determine their power relative to one another and plan future actions. Historically, where large disparities in this power relationship between two countries existed it often prompted the stronger country to start a war against the weaker one. A variety of reasons would be offered to justify their actions but in reality this attitude was often embodied in the phrase "I do because I can". Most of the wars throughout history had been fought as "All Out Warfare". The intent was to subdue your enemy and the conflict was continued until one of them submitted to unconditional surrender or was vanquished.

In 1945 the nature of warfare changed. The world had entered a new era of unprecedented destructive power. This new era had been ushered in by the use of an atomic bomb dropped on a major Japanese city with devastating affect. The destruction from that single weapon was unprecedented. The "All Out Warfare", concept which characterized pre-1945 wars, was now viewed as obsolete. As the possession of this weapon proliferated it became clear to everyone that its' wide spread use could effectively destroy life as we know it on the planet. There would be no winner. All parties to such a conflict would lose.

The first decade of this new era, which followed the end of World War Two, saw the development of a fierce rivalry between the United

70

States and the Soviet Union. The rivalry intensified and expanded from a power confrontation between major powers to a competition to align as many of the other countries of the world as possible into opposing alliances. Relationships by the two major powers with other countries were increasingly viewed from the perspective of "You are with us or you are against us". This attitude became the flavor of international relations for the next several decades. The confrontation, while clearly hostile in intent, did not involve the armed conflict of a Hot War (maneuvering armies on the field of battle). It was thus referred to as the Cold War. This Cold War came to be characterized more by posturing rather than open armed conflict. While armed conflicts continued to occur there was no open warfare (Hot War) directly between the two major powers. Most incidents of armed conflict were supported by one of the major powers with materials and/or troops. The majority of the conflicts were fought in the context of the Cold War but never involved troops from the major powers actually facing off against one another. Unrestrained direct open warfare between the two major powers,   both of whom possessed the new weaponry, was now unthinkable. Military planning on both sides of the divide was viewed through the Cold War lens. Possession of the new weaponry acted as a deterrent to direct action. Several of the armed conflicts that did occur were fought as Proxy Wars. Prime examples of these Proxy Wars were the Viet Nam conflict and the war by the Soviet Union in Afghanistan. In Viet Nam US troops did not face Soviet troops in a direct conflict but the Russians supplied and trained Vietnamese troops that fought the US. In Afghanistan the roles were reversed. The nuclear standoff was seen as a deterrent to the actual use of the weapon. The Military concept for this standoff was referred to as Mutually Assured Destruction or MAD, a clearly appropriate tab.

The nature of intelligence gathering, by the United States, during this Cold War period had also changed. This change was driven by two primary factors. The first, of course, was the changed nature of warfare itself, as described above. Intelligence for strategic objectives became paramount. Tactical battlefield intelligence became less important. The second change was a shift to a heavier reliance on technology. The Second World War had stimulated a dramatic increase in the pace of technological development. The advances occurred in multiple aspects of warfare. The advances in aircraft development in particular were unprecedented and mind boggling. This technological drive continued after the war ended and was further driven by the rivalry between the Soviet Union and the United States.

Intelligence gathering methods, even the clandestine variety, are much easier to conduct in an open society such as the United States. The Soviet Union and its' satellite countries in Eastern Europe became a closed society. It was as if a curtain had been drawn around them to restrict the movement of peoples and information into or out of. This curtain like barrier became popularized in the press and in the minds of our leaders as the Iron Curtain, a term coined by Winston Churchill in a speech he gave in Missouri. (1) This situation gave the Soviet Union a distinct advantage in the intelligence gathering aspect of the confrontation. In hindsight, we have to admit that the Soviets' espionage efforts had been highly successful. At the conclusion of World War Two the United States was in sole possession of this new weaponry, nuclear (atomic and hydrogen) bombs. This provided us with a huge advantage in this developing rivalry. The Soviet Union had negated this advantage by the early 1950s. They had acquired the technology, through highly successful espionage efforts within the United States, to produce nuclear weapons. The potential for Mutually Assured Destruction became a reality and drove the politics of the two countries for the next several decades.

The United States faced a more difficult task in its intelligence gathering activities. Penetrating the Iron Curtain presented a huge problem. Without the ease of moving agents (spies) in to position, an advantage the Soviets enjoyed in the United States, we came to rely more on technology. Intelligence gathering by air assumed a major role. During the late 1940s and early 1950s the Air Force conducted numerous flights around the periphery of and occasionally penetrating Soviet territory for the purpose of gathering data on Soviet military postures and capabilities. The flights, which penetrated Soviet airspace, focused on areas where their defenses were minimal. The U-2 aircraft, developed by the Lockheed aircraft company, could fly high enough to avoid all of the Soviet defensive systems. The U-2 program conducted flights over the Soviet heartland. The Soviets, of course, responded to these activities. Several US aircraft were attacked both within and near Soviet airspace. The incidents were, however, sporadic. Some US aircraft were shot down and numerous aircraft returned to base with bullet holes.

Soviet defensive systems improved over time. On May 1, 1960 a U-2, flown by Francis Gary Powers, was downed over the Russian heartland by a Soviet Surface-To-Air (SAM) missile. (2) By the early 1960s, most of the flights which penetrated Soviet airspace were discontinued. Peripheral flights just outside of Soviet airspace were continued. Technology continued to improve. Within a few years satellite technology allowed unfettered over flight surveillance which provided intelligence far beyond the level of the 1950s and 1960s. During the last decade or so, Unmanned Aerial Vehicles (UAVs) have assumed a major role. In the period which preceded the development of satellites, the period that is the subject of this book, aerial reconnaissance by manned aircraft bore the heaviest burden.

Agencies involved in intelligence gathering activities tend to specialize in a certain area. Each of these areas requires a separate set of skills and resources. It would be impracticable to try to cover multiple areas. Each is, of necessity, kind of a niche activity. The names of these niche areas are often shortened to an acronym. For example, the collection of electronic emissions is known as Electronic Intelligence and uses the acronym, ELINT. The collection of radio communications is know as Communications Intelligence and uses the acronym COMINT. Intelligence gathered by human agents (the popular notion of the spy) is know as Human Intelligence and uses the acronym HUMINT. These acronyms are in common usage within the intelligence community as well as in documents and conversations by persons involved in the activity.

Aerial Reconnaissance

The unit I was joining, the 55ᵗʰ Strategic Reconnaissance Wing

(SRW), was involved in aerial reconnaissance. Its' niche area of the intelligence gathering community was electronic emissions or ELINT. In 1963, the majority of the aerial reconnaissance conducted by the United States was done by the military using military aircraft. Satellite technology was still a future development. All three major branches of the military had units devoted to this effort. The Air Force also had several different units each devoted to a specific unique mission. The majority of the aerial reconnaissance conducted by the military, both in the 1960s and today, is primarily conducted to directly support military objectives. The 55th SRW specialized in strategic rather than tactical reconnaissance. The 55th s motto, which appeared on the patches worn on their flight suits, was Videmus Omnia which is Latin for "We See All".

Forbes AFB was the home of the 21st Air Division. In late 1963, the Air Division had two wings assigned to it, the 40th Bomb Wing and the 55th Strategic Reconnaissance Wing (SRW). Both wings were equipped with the B-47 aircraft. The 40th Bomb Wing had 30 plus B-47E model aircraft. Its' mission was as part of the Strategic Air Command's nuclear strike force. A percentage of their crews maintained a constant alert posture. Combat ready crews consisted of a Pilot, a Co-pilot and a Radar Navigator-bombardier.

The 55th SRW had 35 RB-47H and 3 RB-47E model aircraft in several different configurations. The configuration differences mainly involved the type of reconnaissance equipment on board. The majority of the wing's aircraft were configured with similar reconnaissance equipment. This configuration of equipment was referred to as the standard RB-47H. The crew configuration was designed to match the standard RB-47H operation. The standard combat ready crew consisted of a Pilot, a Co-pilot, a Navigator and 3 Electronic Warfare Officers (EWO) known as Ravens.

The wing's mission involved the collection of Electronic Intelligence (ELINT) data from enemy nations. The data was used to maintain and update the Strategic Air Command's (SAC) data bases concerning enemy offensive and defensive equipment and capabilities. These data bases were used in formulating SAC's war planning. The 55th SRW conducted operational flights to collect the data by listening to and monitoring enemy electronic emissions. Operational collection flights were conducted in or near these countries. During the 1950s, as mentioned above, some over flights were conducted. The RB-50 (an updated version of the B-29 configured to conduct reconnaissance) was used during the early 1950s. They were replaced by the RB-47s in the mid part of the decade (3). The delivery to the 55th of the last version of the B-47, the RB-47H began in 1955 (4). The practice of over flying Soviet territory had generally been discontinued prior to the arrival of the RB-47s but there were rare exceptions where the aircraft did engage in over flights. The front line Russian fighter aircraft at the time (MIG-15s) had some difficulty intercepting and engaging the B-47. The introduction of the MIG-17 in the Soviet operational squadrons changed this situation. The MIG-17 was much more capable of engaging the B-47. The 55th SRW's operational reconnaissance flights were, hence forth, generally restricted to operating on the periphery of these countries.

Operating Locations (The OLs)

The operating range of the RB-47H made it impracticable to conduct operational flights directly from Forbes AFB, the wing's home base. The aircraft was capable of mid air refueling, but it would have required multiple mid-air refuelings and exceptionally long sorties. The B-47 was not a comfortable aircraft to fly in. The seats were uncomfortable, crew members were required to wear heavy parachutes at all times and quarters were cramped. The solution to this problem was to forward deploy the aircraft and crews. The sorties would be launched from these forward operating locations.

In late 1963, the 55th SRW had four regular forward Operating Locations (called OLs). Special situations would from time to time require additional temporary sites. The periphery around the entire communist block of nations was divided into four parts. Each part was assigned to one of the four regular Operating Locations. This was their area of collection responsibility. These Operating Locations were;

-Operating Location 1 (OL-1) was based at Brize Norton AFB in England. Brize Norton is located near Oxford, England and was about 50 miles west of London. OL1's area of responsibility was from the west side of Novaya Zemlya Island (a large north-south oriented island several hundred miles north and east of Norway) to the northern edge the Mediterranean Sea. This included all of the Communist block countries of Eastern Europe. We referred to Novaya Zemlya as Banana Island because it was shaped like a banana.

-Operating Location 2 (OL2) was based at Yokota AFB in Japan. Yokota is near the town of Fusa just north of Tokyo. OL2s area of responsibility was from the Kurile Islands to Indo-China. This included the Sea of Okhotsk north of the Japanese island of Hokkaido. The Sea of Okhotsk is between Sakhalin Island and the Kamchahkta Peninsula, both of which were Soviet territory. This area between the two and which was more than 12 miles off shore was considered international waters.

-Operating Location 3 (OL3) was based at Eielson AFB in Alaska. Eielson is located about twenty miles east of the city of Fairbanks. OL3s area of responsibility was from the Kamchahkta Peninsula over the north side of the Soviet Union to the east side of Novaya Zemlya Island.

-Operating Location 4 (OL4) was based at Incirlik AFB in Turkey. Incirlik is located near the Turkish city of Adana. It was a joint use base between the Turkish military and the U.S. Air Force. OL4s area of responsibility was from the Mediterranean Sea to the Pakistan-China border.

The 55th had a crew and a standard RB-47H aircraft deployed to each of the four regular Operating Locations at all times. These deployments were from three to four months in length. The deployed crew would fly from 10 to 12 operational sorties during a deployment. They would deploy with an aircraft from Forbes. That aircraft would be used for all of their operational sorties. When the time came to be replaced, another crew and aircraft would arrive. The aircraft were maintained, while at the Operating Location, by a detachment of maintenance personnel from Forbes AFB.   The detachment did not have the full capability that would be available at Forbes. The maintenance division of the 55th SRW was divided into two squadrons. The first was called the Operational Maintenance Squadron or OMS. The OMS personnel handled the task of preparing the aircraft for flight and doing the minor maintenance that could be accomplished while the aircraft remained on the ramp. The second squadron was called the Field Maintenance Squadron or FMS. The FMS personnel worked in the hangers and handled the major repairs to the aircraft. The OMS personnel were the only ones deployed to the forward operating locations. This meant that only minor maintenance and servicing would be available at the OL. To identify and fix maintenance problems, the crew that was scheduled to deploy with the aircraft, would fly about three training sorties at Forbes prior to deployment. These were called Shake Down flights. These flights were to ensure the aircraft was in good mechanical condition when it was deployed. This aircraft would be used for all their flights flown during their deployment. When the crew returned to Forbes, the aircraft would return with them. If an aircraft had major mechanical problems during a deployment beyond the ability and resources of the detachment, a replacement aircraft would be flown in from Forbes by another crew. This crew would return with the troubled aircraft. When a deployed crew was replaced by a new crew there would be about a week's overlap.

The 55th SRW was commanded by a full Colonel. The deputy commander was also a full Colonel. Colonel Marian Mixon was the Wing Commander and Colonel Charles Paxton was the deputy when I joined the wing in late 1963. The wing was divided into two major functional areas. These were the operations area and the maintenance area. Each of these areas were also commanded by a full Colonel and reported to the Deputy Wing Commander. The head of the operations area was know as the Deputy Commander for Operations (DCO). The head of the wing maintenance function was known as the Deputy Commander for Maintenance (DCM). The maintenance area was further divided into two squadrons, OMS and FMS, as described above. Both squadrons were commanded by a Lt. Colonel. Each aircraft was assigned a Crew Chief who coordinated maintenance activities on that aircraft. Crew Chiefs were assigned to the OMS.

Each of these Operating Locations had a permanently assigned staff and the detachment was commanded by a full Colonel or a Lt. Colonel. The detachment commanders were subordinate to the 55th Wing Commander. Aircraft and flight crews from the home base at Forbes were assigned in temporary duty (TDY) status. The mission profiles and specific requirements for each of our sorties were developed at SAC headquarters. They would be disseminated to the field in the form of Fragmentary (FRAG) orders. There was a permanent operations order that directed our general operational procedures. FRAG orders were amendments to this order devoted to specific sorties. The FRAG orders detailed the route and collection requirements.

The Ravens operated the collection equipment. There were general tasks and each Raven might additionally have some specific tasks. The standard aircraft (RB-47H) included an appendage on the left side of the aircraft. We called this the POD. The POD was an automated collection device. It collected most of the electronic emissions in the area of operation but did not record the details that the manually processed intercepts did. It was, in effect, a garbage collector. The Raven One would turn it on and monitor its operation. The Ravens were given specific manual collection requirements for the mission for more detailed analysis of assigned emissions if intercepted.

The 55th had about 20 to 25 combat ready crews. A combat ready crew was one in which each member of the crew was properly certified and ready for immediate use to meet the wing's operational commitments. The standard crew had six members. The only exception to the standard was Tell-Two special project crews which had five members (minus one Raven). The flight crews were assigned to one of two squadrons, the 343rd and the 38th. Each of the squadrons was commanded by a Lt. Colonel. Staff activities such as supply and administration were centralized under the Deputy Commander for Operations (DCO). Three flight crews were tasked to provide periodic evaluations and certifications on the crews of the 55th SRW. These crews were called Standardization or Standboard crews. Each combat ready crewmember received a periodic flight evaluation (called a Standboard) once a year. These Standboard crews were also required to support the deployments to the forward Operating Locations. The wing also had several special projects. Special projects were normally ongoing rather than one-time efforts. Each project was devoted to a unique type of collection activity and had resources in the form of aircraft and crews assigned to it. I will discuss the Special projects later in the chapter.

The majority of the crews stayed at Forbes AFB. Only a quarter to a third of the wing's crews would be deployed at any point in time. Time spent at Forbes was devoted to crew training, certification and administrative tasks. Training missions would normally include a mid-air refueling. The Ravens would practice collecting US radar data. Many of the training flights would involve instructional activity, periodic evaluations or certifications. These were generally done on an individual basis. For example, the Raven One may be getting a Standboard (annual evaluation) while the Navigator might be getting instruction leading to certification. One of the crew's Ravens would be dropped to make a place for the evaluator (Standboard Raven) and an Instructor Navigator would be added. The wing was also subject to evaluations by higher headquarters. The 21st Air Division was part of the 8th Air Force with headquarters at Barksdale AFB in Louisiana. The 8th Air Force had a unit called the Combat Evaluation Group (CEG). They would do spot evaluations on individual crews in the wings assigned to 8th Air force.

Spot Promotion Program

In the 1950s the Air Force initiated a spot promotion program. It was restricted to combat ready crews within the Strategic Air Command (SAC). It included both officer and enlisted personnel. General Curtis LeMay, the Commander of SAC at the time, had been its architect and the prime mover in establishing the program. The program allowed selected individuals, who had served a minimum time (normally a year) at their present rank, to temporarily assume the next higher rank. During the early years of the program there were some double-spot or even triple-spot promotions. This meant that it was possible for a First Lieutenant to have a spot promotion to Lt. Colonel three years after being promoted to First Lieutenant. Though it was rare, there were a few 25 year old Lt. Colonels. The program continued into the 1960s but allowed for only a single spot promotion. Several crews in each of SAC's flying wings were designated as Select crews. Those members of Select crews who were eligible would receive spot promotions. They retained the spot promotion as long as they remained on the Select crew. In most SAC wings the standardization crews were the ones designated as Select crews. When an individual left the Select crew they returned to their permanent rank. The time spent in the higher grade would be credited as time in grade if they were subsequently promoted to the spot rank they had held. Spot promotions in the 55th were handled differently. The Standboard crews were designated as Select similar to the practice in other SAC wings. In addition, the 55th crews that were deployed to one of the Operating Locations were also designated as Select crews for the period of their deployment. When a crew deployed and flew their first operational sortie, those members of the crew who had the required time in their present rank received a spot promotion. They held this rank until the deployment was completed. At the time I joined the 55th, SAC's Spot Promotion Program was still in use. The program ended in December of 1965. I was clearly aware of the program's demise because my crew was deployed to OL2 at Yokota AFB in January of 1966 and as a result would have received temporary spot promotions. We did not receive them.

Special Projects

In addition to the standard RB-47H configuration the 55th had several special project aircraft. When I joined the wing in November of 1963 they had three on-going special projects, namely the Tell-Two, ERB and Iron Lung projects. In 1965 the Fire Fly project was added. I will give a brief description of each here and cover the ones I was a part of in more detail later.

The Tell-Two project was devoted to tracking Russian missile activity, particularly the down range telemetry of their test launches. The Russian Ballistic Missile test activity was confined to two facilities. The first was at the Bakinour facility located near Tyuratam in Kazakhstan. The second site was at Kapustin Yar near the city of Volgograd in Russia (5). These facilities were the Russian's launch sites for their Intercontinental Ballistic Missile (ICBM) and Medium Range Ballistic Missile (MRBM) tests. The Tell-Two missions were flown from Incirlik AFB (OL-4) in Turkey. They would fly to and maintain an orbit as close to Soviet territory as possible without entering it. The orbit area was normally along the Soviet-Iranian border or over the Black Sea. The Tell-Two program had three aircraft assigned to it. The aircraft were specially configured RB-47E model aircraft. A minimum of two but generally three Tell-Two crews would be deployed at Incirlik at all times. One of the crews would be kept on constant Alert status. That means that one of the crews must be ready to respond immediately when alerted. I would later be involved in this special project but not at Incirlik AFB.

In the fall of 1963, the ERB program had a single aircraft and one crew assigned. It was an ERB-47H aircraft. Their operational sorties were flown from one of the four regular forward Operating Locations (Incirlik AFB, Brize Norton AFB, Yokota AFB and Eielson AFB) and often in conjunction with one of the standard RB-47H operational missions. My knowledge of their mission purpose was quite limited. Their task often involved monitoring and collecting data on the new and more sophisticated radars. I was never involved in this project but did fly a joint mission with them during the summer of 1964. It turned out to be one of the more tense missions that I had been on.

The Iron Lung program's purpose was to conduct and record very precise aerial power measurements on a specific enemy radar system. The data was recorded in digital format. The use of the digital format was uncommon in 1964. The recorded data was used to update the Air Force's knowledge of enemy radar systems. Frequently the data would be used to construct a working copy of the enemy radar. The copied system would then be installed at a site in the Nevada desert and we would conduct power measurements on the copied site to verify its similarity in function and signature. The Iron Lung program had a single aircraft and one crew assigned. The aircraft was a specially configured RB-47H. The crew consisted of the standard six crew positions. The <u>Iron Lung</u> program was an ongoing one, but the task changed frequently. Each task focused on a specific enemy radar system. The aircraft would often be re-configured for each new task. Reconfigurations normally involved a change in the Raven's electronic equipment. Occasionally a change in the exterior of the aircraft was needed. These external changes normally were in the form of antennas. Each project was tasked, directed and the contractual portions funded by the CIA. The aircraft and crew belonged to the Air Force. The project equipment, data analysis and technical support were provided under contract by ITT research labs in San Fernando, California. Airframe modifications were contracted to Lockheed Aircraft Company in Ontario, California. I participated in this special project during two different periods of time.

The <u>Fire Fly</u> project was initiated in 1965 in response to the Soviet's deployment of their first major Surface-To-Air missile system, the SA-2. The SA-2 system was initially deployed around several of the major cities and strategic sites in the Russian heartland. One of the sites had reportedly downed the U-2 flown by Francis Gary Powers in May of 1960. Initially, our Intelligence Services' knowledge of its' capabilities was limited. During the summer of 1964 they had evidence that it was being further deployed to the countries of Eastern Europe and by the end of the year to North Viet Nam. My crew provided some of this evidence with an intercept of an electronic emission from a new site in Poland. I will address this in more detail in a later chapter.

The RB-47H Aircraft

The B-47 aircraft model was developed and predominately used as a bomber. Positions for the pilots and the navigator were in a pressurized compartment toward the front of the aircraft. The pilot's seats were configured in tandem and on an elevated platform which extended the upper parts of their bodies through an opening in the top of the airframe. The opening in the top was covered by a bubble type canopy. The pilot's upper bodies projected up into the bubble canopy. This provided them with excellent visibility. The canopy could be opened hydraulically by lifting one end. A series of pins locked it in place when the canopy was closed to form a seal so the compartment could be pressurized in the air. The navigator was located in the nose of the aircraft. The entry door was on the left side of the aircraft and equipped with a retractable ladder. A separate pressure door was located about three feet above the entry door which allowed the compartment to be pressurized in flight. There was a narrow aisle along the left side of the pilot's platform from the pressure door to the nose area to provide access to the navigator position. Ground entry for all positions was through the entry door. The B-47 was initially equipped with twin 50 caliber guns on the tail of the aircraft. The later models (including the RB-47E and the RB-47H used by the 55th) were equipped with two 20 millimeter canons (6). The guns were operated by the co-pilot. The controls for the guns were behind him. He would rotate his seat toward the rear of the aircraft to operate them.

The 55th s two versions of the B-47, the E and H models, used the same basic airframe and the pilot/navigator compartment was configured the same as other versions. The difference was the addition of a separate pressurized compartment for the three additional crew members (ravens). The new pressurized compartment replaced the bomb bay of the bomber versions. The compartment was formed by removing the bomb bay doors and replacing them with a plexiglas dome. A crawlway allowed access to the rear raven compartment. The crawlway went from the entry door to the pressure door of the rear crew compartment. It was about three feet high and it was a tight fit for the larger crew members with a parachute pack on their back. The plexiglas dome was affixed to the aircraft but had a large hatch which was mounted to the dome with a ring of screws. The hatch was removable on the ground to provide maintenance personnel easier access. Routine ground entry to the rear compartment by the crew was through the entry door and down the crawlway on your hands and knees.

Each of the raven positions had an ejection seat to allow emergency egress from the aircraft. The rear compartment was configured with three raven positions and related equipment. The ravens remained in the forward compartment during the takeoff and landing phases of a flight. There was a seat at the rear of the aisle in the forward compartment for the Raven One to sit. The seat was beside the copilot facing forward but well below the copilot's seat. The ravens two and three sat in the aisle leading toward the navigator's position. They faced aft in slings. Once the aircraft was airborne the ravens would transfer to the rear compartment. This transfer had to be completed before the aircraft climbed above ten thousand feet. To complete the transfer quickly two of the three ravens might be in the crawlway at the same time. Once the transfer was complete both crew compartments could be pressurized. While we were transferring, the forward compartment would be unable to communicate with us. The pilots had to wait until we plugged into the interphone system in the rear compartment to communicate with us. Then both compartments were pressurized and the aircraft could continue the climb above ten thousand feet.

The parachutes we wore were of the back pack type and were bulky. Each crew member had a survival pack at their enroute position that they sat on and attached by webbed straps to their parachute harness. Each position also had a lap belt and shoulder harness. Crew members were required to wear their parachutes and helmets, sit on top of the survival kit and remain strapped in with the belts and harnesses at all times except for short periods when they would need to perform a special task. When we made the transition from the forward compartment to the rear compartment we did so with the helmets and parachutes on. This made the clearance as we crawled down the crawlway quite tight, particularly for the bigger men. The net result was an uncomfortable situation.

We took all of this in stride but occasionally things would happen and the only way to deal with them was to laugh. A couple of examples will illustrate. Parachutes are deployed (opened) by pulling a lanyard. It removes the pins that hold the parachute in the pack. Once the pins are pulled a spring pops the parachute canopy out of the pack. The lanyard is on the outside of the parachute pack so that it is accessible when needed. Given the tight quarters in the crawlway it was possible to accidentally catch the lanyard on something and deploy the parachute in the crawlway. This, in fact, did happen a few times. It only happened once while I was flying. In this instance, two ravens were in the crawlway. I was the second one. The lead man, in front of me, had his parachute deploy. All I could see was parachute canopy. It covered the crawlway in front of me and enveloped me. I had to wait for the guy in front to push forward, find the pressure door to the rear compartment's handle, open the door, push some of the canopy through the door ahead of him, get into the rear compartment and pull the rest of the parachute canopy into the compartment. Only then could I see much less continue. Fortunately I was not claustrophobic.

The pilots could see us leave the front compartment so it was not a difficult task for them to predict when one or two of us was still in the crawlway. A slight forward pressure on the control column would force the aircraft's nose down and our upward momentum would temporarily pin us to the top of the crawlway with enough pressure that we would not be able to move. We were never sure if it was intentional or not. It happened to me a few times. I am not a large fellow so my finger tips could barely reach the bottom of the crawlway. I could not continue until my upward momentum abated.

Emergency Egress from the Aircraft

There were two different methods available to crew members to bail out of the aircraft if it became necessary. The first was to drop through the entry door opening. This method was not very practicable given the high speeds of jet aircraft and would not normally be used in an emergency. When the entry door was opened in flight a spoiler (a slab a few feet long), located just in front of the door was extended a few feet into the slipstream (the flow of air along the bottom of the aircraft). This would allow the exiting crewmember to get a few feet below the aircraft before the slipstream literally whipped him away. There was a good likelihood that this would result in the exiting crew member bouncing along the bottom of the aircraft. I had not heard of anyone using this method of exiting the B-47 except at lowered airspeeds. The KC-135 aircraft, used for mid air refueling, did not have ejection seats and used this method exclusively in emergencies. Dropping through the entry door was the only way out. The only instance where this method was actually used to exit the KC-135 while at the higher airspeed, to my knowledge, did result in all crew members bouncing along the bottom of the aircraft. Each of them had their helmet torn off their heads. Only one survived.

Each of the crew positions on the RB-47 aircraft was equipped with an ejection seat to provide for emergency egress from the aircraft. Ejection seats use an explosive charge to propel the seat, with the crew member in it, clear of the aircraft. The crew member would be strapped into the seat. Both of the pilots ejected upward. The navigator as well as the ravens ejected downward. Downward ejections could obviously not be used at low altitudes. When one of the pilots initiated their ejection system the first step in the sequence blew the canopy clear of the aircraft using an explosive charge. A split second later the seat was blasted clear of the aircraft. Ejections from the pilot seats in the B-47 had been successfully done on several occasions. When the navigator initiated his ejection sequence the first step was to blow a pressure hatch cover located just below his seat. Then two leg restrains would snap around his ankles. These would prevent his legs from flailing around. The seat would follow a split second later. The web straps (seat and shoulder) of the harnesses kept him in the seat during exit from the aircraft. He faced forward. This system had also been used successfully. The ravens' ejection sequence was a little more complicated. Their seats faced aft and ejected downward. The plexiglas dome below the seats did not have a hatch that could be blown clear. A hole had to be created for the seats to pass through. When each raven initiated his ejection sequence, an explosive charge would propel a knife deck, located just below the seat, through the plexiglas dome blasting a hole in it for the seat to pass through. One end of the knife deck was hinged to the aircraft so it pivoted as it blasted through the dome. Theatrically, this would clear the path of debris when the seat followed it. The seat followed a split second later. To my knowledge, this system had never been used successfully. Rumors circulated among the ravens of the wing that our ejection system had been extensively tested during the development phase of the aircraft using dummies. The results had been dubious. The flat back of the seat facing the slipstream had caused the seat to go through violent gyrations. All of the dummies heads were missing when the seats were recovered.

A few seconds after the seat was clear of the aircraft another light charge would separate the crew member from the seat. A webbed strap ran from the top of the seat, down the back of the seat, under the survival kit (on which the crew member was sitting and attached to). The charge would tighten this strap expelling the occupant from the seat. When the falling crew member reached 14,000 feet the parachute was automatically deployed. This sequence of events would save the occupant even if they had been rendered unconscious.

Flying the B-47

Our training and operational flights generally followed a similar sequence of events. Each sortie would be extensively planned in advance. The planning was generally done a day or two prior to the flight. Celestial computations by the navigator were done at this time. Ravens would review their requirements. The day of the flight would begin with a detailed pre-flight inspection. We would check all of our equipment for proper operation. The engines would be started using an external electric power cart. The external power cart would pre-rotate the engine turbines (modern jet aircraft are equipped with an onboard Alternate Power Unit [APU] which is used in place of the external power cart). When the prescribed RPM was reached, ignition was applied and the engine was started. This was normally done one engine at a time using the power cart for each. <u>Alert</u> engine starts were different. One engine was started using the power cart. That running engine was then advanced to a high RPM. It could then provide sufficient power to pre-rotate the other engines. The remaining engines would be gang started. If a power cart was not available the engines could be started using a cartridge. The cartridge was an explosive charge. One of the engines had a chamber for this purpose. The charge would be triggered, producing a large cloud of smoke, to pre-rotate the engine. The rest of the engines were then started one at a time using power from the running engine. During the three plus years that I was on a B-47 crew we used this technique twice. Both times were for practice. I clearly remember the ground crew standing by with their fire extinguishers at the ready.

The B-47 aircraft required a lot of runway to take off. Our aircraft were considerably heavier than the original aircraft design had called for. The Strategic Air Command (SAC) had to lengthen the runways at all of their home bases to accommodate the long take off rolls of the B-47 and the B-52 aircraft. The lengths of SAC runways ranged from 11,200 feet to as much as 15,000 feet. This was longer than the average of 7,000 to 10,000 feet used, even today, by most civil and military jet aircraft. The B-47 was somewhat under powered. Additional thrust was added to be used during the takeoff run. A water/alcohol system was added to provide this additional thrust. A mixture of water and alcohol would be misted into the exhaust of each engine. It would produce additional thrust. The water/alcohol would last long enough to get the aircraft airborne and would run out during climb.

Even with the longer runways and the added thrust a fully loaded B-47 could not accelerate to near takeoff speed, abort the takeoff, and stop the aircraft on the existing runway. A special technique, an acceleration progress check, was used to ensure that the aircraft was accelerating normally. This check was a timed speed check at a precise point in the takeoff run. The check was designed to allow the pilot to abort the takeoff and stop on the existing runway if the acceleration was not right. Beyond this point the aircraft could not be safely stopped on the existing runway and the takeoff run had to be continued what ever the circumstances. Once started the water/alcohol would continue until it was exhausted. It could not be stopped and re-started. This was the reason the pilots waited to activate them until they were rolling on the take off run. When the water/alcohol ran out during climb you could feel the change. A more detailed explanation of the B-47s flying characteristics is covered in Appendix B.

Once the aircraft had established a climb and the gear and the flaps were retracted, the pilot would clear the ravens to transfer to the rear compartment. We left the slings and crawled down the crawlway to our compartment. The raven three was normally the closest to the door and was the first one down the crawlway. Once in position the

Raven One would notify the pilots by interphone and both compartments were pressurized and the climb to altitude continued.

Nearly every flight, training or operational, involved a mid-air refueling. The training flights that included a refueling were about seven hours in length. All crew members generally remained in their seats strapped in until it was time for the ravens to return to the front for landing. Then the transfer sequence was reversed.

Operational Sorties

The typical operational sortie would involve the standard RB-47H configured aircraft. Each of the sorties would be launched from one of the Operating Locations (OL). When a new crew arrived at an OL, they would be briefed on the missions that they would be flying. The crew that they were relieving would remain at the OL for about a week. While the Spot Promotion system was still in effect, the new crew wanted to get their first operational mission completed as quickly as possible. This would trigger their spot promotions. The crew would spend three to four months at the OL and fly about 10 sorties during that time. The sorties were dictated by SAC headquarters in the form of Fragmentary (FRAG) orders. The routes would be somewhere within the OL's area of collection responsibility as described earlier. Each sortie had specific requirements and each of the raven positions had specific tasks.

The flight paths during the collection phase of the sorties were along the periphery of one of the Communist countries (Red China, Russia, North Korea, Eastern Europe or North Viet Nam). All of these countries, at that time, claimed the first 12 miles off their coast lines as their territorial waters (their sovereign territory). Our flight paths were normally planned to fly at least 15 miles off their coast lines to remain clear of their sovereign territory. Things would get pretty sticky if we got closer. We flew these tracks with considerable regularity. The sporadic attacks by Soviet aircraft, that had been relatively frequent during the previous decade, had diminished by the time of my arrival in the unit. Our mode of operation and their response had become somewhat routine and a defacto mould had been established. As long as both sides continued in this mould things tended to stay pretty routine. They, particularly the Soviets, would occasionally launch a fighter aircraft to identify us. The fighter would often stay with us for a period of time flying formation just off our wing tip. Close enough that you could see the pilot and tell when he moved his head. It had become a cat and mouse game. When the Russian pilot broke off and returned to base he would often wave and we would wave back. We, of course, didn't kid ourselves, we knew that if he were ordered to shoot us down, despite the seemingly friendly gestures, he would not have hesitated.

There are several interesting stories related to this cat and mouse game we were playing with the Russians. The B-47 had a bubble canopy on the top of the aircraft. The pilot's upper bodies projected up into the bubble canopy. This gave them excellent visibility. On several occasions the Russian fighter pilot would go beyond flying formation off the B-47's wing tip. Many of their fighter aircraft also had bubble canopies. He would roll inverted and fly just above the B-47's bubble canopy looking straight down on our pilots. They in turn could look straight up at him. They could literally "see the whites of his eyes". On another occasion while the Russian fighter was in formation just off our wing tip, our pilot started to slow the B-47 down in what is known as slow flight staying above the stall speed. The Russian fighter would maintain his position also slowing down. The fighter, of course, had a higher stall speed and would eventually have to drop off to keep from stalling. Our pilot then increased the airspeed and the Russian pilot re-joined the formation. The process was again repeated. The cat and mouse game remained seemingly friendly as long as each of us stayed in this routine mould. This mould was not as well established with the Chinese and was very unpredictable with the North Koreans.

Our mission was to gather and record data on electronic emissions, primarily radars, from the country of interest. This data was used to verify and update the SAC's data bases. These data bases were used to develop war plans especially those under the Single Integrated Operations Plan or SIOP (the master plan in the event of an all out nuclear conflagration.). The Russians and the Chinese were not naïve about our reason for being there. They knew we were listening and that we could only gather information on those facilities that were transmitting at the time we passed an area. So if they kept some of their radar facilities off the air we would not be able to glean any data on them. They were, however, very interested in keeping track of us. So they would turn on only those radars that were needed to track us. These were long range types that were known as search radars. As long as we behaved in accordance with this routine mould that was all the radar facilities we would ordinarily see. As a result we would see the same radars each time our track took us by an area. The planners at Strategic Air Command (SAC) headquarters needed data on all of the enemies' radar facilities. To serve this purpose the planners would occasionally create a situation in which we would break the routine mould and became somewhat more provocative. The intent was to cause them to become concerned enough to turn on additional radar facilities but not so concerned that they would become hostile and attack one of our aircraft. This was a fine line that had to be crossed cautiously. We were normally out there by ourselves and were no match for even a single attacking fighter aircraft. One of the sorties that my crew flew during my first deployment during the summer of 1964 crossed that line and created a very tense and dangerous situation. That event is described in detail later

Operational missions, even when launched from an operating location, would still require from an hour to several hours of flight time to reach the collection area. During this time the ravens had no specific duties. Once the collection area was reached they would operate their assigned tasks until the flight left the collection area. The time in the collection area was known as <u>On Watch</u> time. We would sign on to our recorders with the phrase "On Watch". Each raven had specific tasks in accordance with the <u>Frag Order</u> for the mission. Often they were assigned a specific radar emission to search for. They would continuously search the assigned frequency bands. Each raven position was equipped with a tunable receiver capable of scanning the entire spectrum of frequencies. It had a series of buttons. Each button was for a specific segment of the spectrum of frequencies. The receiver would be tuned up and down in frequency, within the band, similar to tuning an AM or FM radio dial. The receiver was connected electronically to several other pieces of equipment. When a radar signal was intercepted the signal would be routed to each of them from the receiver. One of these pieces of equipment was a Pulse Analyzer. A Pulse Analyzer displayed the shape of the pulse of radar energy. Radars operate by transmitting a short burst of energy. This burst is called a pulse. The length of the pulse depends on how long the transmitter is on. The radar system then listens for a much longer period of time for any return of this energy that bounced off a target. The length of the pulse depends on the length of time the transmitter was on before the period of listening. The Pulse Analyzer displays the pulse. The length of the pulse (known as the pulse width or PW) and the number of bursts (pulses) that a radar emits per second (known as the pulse repetition frequency or PRF) can be determined from the Pulse Analyzer. The signal is also routed to a recorder that is capable of recording the display on the Pulse Analyzer. It also records the time on the recording as well as any voice comments the raven makes to add detail to the intercept. When the intercepted signal is one of interest the raven turns the recorder on. Finally, the signal is routed to a direction finder. The raven can use it to determine the direction to the radar site from the aircraft. Each raven keeps a log of all the signals (emissions) of interest that were processed and recorded. These parameters (PW and PRF) are key features that determine how and for what purpose a radar system is used.

Covert Missions

All aircraft flights are conducted using one of two sets of rules, Instrument Flight Rules (IFR) or Visual Flight Rules (VFR). The larger and higher performance aircraft predominately use the former, Instrument Flight Rules. IFR rules require the aircraft to maintain constant radio communications with air traffic controllers on the ground and use onboard instruments to ensure control of as well as to navigate the aircraft. This allows them to operate in almost all types of weather and be provided separation from other aircraft in their vicinity, both advantages not available to aircraft using the latter rules, Visual Flight Rules. These two sets of rules apply to flights within the United States airspace, referred to as domestic, as well as over international waters. The <u>Federal Aviation Administration</u> (FAA) governs domestic flights while a body known as the <u>International Civil Aviation Organization</u> (ICAO) provides rules for participating aircraft flying within international airspace. The majority of the countries of the world recognize their domestic airspace to include oceanic areas within 12 miles of their coastlines. The United States was one of the few exceptions. In 1963, we recognized our domestic airspace to include areas within 3 miles of our coast line. Three miles had been the effective range of the shore battery cannons during the 19th century and was the rational for this three mile limit. Several years later we expanded this to 12 miles, to match the rest of the world, which is what we recognize today. International airspace is open for use by all countries similar to the concept of the open seas for maritime vessels. The ICAO rules were guidelines that the majority of countries had agreed to. There was no enforcing authority. Those aircraft that choose to participate (they were on their own if they did not) were provided with air traffic services, emergency search and rescue if needed and would not risk being identified as hostile by the country whose domestic airspace they might be approaching. Military flights generally fly under IFR rules both domestically and internationally. The operational missions flown by the crews of the 55th were an exception to the above. Radio silence was maintained throughout the flight often including the takeoff and landing phases of the flight. A green light from a light gun operated by control tower personnel cleared us for takeoff. The rational for this procedure was to not alert the subject of our surveillance that we were coming. It was to our advantage if they identified us as potentially being hostile. They would have to track us with their radars which would in turn allow us to monitor and record these emissions. This practice was known as <u>Covert</u> operations. Since the entire en-route portion of the flight would be conducted over international waters (at least 15 miles from any coastline) we were operating legally as a non-participating aircraft.

Mission Monitor

During the first decade or so following the end of WWII, reconnaissance sorties were not closely monitored by their unit operations personnel. If the aircraft was attacked the earliest indication that something was wrong was if they did not return to base. It was often days before any concrete information concerning the missing flight was available. Over time, the Air Force responded to correct this situation. The first change was to provide a <u>Mission Monitor</u> for each sortie. The <u>Mission Monitor</u> was an officer from the unit's operations staff. He would be in the <u>Command Post</u> (the base communications center) throughout the reconnaissance aircraft's sortie. The flight plan for the sortie would be given in advance to the appropriate air traffic facilities and the <u>Command Post</u> at the aircraft's point of departure.

The flights were flown as <u>Covert Missions</u> (radio silence) as explained in the previous section. The mission profile generally called for the crew to briefly break radio silence to make a position report at a few prescribed points along the track. The coded position report was brief and would be made on the High Frequency (HF) band radio. All domestic flights normally use either the Very High Frequency (VHF) or Ultra High Frequency (UHF) band radios to communicate with ground sites. Both of these radio bands have a limited range known as <u>Line Of Sight</u>. Line of sight means that their signal only travels in a straight line. Due to the curvature of earth this straight line will eventually carry into space and well above any possible receiver. A ground based radio beyond this line of sight distance would not be able to receive the signal. Aircraft operating over international waters are generally beyond this line of sight distance. As a result, most flights over international waters are equipped with an HF band radio. The HF band signal has a much greater range because its' signal bounces off the ionosphere. This bouncing of the signal between the ionosphere and the ground, a skipping behavior, means it can often be received half way around the world. For example, we might be flying off the Chinese coast and our transmission would be received by an Air Force operations center outside of Boston. They would then pass the coded position report to

94

the operations center (Command Post) at the aircraft's point of departure.

The <u>Mission Monitor</u> would remain in the Command Post throughout the mission. He would compare these coded position reports to the planned track and update the air traffic facilities with the missions' timing. These updates would be passed via a secure telephone line. If the planned position reports were missed he would notify the unit's commander and Search and Rescue. I would have the opportunity to act as a mission monitor for several missions at Yokota AFB in Japan.

Early Warning

By the decade of the 1960s the support for these <u>Ferret</u> flights (a colloquial term applied to the covert peripheral type missions that we were flying) had expanded to include an <u>Early Warning</u> platform. In the book <u>By Any Means Necessary</u>, written by William Burrows, he describes in detail many of the incidents where the Russians shot down one of the U.S. reconnaissance aircraft during the 1950s. The aircraft's crew had no way of knowing if the Russian aircraft that was intercepting them was there to just identify them or to attack them. There was no way to get an advance feeling to tell if on this particular day the Russians would respond with hostile action. The crews could not be warned. The <u>Early Warning</u> platform was developed to address this gap. It consisted of another airborne aircraft that was monitoring Russian communications including those between the aircraft intercepting ours and their controllers on the ground. If the communications seemed exceptionally belligerent in nature the supervisor on the <u>Early Warning</u> aircraft would issue a <u>Condition One</u> alert to the reconnaissance aircraft. A <u>Condition One</u> alert called for the reconnaissance aircraft to abort the mission and exit the area as fast as possible. These alerts may have prevented several earlier hostile actions that resulted in a downed aircraft.

Hostile Intent

The countries that were the object of the 55th SRW's surveillance missions were not countries that had friendly relations with the

United States. They included the Soviet Union, Communist China, North Korea, North Viet Nam and the communist block countries of Eastern Europe. We were technically not at war with these countries. The period, as described earlier, was known as the Cold War. William Burrows, in his book By Any Means Necessary, describes the role of reconnaissance crews during this period as follows; (7)

> *"Since they couldn't do their jobs unless they got close Enough to their armed quarry to invite attack, reconnaissance crews were effectively the only units in the armed forces that continuously engaged in actual combat operations. Others practiced fighting the bear and the dragon. But out of sight of the rest of the world, recce crews actually tweaked their tails, and many were severely mauled for it."*

In September of 2004 the Air Force Museum dedicated the Cold War Memorial to honor the contributions of the reconnaissance crews during this Cold War period. The Air Force Museum is at Wright Patterson AFB located near Dayton, Ohio. The center part of the memorial has more than 50 names engraved on it. These are the names of the men who lost their lives due to hostile actions while engaged in the Cold War reconnaissance activity. The 55th had its share. The majority of the casualties were suffered in the decade of the 1950s. Their stories are covered in detail in the Burrows book. The toll of losses in aircraft and crews continued into the 1960s but fortunately at a slower pace.

It is fair to say that those countries that were the subject of our surveillance did not want us to be there. They occasionally challenged our right to be there even though we might be over international waters. When they chose to challenge our presence with hostile actions it was normally an unequal contest. We were a sitting duck. During the decade of the 1950s the United States did engage in several actual penetrations of Soviet airspace. Hostile actions were far more numerous as a result. Those reactions, however, were not solely directed at our aircraft engaged in over flights but also at our aircraft on peripheral flights over international waters. Both Air Force and Naval units suffered casualties. Hostile actions, though diminished by the 1960s, were still a constant threat. The informal rules of the cat and mouse game had been loosely established by this time but the potential for hostile action was still clearly there. In fact, the 55th SRW aircraft and crews were the subject of two hostile actions during the decade of the 1960s. The first occurred on July 1, 1960 when an RB-47H was attacked by a Russian Mig-19. The second occurred on April 28, 1965 when an RB-47H was attacked by a pair of North Korean Mig-17s. These incidents are covered in more detail in the next chapter.

A Heavy Veil of Secrecy

The activities of the entire aerial reconnaissance community (air crews, operations personnel and the data handling personnel) were shrouded under a heavy veil of secrecy. In the event of capture our cover story was that we were conducting weather reconnaissance. The veil of secrecy continued for several decades. It extended to discussions with friends and family. Government and military officials were generally evasive and guarded in their public responses when incidents occurred. Public commentary was virtually non-existent and then only very limited when an incident did occur which had been elevated to international attention. Many of the families who lost loved ones were not told what actually happened until decades later (8). The first authorative public commentary on the subject was the Burrows book which was not published until the early 2000s, some three to four decades after the fact. The book details the events of the community from the early 1950s through the 1970s.

Chapter 7   The High Price in Men and Equipment

The 55th SRW was flying the RB-47H aircraft in the period from 1956 thru 1967. The aircraft was retired from service in 1967. During that period six of the Wing's RB-47H and two of its' RB-47E aircraft were either destroyed or damaged. Eight out of a total of 39 aircraft is a high number for a <u>Cold War</u> operating environment. All of the damaged aircraft were subsequently retired from service as a result of the damage. The causes ranged from mechanical failure to hostile actions. Many crew members assigned to the 55th SRW lost their lives as a result of these incidents. Four of these incidents occurred prior to my joining the wing in November of 1963. One to hostile action by the Russians that I describe in the section entitled <u>The Little Toy Dog</u>. Two of the accidents occurred during the Cuban Missile Crisis and are described in the segment on the <u>Cuban Missile Crisis</u>. The fourth was during a training flight. I have included a brief description in the segment entitled <u>A Training Accident</u>. In all four of these cases the aircraft was destroyed and all but two of the crew members on board were killed. I do not know the exact number of crew members who perished on these incidents but it was at least twenty.

The final four incidents occurred while I was a member of the wing. The first was a landing accident at Incirlik AFB in Turkey. The aircraft was destroyed and two of the five crew members on board were killed. I describe this accident in the segment <u>Accident at Incirlik</u>. The second one was a mid air refueling accident. The aircraft was damaged but was able to land. One of the four crew members on board was killed. This is described in the segment <u>Tragedy Over Mattoon</u>. The third incident was another landing accident. I was on board this one. It occurred at Shemya AFB at the end of the Alaskan Island Chain and is described in detail in the segment entitled <u>Over The Cliff</u>. The aircraft was damaged but all five crew members, obviously including myself, survived. The final one was due to hostile action by the North Koreans. The aircraft was damaged but all six crew members survived. It is described in the segment entitled <u>North Korea Attacks</u>. Each of these incidents is dealt with in this chapter except the one entitled <u>Over the Cliff</u>. I deal with that in a later chapter.

The Little Toy Dog

The first of these hostile actions against a 55th aircraft during the decade resulted in the loss of the aircraft, the death of four of the crew members and the incarceration of the remaining two crew members. The action occurred on July 1, 1960. The aircraft was an RB-47H. The pilot and the aircraft commander was Major Willard Palm. The flight was the initial flight of the crew's deployment to Brize Norton AFB (OL-1) in England. This incident occurred prior to my joining the 55th. SRW but the entire incident was later the subject of the book The Little Toy Dog by William White. The book was my primary source of information concerning the incident. The name of the book was derived from the fact that Major Palm carried a little toy dog, which had been given to him by his young daughter as a good luck charm, on the flight.

A U-2 reconnaissance aircraft flown by Francis Gary Powers, was shot down near Sverdlovsk in central Russia, on May 1, 1960 (9). It created an international furor and sabotaged a scheduled summit meeting between Premier Khrushchev of the Soviet Union and President Eisenhower of the United States. Powers was captured by the Russians and held in prison. It was an embarrassment to the President and as a result he had suspended all aerial reconnaissance activities. Major Palm's flight from Brize Norton, two months after Powers was shot down, was the first flight when reconnaissance flights were resumed (10). Due to the sensitivity of the situation, the flight path was designed to keep the aircraft at least 50 miles from any shoreline. This was much farther from Russian territory than had previously been the practice.

The flight departed from Brize Norton in England accompanied by a KC-135 tanker aircraft and proceeded north staying well off the Norwegian coast. The aircraft completed a mid-air refueling along this part of the route. It then turned east some 30 miles north of Norway into the Barents Sea. The Barents Sea is north of the Kola Peninsula in the Soviet Union and west of the island of Novaya Zemlya which is also Soviet territory. The Russians had launched a fighter aircraft to intercept and identify them. The RB-47H was due north of the Kola Peninsula and was approximately 60 miles off shore from Russian territory when the Russian aircraft joined them in formation off their right wing. At that point the route called for the RB-47 to make a 90 degree left turn back to the north to avoid over flying Russian Territory (11). The left turn, however, placed the Russian aircraft in the RB-47H's six o'clock position. This placed him in line with the twin 20 millimeter guns on the tail of the RB-47. At this point the Russian aircraft opened fire. The American aircraft was severely damaged and became uncontrollable. The crew was ordered to bail out. Two of the crew members survived to tell their story, Capt. John McCone the Navigator and Lt. Bruce Olmstead the Co-pilot. They were both picked up by a Russian fishing trawler some six hours after the incident. They were incarcerated in the infamous Lubayonka prison in down town Moscow, the same one where Powers was being held. The United States protested the action on the floor of the United Nations. Ambassador Henry Cabot Lodge put the route on display on a large board which demonstrated that the aircraft was over international waters and well clear of Soviet territory (12). McCone and Olmstead were incarcerated for about nine months and then released. Their experiences in prison were used in the development of the Air Force survival training curriculum at Stead AFB.

Cuban Missile Crisis

The 55th had a major involvement in the Air Force's activities during the Cuban missile crisis in 1962. The wing played an important role by providing up to date intelligence to the national command structure during the crisis. The wing paid a high price in terms of men and equipment for its participation. I was not assigned to the wing during this period. I would join the wing about a year later. The information related here was gleaned from discussions with crew members who were members of the wing during that period. The wing's aircraft and crews were dispersed to several locations, among them Kindley AFB in Bermuda and McCoy AFB in Tampa, Florida. During these operations the wing lost two aircraft and their crews. Both accidents occurred during takeoff. The first was at Kindley AFB in Bermuda. The wing's RB-47 aircraft were considerably heavier at take off than the original design had called for. The additional weight required additional thrust and a longer takeoff run. Additional thrust was provided by a water-alcohol mixture that was atomized into the exhaust during the takeoff run. The water-alcohol mixture added additional thrust similar to an afterburner in fighter aircraft. The water-alcohol would be depleted after about 120 seconds, long enough to get the aircraft off the ground. A specific ratio was required for the mixture. This particular aircraft was serviced with the wrong mixture. The result was a loss, due to excessive cooling, rather than an increase in thrust. The aircraft became airborne but could not clear the terrain on the opposite side of a small bay. The aircraft was destroyed and all crew members aboard were killed. The second accident was at McCoy AFB near Tampa, Florida. The aircraft lifted off but went through some rapid attitude changes and crashed. Again, all aboard were killed. The cause was listed as unknown.

When the Cuban crisis was over the aircraft and the crews returned to Forbes. The national command structure felt that continued monitoring of Cuban activities was needed. This resulted in a new operational requirement. It was called Common Cause. Common Cause sorties were directed at Cuba. These sorties were also peripheral in nature and were conducted much the same as these from the regular Operating Locations. The difference, of course, was that they could be launched and recovered from Forbes. From late 1962 on, operational Common Cause sorties were added, in addition to the training activity, for the crews remaining at Forbes

A Training Accident

The outboard engine, on each of the wings of the B-47, is located well out on the wing. When the outboard engine on one side loses power a serious case of asymmetrical thrust differential is created. This thrust differential is most critical at slower air speeds. The point of lift off is the most critical point. The pilot must counter act this thrust differential with the rudders. I remember one of the pilots in the wing telling me how difficult it was to control the aircraft at lift off with the loss of an outboard engine. He said that the pilot would have to recognize the loss of thrust and apply full opposite rudder within three seconds of lift off or the roll in the direction of the lost engine could not be stopped and the aircraft would likely crash. The task of quickly recognizing the loss of thrust on an engine was more difficult on the B-47 aircraft than most jet aircraft that were developed later. The pilot who was not making the take off would be monitoring the engine instruments. The most sensitive instrument on the modern jet engine is the Engine Pressure Ratio or EPR gage. This instrument compares the pressure between two parts of the engine. A loss of power immediately affects the pressure allowing the pilot quick recognition. The B-47 did not have EPR instruments. The second most sensitive instrument is the Exhaust Gas Temperature or EGT gage. It reads the temperature of the exhaust gases in the tail of the engine. A cooling in the EGT reading would indicate the loss of power. At 700 plus degrees this happened fairly quickly but not immediately. This same pilot advised me that he was aware of two instances where this situation had occurred on 55th aircraft. On one the pilot had successfully responded while on the second he had not. The cause of this training accident was listed as unknown but due to the flight path prior to impact many of the wing's pilots felt that the probable cause was the loss of power on an outboard engine. The aircraft was destroyed and all crew members aboard perished.

Accident at Incirlik

I had been at Forbes a little over a year and a half when an RB-47E aircraft assigned to the Tell-Two special project crashed at Incirlik AFB in Turkey. The accident occurred on April 3, 1965. The aircraft was destroyed and two of the five crew members perished. Alwyn Lloyd, in a book chronicling the development and use of the B-47, indicated that this sortie had fought a running gun battle with MIGs and crashed on landing. (13) I had not previously heard of the encounter with MIGs. Major Walt Savage was the aircraft commander. Capt. Albert Parsons (Albie), who had lived in the house next to me at Mather AFB, was the Raven Two on the crew. Several members of the crew, including Albie, had spot promotions. The crew had been the alert crew for the day and had taken off in response to an alert launch. They had completed the mission and were returning to Incirlik to land. The surface winds at Incirlik were strong. The steady cross wind was close to 25 knots with occasional higher gusts. As I describe in Appendix B, the B-47 aircraft had a limited tolerance for cross winds and the maximum it could tolerate was 25 knots. Had the flight been operating from its home base at Forbes it would, in all likelihood, have been diverted to wait out the winds. There were, however, few acceptable places to divert to from Incirlik given the need for the security of the aircraft once on the ground. The decision was made to attempt a landing at Incirlik. At the moment the aircraft flared to touch down on the runway a gust of wind near 35 knots pushed it toward the side of the runway. In danger of going off the runway Major Savage attempted a go around. He lost control of the aircraft and it crashed. I had heard, somewhat later, from several sources that when he advanced the throttles one of the out board engines did not spool up normally. If true this meant that he was dealing with excessive cross winds as well as asymmetrical thrust problems at the same time. The wings were sheared off and the fuselage came to rest on its side. The canopy was gone and the aircraft was on fire. The opening in the top of the aircraft was close enough to the ground so a short jump out of the aircraft was possible. The Navigator, Captain Jacobs in the front of the aircraft, had been killed on impact. The Pilots and the Raven One, Captain Barry Hammond, exited the aircraft. Captain Parsons, who sat in the aisle strapped into a webbed sling for landing, got out of the aircraft and was standing on the ramp. He was tangled in the web straps of the sling which were still attached to the aircraft and he was unable get away from the aircraft. As he struggled to free himself from the straps he was severely burned. The Turkish firemen finally freed him by cutting the straps. They also went into the burning aircraft and bought the Navigator's body out. Albie survived for a couple of days but died from his burns.

Tragedy Over Mattoon

During the summer of 1966 a 55th SRW aircraft, on a routine training flight, was involved in a mid-air refueling accident. When the

103

incident occurred the aircraft was over Mattoon, Indiana. I have not been able to find any record, in the publications I've reviewed nor in my own notes, of the exact date, so my time reference is not specific. My notes did cover the accident itself quite well. The flight was a training flight. There were four crew members on the flight. Captain Tom Hoose, the Copilot on my first crew, was in training to upgrade to an Aircraft Commander. The Deputy Wing commander, Colonel Charles Paxson, was going along for flight proficiency. The Instructor Pilot was Lt. Colonel Wayne. Colonel Wayne was part of the Wing staff. The Navigator was Captain Bobby Bates, the Navigator on my first crew. At the time of the incident Tom Hoose was in the front seat flying the aircraft. Colonel Wayne was in the rear seat as the Instructor Pilot and Colonel Paxson was down in the aisle, awaiting his turn to fly the aircraft. They were in the middle of a mid-air refueling. It had gone very smoothly. When the incident occurred the aircraft was approaching the forward limit of the refueling envelope.

Let me digress and describe to the reader what the refueling envelope is. The tanker aircraft has a movable refueling boom that is approximately 16 feet in length. It can be hydraulically extended an additional 16 feet. The boom has a pair of fins that allow the boom operator to control its movement. These fins allow the boom operator to literally fly the boom within certain limits. When the receiver aircraft is in the proper position the boom operator extends the boom to enter the refueling port on the receiver aircraft. It is locked in place so when fuel pumping is begun there will not be leaks. The system in the tanker aircraft senses the receiver's position by monitoring the position of the boom. It has an imaginary envelope. When the receiver moves outside of this imaginary envelope the boom system automatically disconnects from the receiver aircraft. This prevents damage to the boom. There are six limits, forward and aft, side to side and up and down. On this day the receiver aircraft (the RB-47) was approaching the forward limit of this imaginary envelope. One of the techniques that boom operators frequently use, when a receiver aircraft is approaching a limit, is to apply a little opposite direction pressure with the boom, both in direction and hydraulic extension, to slow the receiver aircraft's movement toward that limit. It works quite well as long as the boom is still connected. The boom operator on this day was apparently using that technique. Unfortunately on this day, just before the boom operator applied this opposite pressure the limit had already been reached and the boom had automatically disconnected. The actions of the boom operator suddenly extended the boom with out the resistance of a connected receiver aircraft. The boom hit and penetrated the bubble canopy of the B-47. The boom hit Captain Hoose in the head killing him instantly. The boom broke away from the tanker aircraft and with the B-47s bubble canopy tumbled over the B-47 aircraft's wing. The contact with the boom flipped the B-47 toward the damaged wing and it entered a steep dive. Colonel Wayne was able to recover the aircraft but at the expense of the loss of almost 20,000 feet in altitude.

A brief description of the situation facing Colonel Wayne is warranted. As mentioned earlier, the pilot's upper bodies extended above the fuselage in the B-47. With the canopy gone the pilots would be exposed to the slip stream (the flow of air around the fuselage). The aircraft's indicated airspeed had been about 270 knots during refueling. In the steep dive that resulted from the accident the airspeed would have increased dramatically. This would have had a disabling affect on the pilots and prevented them from any effort to recover the aircraft. Fortunately the rear seat of the B-47, where Colonel Wayne sat, has an equipment rack that is right in front of the seat. The equipment rack effectively blocked the impact of the slipstream. It also did not allow him any vision straight forward without exposing himself to the slipstream. This fact protected Colonel Wayne from injury. The aircraft was flown back to Forbes using the cockpit instruments. The existence of the equipment rack, however, made normal landings (with the canopy in place) from the rear seat a little more difficult. It required the copilot to peer along the sides of the equipment rack directly in front of him. Even then, they could only see the edges of the runway. They had to move the head from side to side to track both sides of the runway. In this case any attempt by Colonel Wayne to do this would put his face right in the slip stream. He would not be able to do that at normal flying speeds. Even at the slower landing speeds a quick peep would have been difficult. He had to land the aircraft almost blind. A fighter aircraft was launched to pace him in and talk him down. This was done successfully. Colonel Paxson, who had just been through a harrowing experience down in the aisle, went immediately to inform and console Tom's wife, Phyllis.

North Korea Attacks

On May 25, 1965, a 55th SRW aircraft was flying an operational sortie off the North Korean coast. It was one of the standard RB-47H configured aircraft. The crew commander was Lt. Colonel Matison. He was an old head in the 55th. The crew had deployed with a different aircraft which had experienced some serious mechanical difficulties. A replacement aircraft, serial number 57-4290, had been flown in from Forbes as a replacement. I had participated in the shake down flights of aircraft 57-4290 at Forbes before it was flown to Yokota by another 55th SRW crew. This was the aircraft they were using on this day.

The sortie had begun its day departing from Yokota AFB (our OL-2) in Japan. It was expected to be a routine sortie similar to dozens that had been flown before it along the same route. While they were flying over international waters off the coast they were intercepted by two North Korean MIG-17s. The MIGs subsequently opened fire making several firing passes at the RB-47. They inflicted severe damage. The Co-pilot, Lt. Hank Dubuy, returned fire. He managed to hit one of the MIGs who started to stream smoke. The MIGs subsequently broke off the attack. Colonel Mattison managed to maintain control of the aircraft. They headed back toward their base at Yokota.

At least two of the aircraft's engines were damaged and had to be shut down. The fuselage had taken several hits. At least two of the fuel tanks had been punctured. They would have to make a landing at Yokota with two engines out. The aircraft's weight and balance was well outside the safe limits due to the loss of fuel. It was questionable if they would make it back to Yokota much less be able to make a safe landing with a seriously out of balance aircraft.

They were able to limp back to Yokota. A landing airspeed that was higher than normal had to be maintained to prevent the aircraft from spiraling out of control. This significantly increased the probability that the aircraft would bounce on landing. A helicopter was in the air to provide emergency assistance if needed. It was hovering over the runway. The resultant bounce by the RB-47 was so high that it nearly came up to the altitude of the hovering helicopter. It was even with the height of the control tower. Colonel Mattison was able to bring the aircraft to a full stop on the runway. It was a superb effort and Colonel Mattison's extensive experience in the RB-47 likely was instrumental in this successful effort.

Survival School – Stead Air Force Base (1963)

My group during the second week of training
Picture taken immediately following the two man Escape and Evasion trek

I'm on the left in the front row – Roger is the second from the right in the front row

Ravens Take Off Positions RB-47H

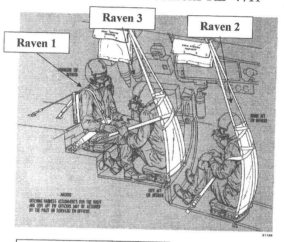

Front of the Aircraft →

RB-47H CREW POSITIONS

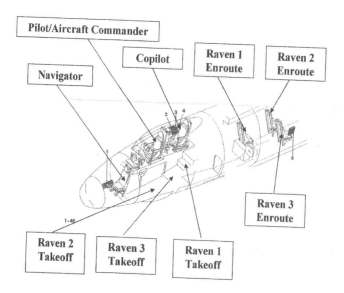

Pilot/Aircraft Commander

Navigator

Copilot

Raven 1
Enroute

Raven 2
Enroute

Raven 3
Enroute

Raven 2
Takeoff

Raven 3
Takeoff

Raven 1
Takeoff

Chapter 8   First Combat Ready Crew

A Place to Live

I had been assigned a room in the Bachelor Officers Quarters (BOQ) when I arrived at Forbes AFB. This was to be my residence for the next couple of months. Each of us had a single room with a bath that was shared with the adjacent room. The officer in the adjacent room was another Second Lieutenant by the name of Don Nolten. His job was in personnel. Don was a quiet and studious type of person. He spent a great deal of time reading and he seldom joined, at least initially, our social forays out on the town of Topeka. Most of us did not want to stay in the BOQ any longer than necessary. A Second Lieutenant's salary, however, didn't afford us many choices unless we found something together. The two of us began to look for something off the base almost immediately. We looked for a two bedroom apartment we could rent. The one we found was not fancy but adequate. It was on Teft Street in Topeka. Coincidently, the apartment was only a couple of blocks away from the Topeka school that had been the subject of a famous court case that had reached all the way to the United States Supreme Court. The case, Brown Vs.The Board of Education decided in 1956, was the legal decision that accelerated the civil rights movement in the United States. By this time, late 1963, that movement was just gathering momentum.

Don and I stayed in that apartment only about three months. An office mate of Don's had located a three bedroom house for rent. Second Lieutenant Tracy Wilson, another personnel officer, joined us in splitting the rent on a house on Mission Street. Tracy was from Massachusetts. He was bespeckled and looked a little like Harry Potter but was quite out going. Tracy often made the statement, in jest we thought (I was never quite sure), that civilization stopped at the Hudson River. About a month later a fourth Second Lieutenant joined us, Mike Hindman. Mike was also a personnel officer and hailed from the Chicago area. He was engaged to be married and needed a place for a couple of months. He slept on our sofa. Mike was a colorful fellow. He had a lively imagination which drove most of our group's capers. On several occasions the neighbors watched as we engaged in mock sword fights with plastic swords in the middle of the front yard.

Mike had been on his college fencing team. It was the first that I was aware of any college that had a fencing team.

Initial Training and Combat Ready Certification

I reported to Forbes on October 30, 1963. Within a week I was introduced to the RB-47H aircraft. I was issued a flight manual and instructed to memorize all of the Warning segments of the manual. These were considered Safety of Flight items and had to be committed to memory by all crew members. My first flight in the aircraft was with Captain Blaisdal's crew on November 7th. I flew two more training flights during November and two more in December. Each crew member had to pass a written test on the Warning or Safety of Flight items in the manual. A score of 100 % was passing. I had successfully completed this step. On January 7, 1964 I was scheduled for an evaluation with a Standboard Raven which could lead to certification and assignment to a combat ready crew. The flight was with Major Don Griffin's crew. Major Harrison Tull was my evaluator. Major Tull was one of a small number of African Americans in the wing. He'd had a storied career. He had been a member of the Tuskegee Airman during the Second World War. He had been a long time member of the 55th and was a member of one of the Standboard crews. He was well known and well regarded in the unit. The flight went quite smoothly and I felt confident that I had passed. The critique was scheduled for the following day. To my surprise I had not passed. Major Tull felt my operations on the equipment were satisfactory. The problem was with my pre-flight checks. I had failed to check the seat separator strap on the ejection seat. This was considered a Safety of Flight item. Any omission or disregard of a Safety of Flight item was an automatic failure. Major Tull was a stickler for Safety of Flight items. It was a good lesson. I had focused on the equipment operation and had taken the pre-flight too casually. It served to re-focus my attention to detail, particularly in checking my equipment. A few years later, during the pre-flight inspection, I found one of the pins on my parachute bent. It was bent far enough that it would likely have prevented deployment of the chute had it became necessary. I had the chute replaced prior to

109

takeoff.

I continued my training with four more flights in February. I was scheduled for re-evaluation on February 27th with Lt. Colonel Rust's crew. Major Bill Allen was my evaluator. The flight went well and I passed the evaluation.

The Crow Shop

The 55th Wing Commander and his staff were located in a separate building from the two operations squadrons. Both operations squadrons, the 343rd Squadron and the 38th Squadron, occupied the same building. The wing had a staff Electronic Warfare Officer. His office, known as the Crow Shop, was in the same building as the two operations squadrons. Major Frank Williams was the Wing Crow when I joined the wing. Major Curly Behrman was his assistant. Frank was close to retirement and was a fatherly type figure, particularly to the young crows like myself, who were new to the organization. Frank had a great deal to say about which crew each Raven was assigned to. Curly was not Major Behrman's first name but everyone called him that. He also did not have curly hair. In fact he was almost completely bald at the time I knew him. He was an affable individual. He was also rumored to be an heir to the Best Foods fortune. Everyone liked and respected our two occupants of the Crow Shop.

Return to Stead

All 55th SRW combat ready crew members were required to attend a special advanced survival training course at Stead AFB in Nevada. The Air Force established this requirement based on the assumption that the nature of our mission meant there was a better chance of our becoming a prisoner of war than in other Air Force flying units. The course focused on prisoner of war issues. Many of the same techniques that we were introduced to during the basic survival course were used in this one. Again, the only one that I found difficult to handle was the water treatment. The class was a week long and started on March 6, 1964. A small group of new 55th officers were assigned to attend this class among them Second Lieutenant Robb

Hoover and myself. We would attend the school and receive a packet of Top Secret documents to return with us to Forbes. I was designated as the Top Secret Courier for these documents. We had driven, as a group, from Topeka to Reno to attend this course. During the return trip we encountered a major snow storm and blizzard in Wyoming. I became concerned that we might be stranded in the storm. I was uncomfortable with the thought of being stranded with these Top Secret documents in my possession. My fears proved to be unfounded. We were able to continue without incident and returned to Forbes.

Assigned to An Operational Crew

On March 21, 1964, shortly after my return from Stead, I had served the required 18 months as a Second Lieutenant and was promoted to the rank of First Lieutenant. I had been assigned to a combat ready crew prior to my departure for Stead. The commander of the crew was Captain Jack Schweizer. Jack was an outspoken, straight forward individual. You never had to guess what he was thinking. He was a good pilot. The Co-pilot on the crew once told me that Jack's landings could be a bit sloppy when the weather conditions were ideal but when the weather conditions were terrible he would make very good and smooth landings. He had to be challenged to put forth his best effort. Jack hailed from St. Paul, Minnesota. The Co-pilot was Captain Tom Hoose. Tom was a short stocky man with an outgoing personality. He was always in a good mood with a good sense of humor. Tom kept things light and easy when he was around. Tom hailed from South Carolina. He would be killed in the mid-air refueling accident described in the previous chapter. The Navigator was Captain Bobbie Bates. The Raven One was First Lieutenant John Lesinski. The Raven Three was First Lieutenant Bill Lewis. I became the Raven Two. Bill was from Arizona. He had been introduced to aviation at a young age. His father had been an early aviation pioneer in Arizona. Bill learned to fly as a teenager. When I first met him he had a private pilot's license but had not flown for a few years. He was just getting back into it. Shortly after I joined the crew, in the spring of 1964, Bill took me with him to a small airport just west of town known as Allen's Air Park. A couple of flights with him fired my interest in getting a license. Unfortunately I wasn't financially prepared to start. I didn't begin my private flight training until December of the same year.

Our crew's first training flight was on March 13th. In late May the crew was notified that we were scheduled for a deployment to Brize Norton (OL-1) in late June. Between early March and mid June the crew flew six training flights and three Common Cause operational sorties. Common Cause sorties normally departed from Forbes in the late evening hours. The return trip to Forbes would be during the daylight hours of the following day. The sorties were approximately nine hours long. On one of the Common Cause sorties we had to lay over for several hours at Little Rock AFB to wait for improved weather. Deviations for weather were normally the result of the B-47 aircraft's limited tolerance of cross winds on landing. The aircraft could tolerate a maximum of 25 knots of direct cross wind and no more. Our commanders always came down on the side of caution so deviations for weather were not uncommon. The wind blows often and briskly over the Great Plains.

The elevated level of security that surrounded our operations made weather deviations more complicated. The aircraft could not be left unguarded. One member of the crew would have to remain with the aircraft until the local Air Police were advised and an armed guard could be provided. This often took some time. The aircraft would have an armed guard until we returned to the aircraft and left the base. We always tried to divert to another SAC base. SAC emphasized security for all of its aircraft to a far greater degree than any of the other commands. The majority of the weather deviations on Common Cause missions were to Little Rock AFB near Little Rock, Arkansas. It was a SAC base and was close to our return route from Cuba. Our stay at Little Rock on this day was about five hours. We hung around the Officers club in our dirty flight suits waiting to fly home.

Collateral Duties

The period between deployments for the combat ready crews at

Forbes were not devoted entirely to flying. Flights required a great deal of planning in addition to the flights themselves. My time between my arrival at Forbes and my certification had been filled with study, training and preparation. It had kept me very busy. Once I joined a crew, the pace slowed to a degree. Our primary duty was flying. Each training flight kept us occupied for only a few days, planning the mission and flying it. Four to six flights a month was a normal crew load. This left some spare time. The squadron filled this spare time by assigning most crew members a collateral administrative type duty. My first collateral duty was as a destruction officer. A destruction officer's duties were to destroy classified documents that were no longer needed. The destruction process followed a very precise procedure. Any carelessness could get you in trouble in a hurry. I vividly recall one of the tasks I had completed as a destruction officer. On this day I was accompanied by a young airman and a master sergeant from the wing. We had several large bags of material to destroy. Each bag was about four feet high and about three feet wide. The bags were stuffed with classified documents. We proceeded to a building that had a special furnace specifically designed for the purpose. The furnace was a large cement enclosure with two flues for the smoke to escape. The flues were about six inches in diameter with screen mesh covering them. The screen was there to ensure that any unburned scrap could not escape in the smoke. The airman and the sergeant did the actual burning. My job was to ensure that the procedures were followed and to certify the destruction when it was complete. The papers had to be fed into the fire individually to ensure they would burn completely. If anything went wrong I would be responsible. It took us about two hours to finish. About six months later I was called before a Major from the Air Police squadron and informed that a partial document that I had certified destroyed had been found. It was partially burned and the control number on the document was clear on the unburned portion. That was how they traced it to the batch that I had certified destroyed. I was concerned that I was in a lot of trouble. The partially burned document had been lodged in the screen covering the flue in the furnace we had used. There would be an investigation. Two days later

I returned to face the same Major. He advised me that the investigation was complete and no further action would be taken. The only thing visible on the unburned fragment was the control number itself. No classified information had been compromised. I was greatly relieved.

Courier Duty

I ended up with another additional duty. Second Lieutenant Mike Hindman was in charge of providing couriers to transport classified documents to and from Forbes for all of the assigned units. He said he was always in need of more couriers so he immediately started to work on me. Much of the material that needed transport by courier was classified as Top Secret, the highest of the general classified categories. He himself, as well as most of his fellow personnel officers, had only a Secret clearance so he could not use them the majority of the time. He knew that I had a Top Secret clearance and since we lived in the same house he had ample opportunity to work on me. I finally consented and was placed on General Courier orders effective May 25, 1964.

Mike put me to work in this additional capacity almost immediately. The majority of the material he needed transported by courier was between Forbes and Offutt AFB which was the headquarters of the Strategic Air Command (SAC). There was a regular weekly run between the two bases by a C-47 aircraft assigned for this express purpose. I made a couple of trips as the lone courier. I would sign for the documents, pick them up and be escorted in an Air Police vehicle to the aircraft. I showed the pilot in command my badge and a letter of instruction. He checked my name against the list and waved me on board. When the aircraft arrived at Offutt I was met by an officer. The pilot and I checked his credentials and had him sign for the documents. He, in turn, had some documents for me. I signed for them and we returned to Forbes. The authentication and transfer process was repeated there. My job was done.

On one of the trips I was accompanied by a Major who was also a courier. The instruction sheet placed him in charge. We followed much the same process except that both of us were issued loaded

114

pistols and a holster. This was special material. It was what was colloquially referred to as the Go Code. The Go Code was the coded documents that were placed on the 40th Bomb wing's alert bombers. When their aircraft were launched on an actual strike mission, which fortunately never came to pass, or an exercise, such as an Operational Readiness Inspection (ORI), they would fly to their planned Fail Safe point and await further instructions. Operational Readiness Inspections were a "no notice" inspection by a team from SAC headquarters. The intent of the ORI was to test a unit's ability to respond to an operational emergency such as a Soviet attack with Inter-Continental Ballistic Missiles (ICBMs). It was the brainchild of SAC's commander, General Curtis LeMay. Operational Readiness Inspections were serious business for SAC units. Unsatisfactory performance by a Wing during an ORI often would result in the Wing Commander being relieved of his job. The Fail Safe point was a pre-planned point part way along the route toward their assigned target under the SIOP (the master plan for a retaliatory nuclear strike on the Soviet Union). It was far enough to be clear of any potential damage from a nuclear attack by the Soviet Union. They would get their instructions from the National Command Authority through the SAC command structure in coded form through a special device on the aircraft. They would authenticate the coded instructions using the Go Code documents that they carried on the aircraft. The instructions would be either to return to base or proceed on course toward their assigned target. They could not proceed beyond their Fail Safe point unless they received properly coded instructions to proceed to their targets and drop their nuclear bombs. The Go Code was changed periodically and that was our task on this day, to transport the new code from SAC headquarters to the 40th Bomb Wing. We flew to Offutt without any documents. We were met at Offutt by a full Colonel and two armed Air Policemen and picked up the Go Code. Both the Major and I had to sign for the documents. When we returned to Forbes we were again met by a full Colonel and two armed Air Policemen. One of the Air Policeman was a young Captain. He and the Colonel both signed for the Go Code.

First Operational Deployment

Our deployment was on June 24th, 1964. The flight to Brize Norton would take about nine and a half hours. A mid-air refueling would be required to make it to our destination. We were to depart from Forbes together with another 55th aircraft that was deploying to Incirlik (OL-4). The commander on the other aircraft was Lt. Colonel Joe Guylavics. His crew was a Standboard crew. The plan was for the two aircraft to fly as a flight of two to a point over Northeastern Canada. There we were to join up with two KC-97 tanker aircraft to refuel. When the refueling was complete the two aircraft would part ways. We would proceed to England and the other aircraft would depart to Spain en-route to Turkey.

Refueling behind a KC-97 is difficult for a B-47 under the best of circumstances. The KC-97 is a propeller driven aircraft and the B-47 is a jet aircraft. There are significant differences between them in their normal operating air speeds and their normal operating altitudes. Jet aircraft operate at higher speeds and higher altitudes. The KC-97 pilot would have to push the throttles to full power and the B-47 would have to slow to near stall speed. The altitude for refueling had to be reduced from about 28,000 feet, where jet to jet mid-air refueling normally occurred, to an altitude under 20,000 feet. To add to the difficulty, weather conditions on this day were less than ideal. The lower altitude and the abundance of moist clouds meant there was a serious potential for icing. Icing is one of the most dangerous problems an aircraft in flight can encounter. It increases drag on the aircraft, deforms the air foil which reduces lift, and adds weight to the aircraft. Ice can build up exceeding fast. There are many stories in aviation of ice building up on aircraft so rapidly the pilots had difficulty saving the aircraft from disaster.

The two 55th aircraft rendezvoused with the KC-97s and the refueling was begun. Both B-47s started to ice up. Colonel Guylavics joined with his tanker aircraft first and completed the refueling. Our aircraft had taken on fuel for several minutes when the nose of the aircraft suddenly plunged down about 20 degrees. Captain Schweitzer had felt the buffet of an approaching stall and broke off with the tanker to prevent it.   A short discussion between the two pilots followed. The Co-pilot, Captain Hoose, seemed to favor aborting the flight. Captain Schweitzer seemed adamant that he wanted to complete it. He needed a few more minutes to have enough fuel to make it to Brize Norton. He mentioned that Colonel Guylavics had gotten his fuel so we should be able to as well. He re-joined the tanker and after a minute or so had to push the nose over again. He asked the tanker to go into a slow descent which would increase its' speed. He re-joined the tanker and finished the refueling. The remainder of the flight was uneventful.

Brize Norton

When we arrived at Brize Norton we found that the ERB special project crew was there as well as the crew we were relieving. Major Tom Moncure was the Raven One on that crew. Major Moncure was very knowledgeable raven and was one of the few wing ravens tasked to evaluate and accept, for the wing, any new reconnaissance equipment. We were scheduled to fly ten operational missions during the deployment, four in July, five in August and one in September. Our return to Forbes was scheduled for mid September. The first mission was scheduled for July 7th. This flight would trigger spot promotions for those of us that were eligible. I was not eligible.

We spent the first week becoming familiar with the routes and requirements detailed in the FRAG orders which described all of our missions. Just before I left Forbes on this trip I had borrowed a copy of the book, The Little Toy Dog, from a friend at Forbes. I didn't get a chance it read it before I left so I bought it with me and read it during the first week at Brize Norton. One of the mission profiles we were scheduled to fly was to the Barents Sea, the same area where they had been shot down. Our route was to be closer to the Russian coast than that ill-fated aircraft had flown. We flew that mission profile on August the 20th. On August 3rd we flew a mission into the Baltic Sea. While we were paralleling the Polish coast line we intercepted a radar signal known by the NATO name of BG-06. The BG-06 was the guidance radar for the Russians Surface-To-Air (SAM) missile system. The system had two radars. The search radar carried the NATO moniker of Fan Song. The Fan Song radar's job was to locate and track the quarry. Once the missile was launched it would be controlled by another radar signal, the BG-06 which would guide the missile to its target. Our presence was obviously not the reason it was on the air since we were flying at least 15 miles off shore. We were beyond the range of the SAM missile. The Russians were most likely conducting tests. When we intercept an emission we use a piece of equipment called the Direction Finder or DF. The DF provides a bearing to the source of the emission. A single bearing would provide a direction only and not a position. If the signal stays on the air long enough, the raven can obtain several bearings from different points on the track. This allows the bearings to intersect and provides the location of the source. Our direction finding bearings on this emission pin pointed its location. We learned later that an earlier U-2 flight in the vicinity had photographed excavations at that precise location. This confirmed that the Soviets were starting to deploy the system to the satellite countries of Eastern Europe. Several months later a 55th SRW crew confirmed that they had also deployed the system to North Viet Nam (14).

First Baltic Mission

One of the sorties during July of 1964 was in the Baltic Sea between Sweden and Russia. The sortie was flown in conjunction with the ERB project aircraft. The ERB aircraft was equipped to do a much more in depth analysis of a specifically targeted radar site. The primary objective of this joint mission was to get the Russians to turn on their Flat Face radar so the ERB project aircraft could record its parameters and assess its capability. Flat Face was the name that NATO had assigned to this Soviet radar system. It was supposedly designed to detect low flying targets. The B-47s and B-52s of the alert bomber force, if they were responding to a Soviet nuclear attack, would be attempting to enter the Soviet Union at a very low altitude staying under radar coverage. Our planners had very little actual data on this radar system. We had been unsuccessful to that point in time of making an intercept. It was always off the air when one of our aircraft was in the area. The plan on this day was to push the envelope to get them to turn it on.

We flew into the Baltic as a flight of two but stayed separated by a few miles so that the Russians could easily see that there were two aircraft. The flight continued to a point close to the Russian coast but still over international waters. We then turned to parallel the coast knowing the Russians were tracking both of us. We then turned back to the west and flew behind Gotland Island which is just off the Swedish coast. This put us out of range of the Russian's radar coverage. While we were behind Gotland Island the ERB aircraft descended down to the deck a few hundred feet above the water. The idea was for the ERB to come in low beneath the Russian's normal radar coverage while we stayed at altitude so they could see us. The Russians could not be sure if the two aircraft had tucked in close so as to appear as a single target or that one of us had left for home or the aircraft they could not see was still out there somewhere and they did not know where. This, we hoped, would prompt them to turn on the Flat Face radar to find the second aircraft. The Russian's first response was to send two fighter aircraft out to look us over. When they found only a single aircraft their concern level obviously went up. They turned the Flat Face on. When fighters were sent to identify one of our aircraft they normally responded with a single aircraft and flew in formation with us off one of our wing tips. On this day the two fighters near our aircraft were zipping in and out in a seemingly agitated manner. Major Schweitzer instructed Captain Hoose to turn on the fire control panel. Captain Hoose rotated his seat and readied the guns.

It was fairly routine for the Russians to send a fighter out to identify us on these types of missions. They always stayed away from the tail area showing respect for the two 20 millimeter cannons we had on the tail. On this day they twice made a pass coming straight from our rear and right up the coverage of our guns. Major Schweitzer later said he had never seen them do that before. At one point he told Captain Hoose "Prepare to Fire". As you might imagine, at this point, the stomach muscles of each member of the crew tightened up. The situation was getting tense. If the firing began and we were lucky enough to hit one of the fighters the other fighter would surely get us. It was at this point we received a Condition One message from our Early Warning platform. This was our orders to get ourselves out of there as quickly as possible. We immediately aborted the mission, turned perpendicular to the coast and started a rapid descent. The fighters followed us for a minute or so and then broke for home. As far as we know they never re-located the ERB aircraft. The mission had been a huge success. We were all thankful when the flight returned to being routine and we were headed back to base.

While in England

The ten missions we flew while deployed left us with quite a bit of spare time. Each flight required about two or three duty days. Occasionally there would be several days between the missions that allowed us to take advantage of being in England. We spoke the same language and shared a common culture. Brize Norton was a few miles from the English town of Whitney and about 20 miles from the city of Oxford where the famous university is located. Several members of the crew, including myself, had purchased an old vehicle which allowed us to get around. It looked like it was right out of the Roaring Twenties. It required constant maintenance which we did ourselves at the base hobby shop. We had to be very careful when we drove it because in England cars drive on the left side of the road. There was a passenger train from Oxford to Paddington Station in down town London. So we would drive to Oxford and board the train to London. There were two large hotels in London where we could stay that catered exclusively to U.S. servicemen and servicewomen. The Columbia House was for officers and the Douglas House was for the enlisted ranks. The rooms were reasonable. The hotel had a dinning room and there were staffed desks for booking a variety of different types of entertainment. The subway system, known as the Tube, provided easy and cheap transportation to any part of London. We had no trouble getting where we wanted to in London in spite of the fact that at that the time it was the largest city in the world.

One of the stops on the Tube was an area known as Piccadilly Circus. Piccadilly Circus has a theatre district. The plays are quite similar to off Broadway type of theatre. It is the place where aspiring actors/actresses get their chance to perform. I was able to attend several of these plays during my trips to London. One was a presentation of the play "Oliver". I also spent several hours of an afternoon at Speaker's Corner in Hyde Park. Speaker's Corner is a storied London forum where a speaker with any agenda can speak his/her mind to an spontaneously assembled audience. If memory serves me correctly, I made three trips to London on this deployment.

Reflex Operations

During the late 1950s and the early 1960s the B-47E aircraft was the mainstay of SACs alert bomber fleet. The aircraft did not have the range that the B-52 had. The B-52 was slowly replacing the B-47s in SACs bomber units. In addition to its greater range the B-52 also carried a heavier bomb load. Toward the end of that decade the B-47 was fazed out entirely. Due to the B-47s more limited range SAC had established a concept know as Reflex. Reflex was a program that deployed the B-47 alert bomber forces to be closer to their targets. Several bases in England were used for this purpose. A bomber crew's tour on a Reflex deployment would be three weeks long. The first week would be in alert status. The second week they were on Rest and Recuperation (R and R) and the final week back in alert status. Then they returned home and were replaced by another crew. They were free to become tourists during that week of R and R. SAC even provided a C47 aircraft which would transport them to a selected tourist area in Europe during their R and R. Each week the Reflex crews would vote on where the C-47 would go. The 55th crews at Brize Norton were included in this R and R program. I was able to take a trip on the C-47 to Copenhagen in Denmark. Bill Lewis and I spent three days there. One of the points of interest we visited was the Tivili Gardens in downtown Copenhagen.

Return to Forbes

The final operational sortie was completed on September 2nd. We had flown 10 sorties in the 3 month tour. A new crew from Forbes Air Force Base (AFB) arrived in early September to replace us. They bought another Forbes based aircraft with them and would be responsible for operational sorties from Brize Norton using that aircraft for the next several months. Our return flight to Forbes was on September 15th with aircraft 57-4286. The flight was lengthy, 10 hours and 45 minutes, included a mid-air refueling; but was otherwise uneventful.

Our operational deployment had been quite successful. The results of our sorties helped to confirm the existence and location of radar facilities that were already known to the Air Force and the US intelligence community. In addition, however, our sorties had helped add significant new information in two areas to this data base and it was done at a significantly increased risk. First, the Russians were known to have a Surface-To-Air missile system (SA-2). They had, to that date, restricted its deployment to sites within the Russian interior. On one of our sorties we had recorded an electronic intercept on the system's guidance radar. This served to confirm the first deployment of the system out side the Russian heartland. The deployment of the SA-2 system led to the 55th s special project program called FIRE FLY in 1965. Secondly, in a joint sortie with the ERB special project aircraft in the Baltic Sea, we had helped add more in depth data on the Soviet's low altitude radar (NATO name FLAT FACE). This sortie had been anticipated as a high risk one. It did indeed elicit an uncharacteristically heavy aircraft response from the Soviets. In order to entice them to put these systems back on the air, so we could record them and learn about them, the mission planners had planned a more provocative profile for us. As I mentioned earlier the objective of these sorties was to raise their level of concern to the point where they would put their systems on the air but not to the degree that they would attack our aircraft. We will never know just how far we crossed that line or what may have happened had we not been recalled when we were. Each member of our crew would later be awarded the Distinguished Flying Cross (DFC) for the accomplishments and risks taken during this operational tour.

Chapter 9   The Iron Lung Project

On October 3, 1964 I was assigned to another crew. Major John Drost was the crew commander. The crew was assigned to one of the special projects, the <u>Iron Lung</u>. The Iron Lung program had a single aircraft and one crew assigned. The aircraft was a specially configured RB-47H. The crew consisted of the standard 6 crew member positions. The program was an ongoing one, but the aircraft was re-configured for each shorter term project. Each project was tasked, directed and the contractual portions funded by the CIA. The aircraft and crew belonged to the Air Force. The project equipment, data analysis and technical support were provided under contract by ITT research labs in San Fernando, California. Airframe modifications were contracted to Lockheed Aircraft Company in Ontario, California. The purpose of the <u>Iron Lung</u> program was to conduct and record very precise aerial power measurements on a specific enemy RADAR system. The data was recorded in digital format. Use of the digital format was uncommon in 1964. The recorded data was used to update the Air Force's knowledge of enemy RADAR systems. Frequently the data would be used to construct a working copy of the enemy RADAR. The copied system would then be installed at a site in the Nevada desert and we would conduct power measurements on the copied site to verify its similarity in function and signature

A single RB-47H, serial number 57-4291, was configured for the <u>Iron Lung</u> program. Each <u>Iron Lung</u> project targeted a specific enemy RADAR. The configuration of the Raven's equipment was changed with each project. Each project task began with the aircraft being flown from Forbes AFB to the Ontario International Airport in California. It would be left there in the hands of the Lockheed Aircraft Company. The crew would return home via commercial carrier. The aircraft would remain there for several weeks while the equipment installation and any needed airframe modifications were completed.

The wing would be notified when the installation of the equipment and the needed airframe modifications were completed and the crew would return to Ontario to retrieve the aircraft. Before leaving the

Ontario Airport, the crew would be briefed on the project by the ITT engineers and receive any needed training. Infrequently the training might include a test flight at Ontario prior to returning to Forbes. The project engineer for ITT Research Labs was a man by the name of Frank Bucher. Mr. Bucher was a man in his mid fifty's and had a highly respectable record in the development of equipment to support aviation. He had been a part of the team that developed the ground based VOR navigation system. This system was then and continued to be until the advent of GPS, the primary navigation tool used by the commercial aviation industry and the air traffic control system in the United States. Mr. Bucher often sat in on the briefings. He would meet and always remembered each crew member. He was a kind of grandfatherly figure to us. The CIA project officer would also be present at the briefings to answer any questions. The aircraft was then flown back to Forbes Air Force Base to prepare for the overseas deployment.

The Ravens on the crew consisted of Captain Bill Henderson (Raven One), Lt. Dick Cain (Raven Three) and myself as Raven Two. I had replaced Captain Stan Rock who was upgrading to Raven One and was assigned to another crew. The first Iron Lung project that I participated in did not involve an overseas deployment. I joined the crew after the aircraft had already returned from Ontario, California. The flights would all be flown against a specific type of RADAR with sites in Cuba. Each mission would takeoff from Forbes AFB, fly to and set up an orbit on the periphery of Cuba, then return and land at Forbes.

This particular project involved several minor modifications to the airframe. A large, retractable boom (about 6 feet in length) was installed on the left side of the aircraft a short distance in front of the horizontal stabilizer. This boom extended down vertically from the point of attachment. It could, however, be retracted to a position horizontally along the fuselage of the aircraft. It would be in the retracted position during takeoffs and landings. It would be extended when we reached our collection area. With the boom in the extended position it allowed for the extension of a long trailing wire with an attached antenna without interfering or contacting the tail sections of

124

the aircraft. The antenna itself was a large (about 1 ½ feet in length) cylindrical object that we called the "Bird". It was connected to a metal cable. The cable would be retracted (wound onto a drum) for takeoff and landing, then extended (spooled out) a couple of hundred feet while in the collection area. When the boom was retracted along the fuselage, the "Bird" would be held in clam shell like metal hands attached to the end of the retractable boom. The cable was fed in through the clam shells so the "Bird" would be drawn into them. A motor was used to reel the cable in or out. It had a toggle switch located inside the raven compartment that was operated manually by the Raven Three. The speed of the motor was quick and it had only two speeds, full speed and off. This meant that you had to toggle the switch in short jerks when the "Bird" approached the clam shells so as to ease it in. If the "Bird" came in too fast, it could hit the clam shells hard enough to break the cable. This would result in loss of the "Bird" (a rather expensive item). Obviously, you had to be able to see the "Bird" approach the clam shells in order to ease it into them. As there were no windows in the raven compartment, the Lockheed and ITT engineers came up with an ingenious way of letting us see the "Bird" coming in. They bored a hole in the left side of the aircraft from the raven compartment and installed a simple periscope. They also installed an exterior light we could turn on as most of our sorties were at night.

As it turned out, a bit of skill was needed to retract the "Bird" successfully. Dick Cain (Raven Three) got quite good at it. The operation typically went like this. We would complete our mission requirements. Turn off the equipment and reel in the "Bird" before we had to go forward for landing. You started by turning on the exterior light. To look through the periscope, you had to get out of the seat harness and bend down over to the side. This, of course, was done with the parachute still on your back. It was an awkward position. The periscope could be turned. You turned it until you had the clam shells in site (the field of vision was very small and the light coverage limited). Then raise it slightly to see the "Bird" as it came through the light into the clam shells. Initially, we held the toggle switch down full. The **instant** the "Bird" came into view you released the toggle switch. Then you eased it in with short jerks. Once in the clam shells, you retracted the boom. The job was done.

As I said, this took some practice. Dick told me he had lost the "Bird" on the first two sorties. The ITT engineer on site was concerned that, at this rate, we would run out of spare "Birds". Dick only lost one more after that. On the final sortie, Dick thought that I should try it. He talked through the procedure twice for me. I must not have raised the periscope enough, because the instant I saw the "Bird" it hit the clam shells and was gone. That was our last "Bird". Fortunately, the project collection phase was finished. We always tried to recover the "Bird" and retract the boom while still over the Gulf of Mexico. The "Bird" could be a dangerous missile to people on the ground if we were back over land.

An interesting situation had come to light when the crew went to Ontario to pick up the aircraft for this project. This story was related to me by Dick Cain (Raven Three) as I had not yet joined the crew. The engineers at ITT were apparently concerned that the flight crew might forget to retract the boom before landing. In the extended position, the boom would have been destroyed when the aircraft touched down. One of the ITT engineers was explaining the system to the crew during the crew briefing at Ontario. He mentioned their concern and explained that they had added a feature to ensure this didn't happen. He advised them that a series of micro switches had been installed that tied into the aircraft's gear retraction system. In short, if the boom was not retracted we would not be able to extend the landing gear. This would serve as a reminder for the crew to retract the boom. Major Drost had jumped to his feet and stopped the briefing. He explained to them in rather sharp language, that if the boom retraction system had problems, as any mechanical system can, the inability to extend the landing gear would result not only in destroying the boom, but the aircraft as well. This would compromise the safety of the aircraft and possibly the lives of the crew. He informed them that the aircraft would not move until all that circuitry had been removed.

At the time I joined the crew in early October of 1964, the crew had already flown several operational Iron Lung sorties in this

126

configuration. Six more sorties were flown during the month of October. The majority of the special project duties in the present configuration fell to the Raven Three (Lt. Cain). My equipment and duties, as the Raven Two, were mostly similar to those on a standard configuration RB-47H. The most interesting part of each sortie, for me, was to watch Dick extend the "Bird" and retrieve it. The periscope was located to his right (we faced aft) about armpit high. The raven compartment in an RB-47 was very cramped. We kept our back pack type parachutes on at all times and remained strapped in to the ejection seat with lap belt and shoulder straps fastened. To look thru the periscope, Dick had to release his shoulder straps and lap belt, stand in the narrow space between the Raven Two and Raven Three seats, twist to the right and crouch down (with parachute still on). From this position if he slipped slightly backward he would be sitting in my lap. He remained in this twisted (and uncomfortable) position until the "Bird" was safely in the clam shells and the boom retracted. He only lost one "Bird" while I was on the crew. On that sortie I heard a loud "Shit". He sat up in the seat. His face was red (normal for that procedure). He retracted the boom and we headed for home. Dick was upset with himself. Since all of the sorties were flown at night we normally returned to Forbes in the wee hours of the morning.

On October 21st we ferried the aircraft (57-4291) from Forbes to the Lockheed Company at the Ontario airfield so that the contractors could make the necessary modifications in the equipment configuration that we would use in the next series of sorties. We returned to Forbes via commercial air.

Private Flight Training

I didn't begin my private flight training until December of 1964. It had been several months since my rides with Bill Lewis. In the interim I had learned of a small flight school north of Topeka called Mesa Verde. The prices at Mesa Verde were much cheaper than at Allen Air Park. Mesa Verde was run by a man by the name of Max Collier. Max and his wife owned a small farm about 10 miles due north of Topeka. The majority of the farm was in pasture. He didn't engage in any agricultural activities. The pasture was his airfield. He called it Mesa Verde. Max was a history professor at Washburn University in Topeka. He had recently obtained his flight instructor rating. He was passionate about flying and had started a flight school. To have the time to start a flight school he had taken a leave of absence from the university. The field was grass and essentially square measuring about 2500 feet in either dimension. He had purchased two Aeronca Champs. Aeronca Champs were older aircraft. They had two seats in tandem with a tail wheel in the rear. The student sat in the front seat and the instructor in the rear. Because the aircraft used a tail wheel rather than a nose wheel the aircraft, while it sat on the ground, was nose high and tail low. Neither pilot could see directly in front of the aircraft due to the nose high attitude. When the aircraft was taxied the pilot had to weave back and forth so he could see what was directly in front of him.

I distinctly remember my first takeoff in the aircraft. The aircraft was steered on the ground by using the rudder pedals which also turned the small tail wheel. I had a lot of trouble taxiing the aircraft. I learned later that the proper technique was to step on the rudder in the direction you wanted to turn and then release it. A few seconds later the aircraft would turn. I would step on one of the rudder pedals and hold it down until the aircraft started to turn. This was too long. I was over controlling the aircraft. The aircraft would turn too far. This, of course, prompted me to step on the opposite rudder only much harder to compensate for my initial over control which caused me to over control in the opposite direction. This continued with huge swerves back and forth. When we reached the point to start the takeoff I expected he would take over. No such luck. He talked me through the procedure and told me to take the aircraft off. I advanced the throttle and the aircraft started to roll. Once the aircraft gained a little speed I raised the tail slightly which followed the procedure Max had explained to me. As we continued to gain speed I was over controlling with the rudders much the same as I had done during taxiing. The swerves got larger and larger until I lifted off. The takeoff was made about 60 degrees to the direction that I had started. I was sweating badly. Max's calm voice from the rear said "Not Too

Bad". I thought to myself "I wonder what a really bad takeoff would look like".

The Aeronca Champ is a slow aircraft. It is also a very forgiving aircraft. By forgiving I mean that a pilot can safely make some mistakes in the Aeronca that would be dangerous in many other aircraft. The instructor can allow the student more leeway before he has to take over. I flew several times during January of 1965. I was able to accumulate only about five hours of flying when the money got a little short. My flight training would be interrupted several times due to deployments and lack of funds. FAA rules required a student pilot to accumulate at least 40 hours before he could take a flight check to receive a Private Pilot License. The average was slightly higher than that. I would take about 60 hours and about two years of on again/off again training to finish and finally receive my Private Pilot certification.

Chapter 10   Smiley's Flying Circus

Smiley Crew

In January of 1965, there were several changes in the Iron Lung crew. The three new members of the crew that occupied the front compartment were also new to the Iron Lung project. Captain Crain Smiley assumed command of the crew. Captain Smiley was a talkative man. He had aspirations of becoming a test pilot at Edwards AFB. He was actively pursuing this aspiration. The Co-pilot was Captain Dick Harriman. Dick was a senior copilot and would soon upgrade to aircraft commander. The Navigator was Captain Paul Miller. Paul was an artist in his spare time and had done some very good work. Captain Stan Rock returned to the crew as the Raven One. Lt. Dick Cain and I were the only holdovers from the previous crew. The pilots gave the crew the name "Smiley's Flying Circus". We had baseball caps made with that on the front.

The next several months were devoted to training sorties and Common Cause missions. The crew averaged four to five flights a month. The Iron Lung aircraft was still in California. In June we flew via commercial carrier to Ontario to conduct several flights against a site in the Nevada desert north of Las Vegas. The aircraft had been moved to nearby March AFB. Lockheed had removed the boom and bird appendage from the aircraft while it was at the Ontario airport. It was then moved to March AFB where the ITT research Lab engineers installed the reconnaissance equipment. This was the configuration that we would use on the series of flights targeting the Nevada site as well as on our next deployment.

The engineers at the ITT research Labs had completed a copy of a radar system that had been targeted on an earlier Iron Lung project. The copied system had been installed in the Nevada desert. We were to fly power measurement sorties against it to verify its signature and function as compared to the data collected on the earlier project. The flights were all flown from March AFB. The flight profiles we were asked to fly were always developed by the ITT engineers. None of the engineers had much knowledge about flying an aircraft. We were frequently asked to do things that the aircraft was not able to do. The briefings they conducted with the crew would bring these problems to light so they could be resolved. On this series of flights they wanted us to fly a circular route at a specific distance from the target site. To maintain the circle would require the aircraft to hold a constant two degree angle of bank. They had thoughtfully done all the computations for us. This, however, presented us with a problem. It would be impossible for the autopilot on the B-47 to maintain a two degree bank. A larger angle of bank was possible but this would invalidate their power computations. A compromise was worked out. We would fly straight and level but change the heading a few degrees every few minutes. They calculated the amount of heading change and the interval between changes for us. It approximated a circle for them.

We stayed in a motel in the city of Riverside for the duration of the test flights and were provided with two rental cars for the crews use. The first test flight was flown on June 15th. We flew four more flights against the Nevada site. On June 29th we returned with the aircraft to Forbes AFB. We would soon deploy to Incirlik AFB in Turkey with the aircraft.

Tour at Incirlik

During July Captain Harriman left the crew to upgrade to aircraft commander. He was assigned to his own crew. First Lieutenant Warren Snyder replaced him as the copilot on our crew. We deployed to Incirlik on August 8, 1965. The first flight was from Forbes to Torrejon AFB near Madrid, Spain. We stayed there over night. The next day we flew on to Incirlik. The 55th detachment at Incirlik was quite a busy place. There were four aircraft and five crews deployed from the 55th. The normal three Tell Two crews were there as well as one Standard RB-47H crew. We became the fifth crew. The Tell Two project had one of its crews on alert. We would not be on alert during our time at Incirlik.

Our missions would use the same orbit areas as the Tell Two aircraft used. Apparently the planners at SAC headquarters wanted us to appear as just another Tell Two sortie. Even though we were not on alert our launches were to appear as if we were. This would add to our appearance as just another Tell Two sortie. When a normal Tell Two flight was launched they would not know which of the orbit

131

areas they were to use. They would get their directions once they were airborne. They received their directions in the following manner. A local commercial radio station broadcast continuous Morse Code. The message would be embedded in the Morse Code. It was the job of the Raven Two to copy and authenticate the message. We would use the same procedures. As a result, part of my personal preparation for this deployment was to learn to copy Morse Code.

We flew three missions in August and nine missions in September. The mission on September 17th had to be aborted early because of a mechanical problem. We tried again on September 20th but the problem reappeared and that mission was also aborted. On the 21st we flew a three hour maintenance test flight. The problem had been fixed. The problem that led to the two aborted flights had appeared soon after takeoff. Each of the aborted flights, however, had lasted more than three and a half hours. A fully loaded RB-47 could not land again immediately after takeoff. It was too heavy. This was a problem because the original design maximum gross weight of the aircraft had been 125,000 pounds (15). The landing gear had been designed to handle that weight. The RB-47 we flew routinely took off weighting in excess of 170,000 pounds. If we tried to land at that weight it would require a much higher landing speed and our landing roll out would be excessively long. Most large military aircraft that were developed after the B-47 had the ability to dump fuel when necessary. Dumping fuel means that the fuel was atomized and then sprayed into the air. This allowed the crew to reduce the aircraft's weight quickly in preparation for landing. The B-47 was not capable of dumping fuel. We had to burn it off. The solution was to fly around and burn off the fuel until the aircraft weight was down to near 125,000 pounds. This was done at low altitude where the fuel burn rate was the highest. It often took three to four hours. A B-47E model aircraft that was assigned to the bombardment wing at Lincoln AFB near Lincoln, Nebraska had attempted an emergency landing shortly after takeoff without burning off fuel. It ran off the end of the runway due to the long landing roll out, crashed and burned. So, unless the situation dictated that an immediate landing was imperative, the fuel was normally burned off before the attempt at landing.

The south and central parts of Turkey, where Adana was located, have numerous ancient castles. We spent the time flying at less than a thousand feet above the ground hunting for castles while we were burning off fuel. The ravens were still in the front compartment but we could not see out of the aircraft so only the pilots enjoyed the view. As you might imagine, three hours of sitting on a metal floor, shoe horned into a sling harness and unable see anything was a very unpleasant experience.

We started our return trip to Forbes on September 28th. The departure flight was from Incirlik to Torrejon AFB in Spain. Fifty Fifth aircraft, returning from Incirlik, routinely used Torrejon as a stop over en-route to Forbes. It was a <u>Reflex</u> base for deployed Bomb Wing B-47s and had B-47 qualified maintenance personnel on the base and SAC type security. Oddly, our aircraft often developed a mechanical problem that required the crew to lay over at least a day at Torrejon. On this trip our aircraft, did indeed develop a mechanical problem when we landed at Torrejon. It would take a couple of days to fix. We would be able to spend some time in Madrid. I had been a fan of Flamingo Dancing and Guitar for several years. I had acquired several records of Flamingo Guitar in my collection at home. This was my opportunity to see some shows first hand. I spent both nights at a flamingo club while I was in Madrid. On October 1st we completed the long flight from Torrejon to Forbes.

Chapter 11　　　　First Stop In Japan

I remained at Forbes for the next three and a half months. I had been able to re-start my private flying training at Mesa Verde during July prior to departing for Incirlik. Unfortunately I was able to accumulate only three more hours of training. When I returned from Incirlik in October my instructor, Max Collier, had returned to his full time job as a history professor at Washburn University. His flight school had not been a rousing success. He was closing it down. He did agree to continue with his old students. So I was able, as weather permitted, to get another four hours in October and early November.

In early November the crew was shuffled again. Stan Rock, the Raven One, had some medical problems and had to be dropped from the crew. Dick Cain had been promoted to Captain and became the Raven One. Captain Ted Pruss replaced Dick as the Raven Three. The Iron Lung aircraft had been flown to March AFB in October. I was not on that trip. I was preparing for my annual flight evaluation. I flew training flights with several different crews. One of the flights was my annual Standboard evaluation. I also flew two Common Cause missions in November. In early December Captain Smiley left the crew and Captain Ray Morris assumed command of it. In January the crew flew commercially to Ontario, California to pick up the aircraft for our next deployment. We flew three training missions from Forbes to clear up any mechanical problems with the aircraft prior to our deployment to Yokota AFB (OL-2) in Japan.

Yokota AFB

On January 14, 1966 we began our deployment. The first flight was from Forbes to Eielson Air Force Base (AFB) near Fairbanks, Alaska. We remained overnight and continued on to Yokota the following day. There were two other of the 55th aircraft and crews at Yokota when we arrived. The first was the Standard RB-47H crew. The second crew was the Fire Fly special project crew. Captain Lloyd Navarro was the Raven One on the Fire Fly crew. He would be with the project through out its entire life. While at Yokota, on this trip, we were fortunate enough to meet General John Ryan. He was the

134

commander of Pacific Air Forces Command (PACAF) at the time and based in Hawaii. He would later become the Air Force Chief of Staff. On this occasion he was visiting Yokota and was apparently curious about our project. He wanted to see the aircraft and meet the crew. We assembled in our best uniforms to meet the general. He talked to each of us briefly and got a tour of the raven compartment. The hatch in the plexiglas dome had been removed by maintenance so he did not have to use the crawlway.

Our mission on this deployment was to do power measurements on the radar system known by the NATO name Big Mesh. It was a long range search type of radar. It used five stacked beams. Each of the beams used a different frequency and was transmitted at a different elevation angle. We flew four sorties in January, seven in February and two in March. The mission profile was slightly different from earlier Iron Lung profiles. We targeted specific known Big Mesh sights. The aircraft would be flown some sixty miles from the shore. We then turned and flew directly at the shore with the selected Big Mesh sight directly ahead of the aircraft nose. The straight in flight path was continued until approximately 25 miles from the coast. We then made a steep 180 degree turn going no closer than 15 miles and flew back out to 60 miles. This was repeated several times. We would be recording power measurements on each of the five beams on each run. We followed this same procedure on each of the flights. Oddly, neither the Russians nor the Chinese sent a single aircraft out to look us over.

Stereo equipment such as tape recorders and amplifiers were very cheap in Japan at the time. Early Japanese electronics had been of poor quality but they had made great strides and by 1966 were of excellent quality. The equipment was being imported to stores in the United States but the prices were about double to those in Japan. We all stocked up on the best and latest stereo equipment. Tape recorders at the time were 10 inch reel to reel types. The base also had a tape club. We could rent tapes from the club and copy them onto our own blank tapes. We had several recorders going most of the time. The three ravens put their equipment in one room and ran three copying operations at the same time. We took turns monitoring this operation.

The equipment, when we returned to the States, was used so customs duty on them was minimal.

The return flight to Forbes was on March 10th which happened to be my 25th birthday. The flight back was eleven and one half hours. Combined with the time zone differences that birthday was almost 35 hours long. After the long flight and the time change I didn't feel much like celebrating.

Chapter 12   The Tell-Two Project

Tell-Two Operations

On July 22, 1966 I was re-assigned to another 55th SRW crew, Captain Walt Bauman's crew. The crew was one of the Tell-Two special project crews. They had just returned from an operational deployment to Wake Island collecting data on Russian missile activity in the Pacific Ocean. As I explained earlier, the Tell-Two program was another of the wing's ongoing special project programs. The project's mission was the collection of down range telemetry data on Russian missile test programs. The Russians launched the majority of their missile tests, including the ICBMs, from the Bakinour facility near Tyuritam located in Kazakhstan or Kapustin Yar in Southern Russia. The test range ran from the launch site to the Kamchahkta peninsula just west of the Alaskan Island chain. Test ICBMs would leave the atmosphere, travel across Siberia and re-enter the atmosphere over Kamchahkta and would impact on the peninsula. The vast majority of the wing's Tell-Two monitoring sorties operated from Incirlik AFB in Turkey. The program focus was normally on the launch end of the range. Captain Bauman's crew deployment to Wake Island had been an exception. They had covered a special series of Russian missile tests that traveled out over the Pacific Ocean. Their deployment had focused on the impact end of the tests rather than the launch end.

Tell-Two crews, as I alluded to earlier, consisted of 5 crew members (Aircraft Commander, Co-Pilot, Navigator, Raven One and Raven Two) rather than the wing's standard six man crew. Like all of the crews assigned to the 55th SRW, they were required to first be certified on the Standard RB-47H configuration. The special project operation became an additional certification. Captain Bauman, the aircraft commander, had been in the 55th for several years as a co-pilot and had recently upgraded to the front seat as the pilot and aircraft commander. The deployment to Wake Island had been his first as a crew commander. Captain Leo Johnson, the Co-pilot, was a graduate of the Air Force Academy. He was from Oklahoma and was a member of the Cherokee Indian tribe. He was the first Native-

American to attend and graduate from the Air Force Academy. Leo was of stocky build and a good athlete. He had been a member of the Academy's varsity football team and had won the base handball championship the year before. Captain Paul was the Navigator. Paul was tall and slender. He hailed from the Boston area. Paul was shy, painfully shy. He never took part in crew banter. Captain Gary Percival, the Raven One, was an affable outgoing person from Mississippi. I was now the Raven Two. I was added to the crew when the previous Raven Two entered training to upgrade to a Raven One. During the month of August we flew three Common Cause missions from Forbes. These sorties were routine and uneventful. I had a short time at Forbes with my new crew before we were alerted for our first deployment.

Shemya Deployment

Toward the end of August we received orders for a deployment to Shemya AFB in Alaska. The location would be a new forward operating location for the 55th SRW. The site would be temporarily designated as Operating Location 5 (OL5). The OL5 designation had been used several years before (Tuele AFB in Greenland) and was being re-used here. Shemya is located at the western end of the Aleutian chain of islands. It is the closest Air Force installation to the Kamchahkta Peninsula, the recovery end of the Russian missile range. There were two Forbes AFB based Tell Two crews to be deployed to Shemya, the Bauman crew and the Wells crew. The Wells crew was commanded by Major Doug Wells. We would have one aircraft, an RB-47E serial number 53-2315, configured for the Tell-Two operation.

When deployed operations are conducted at a new site the crews were given only the information they needed to conduct the operation. This seldom included the reasons for operating from a new site. We were left to speculate. Given our experience, we could normally arrive at a pretty good educated guess. Initially, concerning this latest deployment and the one to Wake Island, our general feeling was that the Wing was now merely covering both ends of the Russian missile test launches. We were not informed how long we would be deployed to Shemya nor did we know whether the wing would be routinely operating from there in the future. We would eventually expand that speculation based on the things we did and saw. Eventually it become clear that our intelligence community had concluded that the Russians had developed a new capability called MIRVing. The acronym MIRV stands for <u>M</u>ultiple, <u>I</u>ndependently targeted, <u>Re</u>-entry <u>V</u>ehicles. In short, this means that several war heads could be carried by a single missile. During the re-entry phase the war heads would separate from the missile and each war head would have a separate target. Each would independently track to its target. The United States ICBMs had had this capability for a number of years but the Russians had not. We felt that we were there to confirm this capability. This could only be done at the re-entry end of the range.

Major Doug Wells was the aircraft commander of the other crew that would deploy with mine to Shemya. He had been a crew commander during the entire time that I had been in the 55th. He was one of the old heads. He was a friendly, very likable man who was slightly overweight. Doug was an easy going man with excellent people skills. He could smooth out many of the tensions that occasionally arose between crew members due to the stresses of constant deployments and alert duty. Captain Larry Bishop was the Co-pilot. Larry was a bachelor. He was part of a group of four bachelor officers assigned to the 55th, which including myself, shared a house in Topeka. Given the frequent number of deployments each of us had done in the past we spent more time in the same location on this and the next deployment than we had in Topeka where we shared a residence. Larry was also part of our bachelor group who owned a motorcycle and spent much of our time, when we were home, climbing hills with our motorcycles, in an area in Topeka known as Burnet's Mound. Major Dixie Howell was the Navigator. Dixie was a big man who hailed from Texas. He had been navigator on a bomber crew during the Second World War. His aircraft had been shot up and the crew forced to bail out. Following his tour of duty during WWII he went to school on the GI bill and received a degree in Pharmacy.

Following graduation he opened his own drug store in Texas. In the 1950s most drug stores were still individually owned. There were, as yet, no corporate chain drug stores. As was the case with many of the demobilized WWII veterans Dixie remained in the reserves for some extra income. He was mobilized for the Korean War and had to abandon his business. He had then decided to stay in the Air Force. The Raven One was Captain Bob Hill. The Raven Two was Captain Mike Popkin. Mike and Bob were avid handball players. They had introduced me to the sport during an earlier deployment at Incirlik. Mike was a member of the Mormon religion. He and I had several very civil religious discussions during the long idle hours of deployments and alert duty at Shemya.

Major Wells' crew was assigned to ferry the aircraft from Forbes to Shemya. I was assigned to fly with them replacing Mike Popkin who would come later. We left Forbes on August 31, 1966. The first leg landed at Eielson AFB near Fairbanks. On September 1st we flew from Eielson to Shemya.

The Remote End of the World

Shemya is a remote, barren and rather austere place. It is an island 4 miles long and 2 miles wide and is part of the Aleutian Island chain. The Aleutian chain of Islands forms the southern rim of the Bearing Sea. Shemya is at the western end of the chain of islands. It is the smallest in a group of three islands, (Attu, Agattu and Shemya). The Island group is called the Near Islands. Attu had a small Navy Facility. Agattu was the largest of the three islands and was unoccupied. It was considered a good wild pig hunting site. The Near Islands lie just east of a major weather system spawning region associated with the Japanese current. The area is generally recognized as having some of the worst and most changeable weather on the face of the earth. The entire island was an Air Force Base. It had a single 10,000 foot runway. There are cliffs on both ends of the runway as well as along one complete side.

The buildings at Shemya were old and weather beaten. There were few private vehicles on the island and they all belonged to the civilian contractors. The military provided vehicles for Air Force personnel.

The majority of the vehicles were vans. Vans tended to be vulnerable to the high winds. They could be blown over. High winds were a common feature of the island. During periods of high winds the vehicles were normally parked in protected areas or in hangers. The Air Force made it easier for us to know what a particular vehicle could tolerate. The maximum cross winds they could tolerate were lettered on the sides of the vans.

There were approximately 1200 men on the island and no women. This number included both military and civilian personnel. The standard tour of duty for military personnel on Shemya was one year. Shemya was classified as a remote location. Air Force policy had established a limit of one remote tour of duty per career. Each member of the military who was permanently assigned to Shemya was allowed a week of uncharged leave at the half way point in their tour of duty. This was called a rest and recuperation week (R and R). This policy did not apply to us because we were there on temporary duty (TDY).

A significant percentage of the personnel on the island, however, were civilians working for various defense department contractors. Shemya was the site of an Early Warning Radar system. The Radar system was part of the United States missile launch early warning system. Shemya was one of the sites that provided the initial warning of a Russian launched ICBM bound for the United States. The radar antennas were very large and were prominent features of the landscape. The civilian contractors were responsible for keeping the system operational at all times. They were very well paid.

The Aleutian Islands were serviced by a commercial air carrier, Reeves Aleutian Airlines (RAA). We referred to them as Reeves Awful Airlines. Shemya was one of their stops. RAA flew older propeller driven aircraft. There were two or three flights a week. The flights would be on the ground only long enough to deplane its arriving passengers and load departing passengers. The flights had stewardesses on board. The stewardesses did not disembark but would occasionally come out onto the top of the boarding ramp. This was the only opportunity that the men of Shemya had to see a woman while they were on the island. There would often be a group of men from Shemya assembled at the retaining fence and the stewardesses would wave to them.

The Air Force tried to make the year-long tour of duty for military personnel as tolerable as they could. The "Chow Hall" served the best food I have eaten at any military facility. There were four meals a day (included a midnight meal.) You could have steak at each meal if you wanted. The cooks were obviously a cut above the normal chow hall type. The Air Force provided hobby shops for use by military personnel. These shops were very well equipped. The shops were, however, not widely used. I met one sergeant whose hobby was collecting glass fish balls. These were glass balls that were used to buoy fishing nets. They would occasionally break loose and wash up on shore of the islands. They were of various sizes and colors. Another sergeant was heavily into radio controlled model aircraft. He would fly them out over the water. He was quite good. He admitted to me that he had one that had flown out of range of his transmitter. Drinking was the pastime of choice for most people, civilian and military. The bars in the clubs were generally full at night.

OL-5 Operations

As one would logically expect, the Russians would not give us any advanced notice when they intended to do a test launch. Our command structure had to rely on available intelligence to predict when this might occur and launch the Tell Two aircraft in time to be in position to monitor and record the data. The window of opportunity was normally short. This fact required a crew to be in Alert Status. I have referred to Alert Status before as it pertained to the Tell-Two project crews at Incirlik. The Shemya operation mimicked the existing operation at Incirlik with some significant differences. Let me discuss the differences. Alert Status at both Shemya and Incirlik referred to both the aircraft and crew. Both had to be prepared to launch (takeoff) as soon as physically possible. This meant that the aircraft had to be ready for immediate takeoff, the crew dressed in their gear and reside in a facility near the aircraft. If they left the area of the aircraft they used a vehicle with a radio and siren so they could be alerted and respond immediately.

At Incirlik there were normally a minimum of two and generally three Tell Two crews as well as two Tell-Two configured aircraft. One of crews would be in Alert Status at all times. A second crew would be in semi-alert status. When notification (the horn sounded) came the crew on alert would get the aircraft airborne as quickly as possible. The second crew, on semi-alert, would be notified to be ready to launch immediately. If the first aircraft had any mechanical trouble the second aircraft would immediately launch to replace it. At Shemya, however, we only had a single aircraft.

Alert Facilities

Alert facilities at Incirlik were not up to the usual Air Force standards and the ones at Shemya were ever poorer. Alert facilities occupied by the Strategic Air Command (SAC) bomber crews were modern specially built quarters for crews to live and work in. They were well equipped to ease the strain of confinement and family separation. There would be areas for families to visit and spend time during the day with their father or husband. Some bases even made arrangements to take college classes while on alert. Each of the crews would be assigned a vehicle, equipped with emergency vehicle type lights, so they could travel around the base and respond immediately to the klaxon (the launch signal or horn). When the horn sounded, the crew would drive themselves to the aircraft with lights flashing. They were required to have the entire Alert Fleet of aircraft airborne within 15 minutes. They would be in Alert Status for a continuous period of from 5 to 7 days. Then they had up to 5 to 7 days off. The facilities at Incirlik were not as modern but were comfortable and well equipped. The alert posture was rotated among the three crews. One crew would be in Alert Status. A second crew would be in Semi-Alert Status. When the order to launch was received the crew in Alert Status went immediately while the crew in Semi-Alert Status waited in readiness in the event the first one had to cancel or return. If the first aircraft aborted or had to return to base the second aircraft launched to complete the mission.

Our facility at Shemya was a bare bones, make shift one. It was a large old aircraft maintenance hanger with individual rooms that had originally been used as offices along either side on two levels. There was a conference room that we used as a recreation room. When you walked out of any of the rooms, the aircraft was right outside your door. When the horn sounded, the aircraft would be towed outside the hanger by maintenance personnel. We would climb aboard and go. Alert status meant being dressed in flying gear at all times. We slept with our flight suits laid out and our boots ready to jump into.

Life on Alert at Shemya

One of our two crews would be on alert for immediate launch when notified. The other crew had to be ready to go in about 6 hours (the length of the present mission plus the turn around time for the aircraft). We would be, at a minimum, on call continuously for several straight months. Air Force regulations restrict flight crew members to refrain from drinking for an 8 hour period prior to flight. This meant we could not use the pastime of choice at Shemya. The lack of drinking may have seriously restricted some. Since I wasn't much of a drinker, I did not find it troublesome.

Each crew had one of the afore mentioned vans. When the crew on alert used theirs the entire crew had to go together. That meant that when one member of the crew wanted to go to the chow hall, all of us had to go at the same time. When the winds exceeded the maximum the van could not be driven and was normally placed inside the hanger. This was not an infrequent occurrence. Since there was only one aircraft, both crews must use it. The crew on alert would fly the mission and recover in about 4 hours. The aircraft would be re-serviced and ready to go in about two more hours. When the alert crew was launched, the other crew became the alert crew. So we would on call for the duration of our TDY tour. We became accustomed to seeing guys in flying suits. It was the standard attire.

Two of the rooms on the second floor of the hanger had been combined and were used as our break and recreation area. We spent a great deal of time in the break room, (there wasn't much else to do.). The major activity was a homemade game we called "Launch-Kill". It was played on a make shift wooden board using marbles. We spent our long idle hours playing this game. The marbles were moved around the board.   Each player would in turn roll a set of dice to determine the length of their move. When their marble landed on a space occupied by another player's marble it was known as a "Kill" and the other players marble would be removed. Whenever a "Kill" was made, the guy making it would shout out "Kill" and remove the other guy's marble. Sometimes the shout "Kill" could be heard across the hanger. The boards had been constructed in the hobby shop. They were unpainted. The game was a carryover from earlier alert facilities that some of our fellow crew members had spent time in. Ironically, I saw the game many years later, played with the same rules, as a Milton Bradley game called Aggravation.   I often wondered if someone who had played the game in a SAC alert facility had passed it along to Milton Bradley.

Flight Operations
   Flight operations out of Shemya were tricky at times. The 10,000 feet long runway was only moderate in length for SAC aircraft like the RB-47E. There was a cliff at either end as well as along one complete side of the runway. The field was about 100 feet above sea level and the terrain sloped right down to the sea off that side of the runway. The base power plant was located near the sea off the cliff side of the runway. It was a large concrete building. The winds could change quickly and alternate landing sites were a considerable distance away if weather demanded. I recall on one of our sorties that we called the control tower to ask for the winds while we were still at altitude. The response was "their gusting to 35 knots, but right down the runway". We continued our approach and landing. When we landed the winds were nearly calm. The time span was about 20 minutes. Our post flight debriefing took a little over an hour. When we left to go to the chow hall following the debriefing the wind was back up to 25 knots.
   The sorties were flown close to the Kamchahkta peninsula. We would stay a minimum of 15 miles offshore. This would keep us outside of the 12 mile limit that the Russians claimed as their territorial waters. This closer distance allowed us to add an additional

145

dimension that had not been possible in the sorties flown from Incirlik at the launch end of the Russian missile range.   The pilots could visually see, weather permitting, the re-entry vehicle from the missile. The co-pilot had been issued a camera and was tasked to take pictures of what could be seen. This confirmed our speculation for the reason behind operating from Shemya. On a clear day our co-pilot could observe and photograph whatever was there.

Air Force operations are generally well planned in advance so that they can be completed as safely as conditions permit. The plans consider a variety of contingency situations. One of these contingencies deals with potential adverse weather situations. To complete a landing the pilot must be able to see the runway. If the lowest cloud layer (known as the ceiling) is too low to allow him sufficient time to visually place the aircraft in the proper landing attitude and properly aligned with the runway prior to touch down he is not permitted to land. The same is true if the visibility is reduced too much by fog. Another common weather situation involves the wind. The winds at the intended destination may be too high to safely land the aircraft. As I mentioned earlier, during the landing phase the B-47 has serious limitations under high wind conditions and Shemya often had high wind conditions. To deal with these contingencies each flight must have a planned weather alternate. A second airport that could be used in the event the intended one is not usable due to adverse weather conditions. The plan must ensure that the aircraft has sufficient fuel remaining to reach the alternate airport. Shemya was a long way from any other Air Force installation that could accommodate the B-47 aircraft. This fact would normally require a larger fuel reserve when the decision to divert to the planned alternate was made.

The level of fuel reserves was complicated by the landing weight limitation on the   B-47's main landing gear. The maximum design landing weight under all conditions other than emergencies was 125,000 pounds. The aircraft often weighted in excess of 170,000 pounds at takeoff so we would have to burn off enough fuel to get below the restricted landing weight prior to landing. The nearest suitable alternate was the SAC base at Eielson AFB near Fairbanks, Alaska. Eielson was nearly 2000 miles away which was about four hours of flying time. The aircraft would normally be near the restricted landing weight at the time the decision to proceed to a planned weather alternate airport was made. In our situation at Shemya we would not have sufficient remaining fuel to make Eielson. There were two airports in the Aleutian Island chain we could use in a pinch. Adak, a Navy installation, had a 7,800 foot runway. This length would be very marginal for the B-47 under the best of circumstances. We would, however, have sufficient fuel remaining to reach Adak if it became necessary. The second one was at Cold Bay, Alaska. This was a civil airport with a 10,400 foot runway. The length of runway was adequate and we could reach Cold bay with our remaining fuel. Neither airport had the security or support services we would require if we landed there. The plan for our operation was to use Eielson as our weather alternate. A KC-135A tanker aircraft at Eielson would be in readiness for an immediate launch if needed. It would meet us half way and off load enough fuel to enable us to reach Eielson. In the event that we could not successfully refuel one of the two airports in the Aleutian Island chain could be used.

There were five alert launches during September. Our crew flew two of them and Major Wells' crew flew three. There was no re-entry activity on any of them. All of them were false alarms. There were four more launches through October 16th. The results were always the same. Major Wells' crew had flown on October 17th which placed my crew on alert. Our next alert launch occurred on October 19, 1966.

Chapter 13   Over The Cliff

Russian Missile Activity

On the afternoon of October 19, 1966, the horn sounded. It was a clear day, late in the afternoon, the sun was low on the horizon. My crew was on alert. The aircraft was towed from the hanger, we climbed aboard, started the engines and took off. There was nothing about this particular mission that indicated that it would be a very unusual flight. It turned out to be a hallmark day in terms of mission results but a harrowing day from a personal standpoint. The trip to our orbit area, off the Kamchatka Peninsula, was uneventful. On this day the Russians had launched a test missile. The pilots observed multiple re-entry targets. The co-pilot was able to photograph them. Our recorders in the rear were eating up the telemetry data. This seemed to confirm that the Russian's had now developed the MIRVing capability. We felt that our tapes and photographs were now very valuable to our intelligence community. It also seemed to confirm our speculation about the reasons for the Shemya operation. Our return trip to Shemya, however, was far from routine. To explain what happened next requires some further background on the aircraft and the pilot.

Walt, our aircraft commander, had spent several years as a copilot in the 55th. He had recently upgraded to the pilot position. This moved his position on the aircraft from the rear pilot's seat to the front pilot's seat. The B-47 aircraft is an unforgiving aircraft, particularly during takeoff or landing, when a pilot makes a mistake or uses sloppy technique in handling the aircraft. Walt had been a good copilot operating from the rear seat but had exhibited some difficulty in handling the aircraft from the front seat. This difficulty had been apparent during his upgrade training as well as during the crew's deployment to Wake Island. His difficulties were in landing the aircraft. A pilot's perspective in the B-47 aircraft from the front seat is markedly different than it is from the rear seat. It is important to have the aircraft in the proper attitude during all phases of flight. During most phases of flight, except the takeoff and landing phases, the pilot can use an instrument in the cockpit to do this. This instrument is called the attitude indicator. During takeoff and landing but particularly during landing the pilot's attention must be focused outside the aircraft to see the aircraft's proximity to the runway. Visual references must be used to ensure the aircraft is in the proper attitude. Both pilot positions are near the front of the aircraft. The majority of the aircraft is behind them and out of their normal view. On most aircraft the visual references used are the line of the aircraft's windshield and the horizon. Comparing the two allows the pilot to ensure the proper attitude for landing. This picture, as well as the view of the runway, is very different from the front pilot seat as opposed to the rear pilot seat in the B-47 aircraft. The nose of the B-47 drops off rapidly and its line in relation to the horizon is somewhat lower in the front seat than the view from the rear seat. I was advised, somewhat later by his co-pilot, that Walt apparently had some difficulty with the difference. Walt's perspective had for years been from the rear seat. He had reportedly had some difficulty with this change in perspective during his transition training checkout for the front seat. I later learned that he had made two unplanned go-arounds in the preceding few months. An unplanned go- around is a nice way of saying it was a botched landing. The first of these unplanned go-arounds had occurred during one of the operational sorties on Wake Island. The second was on a training mission at Forbes. These had occurred prior to my joining the crew. On both of these unplanned go-arounds he had to abort a landing after bouncing the aircraft badly.

To place any aircraft in the right attitude for landing the pilot uses the horizon and the nose (windshield line) of the aircraft as reference points as mentioned earlier. Placing the aircraft in the proper attitude for landing is also much more critical in the B-47 than it is with most other large jet aircraft. The B-47 was a very clean aircraft. This means that it had less drag than other aircraft in its class. It took more time to slow down when that was desired. In addition, as the aircraft sat on the ground it was in a positive angle of attack. The aircraft attitude at touch down would have to be the same as when it sat on the ground. Any aircraft that has a positive angle of attack (while it is still flying above its stall speed) tends to want to continue flying (at least until it stalls). The use of the tandem main gear arrangement on

149

the B-47 gave the aircraft a strong tendency to porpoise when the landing attitude at touchdown was not correct, a very dangerous condition. This characteristic of the B-47 is described in more detail in appendix B. Porpoising is a situation where each of the main gear (forward and rear) has contacted the runway and bounced but not at the same time. The sequence is started when one of the main gear, normally the forward, contacts the runway and bounces. It is now rising. Then the rear main gear contacts the runway and it also bounces. It is now rising while the forward main gear has started to fall. The two are now bouncing down the runway but out of sequence. The solution, for the pilot, is to advance the throttles and make an unplanned go-around. An alternate technique is to deploy the brake chute as the forward main gear begins to bounce (porpoise). The chute deploys about the time the forward main gear again hits the runway. This sudden deceleration keeps the aircraft from bouncing further. This technique often results in hard landings. If the chute deploys before the gear touches the runway again the landing can be very hard. Instructor pilots frown on the use of this technique. It is hard on the aircraft and if the timing was off could be very dangerous.

Our first landing at Shemya that day was after darkness had set in on a moonless night. The approach chute was deployed, as is normal, during our approach to the runway. I will describe what happened next from my perspective in the sling down in the aisle. The aircraft bounced very hard on landing. Then the engine noise increased rapidly as Walt initiated a go around. The aircraft bounced a second time then returned to flight. It seemed from my position down in the aisle on the second bounce that one of the wings dipped significantly which is unusual since the wings should be near level when the aircraft is in contact with the runway. The aircraft completed the go around and circled around for another approach. I could look up from where I sat and see Leo's (the co-pilot) face. He had a concerned look. The second approach and landing also bounced. When the aircraft again touched the runway from the bounce it shuttered but did not bounce again. After a second or two it seemed to lean well sideways. I heard the engines spooling up again. The aircraft felt

150

mushy. Since I could not see anything from my position down in the aisle I was limited to what I could feel. The aircraft soon straighten out again and I could hear the steady roar of the engines. After what seemed like a minute or so, I looked up at Leo again. He had an awful look on his face. No one said a word for a very long time. I looked at Gary sitting in the aisle seat just below Leo. He raised his hands as if to say "I don't know". When the silence was finally broken the two pilots talked about the chances of making a third landing attempt at Shemya. Walt had jettisoned the approach chute on the first go around. He had used the brake chute technique on the second landing. One of the wings had started to rise and he had been unable to bring it down so he initiated another go around. Our situation was now much more difficult. We had used both of our chutes and jettisoned them. A landing without the chutes would require a much longer roll out to stop the aircraft. The aircraft was in the hands of a pilot who had botched two landings and would have to attempt a third one under much more difficult circumstances.

The pilots decided to look at the Dash One (the aircraft operating manual) and see what our stopping distance would be without the brake chute. It was quickly determined that it was in excess of 7000 feet. The runway was 10,000 feet long and it could take as much as 3,000 feet before we touched down even with a well executed approach and landing. So even if the third try was a good one we had a good chance of running off the end of the runway and there was a small cliff there. It was thus confirmed we would not be making a third attempt at Shemya. This meant we would have to fly to our alternate which was Eielson AFB near Fairbanks, Alaska. Eielson had 15,000 feet of runway, one of the longest in the world. This length would provide a much larger margin for error in the next attempt at landing. The flying time from Shemya to Eielson AFB (nearly 2000 miles) away was about four hours. We didn't have enough fuel to make it. The original operations plan for the project had called for us to use Eielson AFB as a weather alternate with the aid of a mid-air refueling. A tanker aircraft crew would have been alerted to standby for this possibility each time we launched on a mission from Shemya. This now became the plan. The pilots called our operations people back at Shemya to inform them of our situation and our plans. A tanker aircraft would be launched. It would have to depart from Eielson and it would meet us halfway. We had about two hours to calm our nerves, digest our situation and prepare for a mid-air refueling.

Gary and I transferred back to the Raven compartment in the bomb bay. We did not want to ride in those uncomfortable slings in the aisle up front for the full four hours. The crawl space between the forward compartment and the Raven compartment in the bomb bay is un-pressurized so we had to make the transfer before the forward compartment was pressurized. Once we were in place both compartments were re-pressurized and the aircraft climbed back to altitude to meet the tanker. During the next couple of hours nobody said much. I had quit smoking a couple of months earlier but gladly accepted Gary's offer of a cigarette.

About two hours later, the time for rendezvous with the tanker was approaching. The pilots established radio contact with the tanker crew. Paul (the Navigator) was picking up their rendezvous beacon on his radar. As the code from the tanker, on Paul's radar scope, approached our position the pilots tried to establish visual contact (the running lights of the tanker). We reached the initial point without visual contact. Paul's signal on his radar crossed our position and continued on by. The pilots still had no visual contact. Confusion and some panic begin to appear in the voices of the pilots and the navigator. For about 60 seconds it appeared that we would not find the tanker. This would be highly unusual. Our crews do a midair refueling on almost every flight. It should have been a routine procedure. Suddenly, Paul jumped in over the interphone. "I got em, their 10 miles ahead". Soon after that the pilots established visual contact and the refueling was completed as scheduled   No one I talked to at Eielson had a good explanation for what had happened. Several said they had seen strange things happen to electronic emissions in the high latitudes.

We continued the flight to Eielson.   As we approached the peninsula that extended out from the Alaskan mainland to meet the island chain and while still at altitude Walt queried each of us in turn

152

giving us the option of bailing out or trying another landing with him. I had not thought of bailing out. The idea didn't appeal to me, but Walt's confidence was obviously shaken and he wanted to give us a choice. We all immediately told him we wanted to try again with him. I was convinced this was the only practical decision. The temperatures outside in the Alaskan wilderness were already below zero and all we were wearing was a light summer flight suit. The chances of survival would have been slim.

We used a GCA approach to the runway at Eielson. GCA stands for **G**round **C**ontrol **A**pproach. This means that we had a controller on the ground monitoring our runway alignment and our descent path on his radar and he was verbally relaying instructions to keep us on track. As we approached the runway threshold the controller advised us the aircraft was much too high. The aircraft touched the runway and bounced. Walt immediately initiated a go around. Landing number three was unsuccessful. The controller asked the reason for the go around. He received no answer.

We came around for another try. Leo advised Walt that we were getting a little ice on the wings. No other words were spoken. The GCA controller talked us in for another landing attempt. The aircraft again bounced but not too hard. It did not bounce a second time and rolled out to a stop. **<u>We were on the ground</u>**. The operations officer in the tower told us to shut the engines down and exit the aircraft where it sat on the runway. After a short delay someone outside the aircraft opened the entry door and we left the aircraft. Once out of the aircraft I stood on the runway and looked toward the end of the runway ahead of the aircraft. It was visible in the lights of the ground vehicles. We had less than 300 feet remaining of a 15,000 foot runway.

The Accident Board

We waited on the runway without much talking. I think we all were relishing the fact that we were back on the ground. The ground crew was attending to the aircraft. In a few minutes a van pulled up to take us to the operations building. An aircraft tow vehicle passed us headed toward the aircraft as we left the runway area. We waited in the operations building for about an hour. The time period immediately following a flight would normally be devoted to debriefing by both operations and maintenance personnel. There was no debriefing on this night. A couple of officers from the detachment at Eielson drew the pilot's aside and talked to them for a while. The rest of our crew just waited for transportation to our quarters. We were assigned two to a room. Leo Johnson and I were assigned to one room. Neither of us got much sleep that night. We were advised that we would be staying at Eielson until an accident board could be assembled and conduct an investigation.

Eielson AFB was the 55th SRWs Operating Location 3, so a crew from Forbes was deployed there. One of the Ravens on that crew was Captain John Freeman. John was also a bachelor, a member of our recreational motorcycle group back at Forbes and a good friend. While at Eielson he had met and was dating one of the school teachers employed by the Air Force to teach at the base schools. The teacher, Patsy, subsequently became his wife and a good friend of mine. Since we had several days of idle time while we waited for the accident board, John and Patsy took me under their wing. We didn't talk about the aircraft incident. While we were at Shemya most of my crew had ignored the length of their hair and I had a good handle bar mustache. I didn't bother to change my appearance the first day. I knew that I would have to before I met the accident board.

The night following our arrival we attended a party on the base given by the Forbes crew deployed to Eielson. It had been arranged before our unscheduled arrival. They said they had a show planned. Patsy insisted that our whole crew sit right down front. As guests of honor she said. The show turned out to be a strip show by an attractive young lady from Fairbanks. We must have been a sight with our long hair, mustaches and our mouths gaping wide open. This was the first woman any of us had seen for more than two months and we were getting what can only be described as a close up look. I'm sure John and Patsy were enjoining the situation. Some time later, Patsy explained to me that she and John had gotten to know the young stripper quite well. She was 24 years old and had been living in San Francisco when she was diagnosed with leukemia and given a year to live. She had decided to live that year to the maximum and headed for Fairbanks. Fairbanks at that time was a wide open town with a frontier flavor.

At first the crew talked little about what we had been through. By the second day we started to discuss it and our feelings concerning it. In conversation with Leo, I had talked about what it was like feeling the gyrations the aircraft was going through but not being able to see anything. Leo made the comment that it was much more frightening to see it all going on and knowing how close we came to ending it right there. I had to agreed with him. My feelings at the time had been concern without real fear. Any fear associated with the incident only came later when I had time to digest what had happened. In a conversation with Walt, he stated that the worst part of it for him was not only worry for his own safety but that he also had four other peoples' lives in his hands. This is what compelled him not to give up and to try again. This gave him the resolve to bolster his shattered self confidence. Several years later I came to appreciate those words. I knew that his confidence was badly shaken by the incident at Shemya. A wise man once said that true courage is when you are scared but face up to the situation anyhow. If you are not scared it is not real courage. I think this fit Walt's performance on that evening.

Several days later the accident board was assembled and convened. Each member of the crew was questioned individually. The board consisted of six officers. All were Lt. Colonels or full Colonels. My turn was a short one and I was the last member of the crew to be interviewed. They asked a very few questions. I think they already had most of the information they needed. They asked me to describe what I had experienced.

During the week at Eielson, I did get additional information on the accident. We had gone off the runway at Shemya at about a 45 degree angle to runway heading. We had plowed deep furrows in the dirt on the side of the runway prior to going over the cliff. Fortunately, we went over the side of the runway that had a cliff. The commander of the other crew at Shemya, Major Wells had been watching the landings from a vehicle along the opposite side of the runway. He said that on the second landing the running light on the top of the

B47's tail had disappeared below the level of the runway. That light is about 40 feet high when the aircraft sits on the ramp. The controller in the tower had grabbed the crash phone to activate the emergency personnel. It had been a moonless night. Leo said that when we left the runway we passed over the concrete power plant near the shoreline. He was able to see it in the landing lights. He also said that when the aircraft leveled out over the water he could see the waves in the landing lights. This was a moonless night so that would have been the only light available. The runway is about 100 feet above the waters. We were obviously much closer than that.

The accident board reconstructed the accident. On the first landing, the aircraft had landed hard and heavily on the right outrigger gear. The outrigger gear is the small wheel assembly under each wing to help support the weight of the wing when the aircraft is on the ground. It is not intended to absorb the shock of a heavy aircraft on a hard landing. The tire on the right outrigger gear had shredded on the first landing. Small pieces of rubber had penetrated the aircraft skin along the right side of the aircraft and the tail area. The aircraft bounced on the second landing and came down hard after the brake chute was deployed. The right outrigger gear was now metal to runway and the resultant drag raised the opposite wing. Walt had not been able to counter the yaw by lowering the wing so he executed the go around. Walt was probably one of the most experienced pilots in the Air Force in dealing with unscheduled go-arounds. I have often thought that this prompted him to initiate it earlier than many would have and this factor may have been just enough for us to survive the incident. The aircraft had sustained a cracked wing spar and would have to be retired to the Air Force's aircraft graveyard at Davis Monthan AFB in Arizona. The aircraft required extensive inspection and a special ferry permit to fly the aircraft to Davis Monthan.

Our crew retuned to Forbes toward the end of October. The crew was classified as non-combat ready following the accident at Shemya. Both pilots were placed back in training. They would have to re-certify. The rest of us remained in Combat Ready status but were not immediately assigned to crews. Walt's training program would focus on landings. His instructor was Lt. Colonel Wayne.

Colonel Wayne had been the instructor pilot during the accident, described earlier, in which Capt. Tom Hoose had been killed several months earlier. He had performed very well in that challenging situation and was credited with saving the aircraft. He would be challenged again during Walt's training. On one of the training missions Colonel Wayne had taken them to Offutt AFB near Omaha, Nebraska for a series of touch and go landings. Offutt was not as busy as Forbes.

On their return to Forbes, the final landing of the day, Walt bounced the aircraft badly. His response was the same as he had used in the past. He deployed the brake chute at the top of the bounce. Colonel Wayne judged that the landing attempt should be abandoned. He applied power and took control of the aircraft unaware that Walt had already deployed the brake chute. The aircraft was now under full power with the brake chute deployed. Colonel Wayne quickly realized the situation. He jettisoned the brake chute and completed the go around. The training was terminated and Colonel Wayne landed the aircraft. Walt was dropped from the training program. He would not fly a B-47 again. He was transferred to a B-52 unit. The B-52 has side by side seating for the pilots and cross wind gear. A couple years later I had a conversation, in Okinawa, with a B-52 crew member from Walt's new unit. He said that Walt had performed well and quickly checked out in the right seat (co-pilot). He had recently upgraded to the left seat (pilot and aircraft commander) and was considered a good pilot by the unit personnel.

Chapter 14   Wheelus Adventure

Creel Crew

Following Walt's training incident the crew was disbanded. The squadron used the rest of us to fill in individual openings on training and Common Cause missions. I flew only once during November. It was a Common Cause operational sortie with Captain Haynes' crew. The six week period was a welcome cooling off period for me. During December my flying activity increased. I flew two Common Cause missions and five training sorties. Each one was with a different crew and each involved a mid-air refueling. I must admit that my stomach muscles tightened up a bit during the landings. Fortunately, none of the pilots bounced their landings. On December 22nd Captain Paul and I were assigned to Captain Ray Creel's crew. This was another Tell-Two crew. Captain Russ was the Co-pilot, Captain Paul the Navigator, Captain Tony Villari the Raven One and I was the Raven Two. Captain Creel was an experienced pilot. He was one of the better natural pilots that I have flown with. He was also an FAA licensed flight instructor and operated a small flight training operation near Topeka on his off time. Captain Russ had been in the wing for several years. He was not considered a particularly good pilot. A few of his contemporaries had been recommended for upgrade to Aircraft Commander but Russ had not. Captain Tony Villari had been in the wing a little longer than myself and had recently upgraded to the Raven One position.

Once assigned to a crew I had expected to remain at Forbes for a few months and the chance to play with some of my bachelor toys (motorcycle, water skiing and a convertible) but that hope was short lived. We were quickly alerted for a deployment to Wheelus AFB the first week in January. The deployment was scheduled to last up to 4 months. The deployment would be in support of the Tell Two program. The location was an unlikely place, Wheelus AFB. Wheelus was located near Tripoli, Libya and was a long way from any Russian missile test activity that we were aware of.

Soviet Testing-Targeting from Space

The mission of the Tell-Two project had always been to monitor

Soviet missile activity. This deployment, it turns out, would be no exception. The Soviets were apparently testing a concept of de-orbiting vehicles from space to hit specific targets on the ground. The speculation among our crews was that they wanted to reduce the time it took to deliver nuclear weapons to targets in the United States by putting them in a space orbit ready to use when needed. The ICBMs launched from ground sites within the Soviet Union would take less than 30 minutes to reach their targets in the United States. Our retaliatory response was to launch our ICBMs and our Bomber Alert force. The Bomber Alert force would have to be airborne within that 15 minute time frame. Constant practice and spot evaluations by SAC headquarters in the form of exercises known as Operational Readiness Inspections (ORIs) assured our leadership that they could respond in less than 15 minutes. In theory this Mutually Assured Destruction (MAD) concept would act as a deterrent to both parties. The use of orbiting weapons could reduce this delivery time significantly and possibly change the balance of the concept. The target area for these tests was near the Russians primary launch facilities at Tyuratam. The de-orbiting process would be initiated over central Africa. The closest Air Force Base we could operate from to monitor the de-orbiting process was Wheelus Air Force Base (AFB) near Tripoli, Libya. Wheelus AFB would be another new and temporary Operating Location for the 55th. They didn't bother to give it a number. Tripoli is on the west side of the Gulf of Sidra along the Mediterranean coast in Northern Africa. The country of Libya, at that time, was ruled by a king, King Idrus. His castle was in the city of Benghazi which is located on the east side of the Gulf of Sidra. The king's grown son, the crown prince, had a castle near Tripoli. The major concern of the United States Air Force, at the time, was that when King Idrus died we would be kicked out of the country. The prince was an avowed communist and had already demanded we leave. Two years later, however, while the king was still alive, Libyan Colonel Muhamar Gadaffi and his band of Colonels, as they were known, overthrew the king and we were booted out. Gadaffi would later describe the line connecting the two northern points of the Gulf of Sidra as the <u>Line of Death</u> and dare any American aircraft to enter it. In the ensuing years there were at least two instances where our F14s crossed that line and shot down every Libyan aircraft sent to enforce the <u>Line of Death</u> with no loss of our aircraft. I guess the <u>Line of Death</u> applied to Libyan aircraft. In 1967, however, the king was friendly to the United States and we were welcome for the time being.

Wheelus AFB

Wheelus AFB was a joint use facility between the Libyan Air Force and the United States Air Force. The U. S. Air Forces' primary use of the base was as an aerial gunnery practice range for the American fighter aircraft based in Europe. The Libyan Air Force, at that time, had only two badly outdated aircraft, a T33 jet trainer and a C47 transport. They seldom flew. Many years later they would buy 50 Mirage jets from France but would have great difficulty finding enough trained pilots to fly them. They also acquired several fighter aircraft from the Russians. While we were at Wheelus, U. S Fighter aircraft, in formations of four, were roaring in and out of the base during all daylight hours. The noise was a fixture and you had to get used to it. The 55th's operation at Wheelus would involve a single RB-47E, Tell-Two configured aircraft. The commander and staff for the operation were temporarily assigned from Incirlik AFB in Turkey, which was the normal operating location for the Tell-Two project. Two Forbes based Tell-Two crews would be deployed together. Captain Creel's crew was one of the two crews assigned. The commander of the other crew was again Major Doug Wells. Their crew flew the aircraft from Forbes to Wheelus. My crew was transported there in a C141. The C141 trip included stops at Charleston AFB in South Carolina and Torrejon AFB in Madrid, Spain. Unfortunately, we did not have time to see the areas. We stopped just long enough to re-fuel.

Wheelus was a very busy place in January of 1967. The majority of Air Force flight crews on the base were there in temporary (TDY) duty status. Most were assigned to joint use bases in the various countries in Europe. Each unit in training would arrive in their own aircraft. Ground attack training seemed to be the primary focus. The normal tactics were as follows; A flight of four fighter aircraft, in formation, would approach the target area. The lead aircraft would peel off and dive toward the target. The other three aircraft would follow at intervals keying on the lead aircraft. The lead aircraft set up the bombing run. The target would be a spot in the Sahara desert south of the base. Just before we arrived a major accident had occurred. An F-4 aircraft had hit the ground during his bomb run. The aircraft had disintegrated and the two crew members were killed. The aircraft that crashed was the last of the flight of four. He had focused on the aircraft ahead of him depending on the lead to set up the proper trajectory to the target. The trajectory had been too low and the last aircraft hit the ground at the bottom of the high speed dive. The last aircraft is often referred to as the "Tail End Charlie." The McDonnell-Douglas Technical Representative that I talked to said that the largest piece that they found was an actuator from an ejection seat, a piece that was about six inches in length.

The primary flying activity at Wheelus was by the U. S. Air Force aircraft. The Libyan Air Force had a total of two aircraft and they flew very little. The base was surrounded by an eight foot high stone wall. The wall had embedded glass along the top. I guess this was designed to keep Libyan people out. The only Libyans that I met while I was there were those that were employed on the base. The maid service was not done by women as would be the norm at most of our bases. It was done by men. They were known as house boys. There was a day room where a coffee pot was kept active during the day. We noticed that we were using a lot of coffee and sugar. A pound of coffee would last only a few days. That's a lot for a group of only 10 people. We felt that our house boy was taking some home. The house boy was a friendly fellow. In fact two of us played a round of golf with him at the base golf course. The golf course was rather unique. The greens were sand. When you putted it left a nice little furrow in the sand. Since we would be in alert status the majority of our time at Wheelus I was not able to get off the base to meet the local population. I was told that they were quite friendly toward Americans.

European and U. S. oil companies had large operations in Libya at that time. The McDonnell-Douglas representative told me that many of the management personnel lived in villas which were surrounded by a stone wall. The British seemed to have the largest presence. He said that there were many young single British girls that worked for the Oil companies as clerical help. He said that it was a good location for a bachelor. Those Air Force personnel that were permanently assigned to Wheelus could bring their families. The Department of Defense (DOD) had provided a full school system for the dependents. The teachers were American certified teachers that were under contract with the DOD. A minimum of two years of teaching in U. S. schools was required to apply for the program.

Crew alert

As was the case with most of the Soviet missile activity, we often had little advance warning. This required a crew and aircraft to be in alert status to launch as quickly as possible. The aircraft had to be ready for immediate launch. The crew had to be dressed in flight gear ready for immediate response. The alert posture for this project was even tighter than normal. The five members of the crew were all required to be within voice range of each other at all times while in alert status. The other crew would be in a semi- alert status. When the horn sounded the aircraft would depart. This meant that the other crew, the one not on alert, would have about four to six hours before they would be in alert status. This would be the time to complete the flight and re-service the aircraft for the next launch. Each crew had a van which had an alert rotating beacon.

We found this requirement somewhat more restrictive than previous alert tours. One of the flaps with this policy involved a religious consideration. Paul and I were both practicing Catholics and wanted to attend Mass on Sundays. Obviously the other three members of the crew did not want to go with us. The detachment commander made an exception for us. Paul and I were permitted to take the crew vehicle to church. We had to go in flight suits and take

162

an alert beeper into church with us. We sat in the rear of the church so as to be ready to leave at a moments notice.

The Lady Be Good

In front of the base operations building at Wheelus there were four large four bladed propellers. They were secured in mounts and separated so that they spanned the entire front of the building. The propellers were from a B-24 liberator aircraft that had crashed in the Sahara Desert during the Second World War. The Army Air Corp had sent bombing raids to targets in Europe, mainly Italy, from a base at Benghazi, Libya on the East side of the Gulf of Sidra. On one these bombing missions in 1944, conducted at night, a B-24 named the "Lady Be Good" was part of the group. On this particular night there was an exceptionally strong un-forecast wind from the north. On its return flight from its bombing run, with a strong tail wind, the "Lady Be Good" over flew its destination. It flew well inland over the Sahara desert. At night in the moonlight the desert appeared the same as the Mediterranean Sea. They ran out of gas and crash landed in the desert. Most of the crew survived the crash landing. All hands died trying to walk out the desert. The aircraft wreckage and the remains of the crew were later discovered by searchers. The four props from the "Lady Be Good" were returned to Wheelus and displayed in front of the base operations building with a plaque describing their story. We had spent time reading the plaque and absorbing the story of the ill-fated aircraft.

Aero club activity

Several Air Force bases in the United States had aero clubs. These are membership clubs which own small aircraft. Occasionally an aircraft is donated by the Air Force, but generally they are purchased by the club. The aircraft may be rented by the members. Membership was generally restricted to military personnel and civilian employees of the Department of Defense. The clubs were located on military installations. Flight operations were based at or in the vicinity of the military installation. Most clubs also had members that were qualified flight instructors. They would be available to provide flight instruction for a fee. Occasionally a club would hire a full time instructor. The rates for both the aircraft and the instructor were often well below local commercial rates. The activity in most clubs was heavily focused on basic flight instruction leading to a Private license. The majority of aero clubs were located in the contiguous United States. Aero clubs were rare at overseas installations. Private flight privileges to foreigners are normally restricted in most countries.

Within a week of our arrival at Wheelus, Tony and I discovered that they had a well equipped aero club. The Libyan government allowed American private aircraft and pilots a free run of their airspace. They weren't using it anyhow. The aero club actually owned more aircraft than the Libyan Air Force at that time. Most of the aero club aircraft were routinely tied up in flight instruction. One of the aircraft the club owned was a Piper Comanche. It was used mainly for cross country flights by pilots who already had a Private license. The Comanche was classified by the FAA as a complex aircraft. A complex aircraft, by FAA definition at the time, had either an adjustable propeller (called constant speed) and/or retractable landing gear. The Comanche had both. Complex aircraft are not normally used in basic flight instruction. Since both Tony and I already had our Private licenses and the Comanche would be available more often than the other club aircraft we elected to fly it. The problem we faced was that the club required 150 hours of total time or 15 hours in aircraft type to be able to fly it without an instructor. Neither of us had flown a Comanche before and we both had about 120 hours of total time. We needed an instructor and the majority of the club's instructors were tied up with student pilots. They had to be scheduled well in advance. Our window of opportunity to fly was tied to our alert posture. Opportunities would only come on short notice.

Ray, our Aircraft Commander, had a flight instructor rating and ran a flight school back home in Topeka. The aero clubs normally charged an entry fee as well as monthly fees to members. The Wheelus club waived the fees for those with a flight instructor rating.

We approached Ray to help us build the 15 hours in the Comanche. He agreed. He wouldn't charge us but we had to pay for the aircraft rental. It was a good deal as far as we were concerned. During the times when the other crew was on alert our crew would be free to engage in other activities. We would have to be ready to go on alert within a few hours of the other crew's launch. This allowed us time to fly the Comanche. If the other crew was launched it would take about 4 to 5 hours before we might have to do the same. It would take about two hours to complete a flight in the Comanche and return to the barracks.   Most small aircraft used for basic flight instruction are forgiving. They tend to float during the landing phase. Students are taught to land with the throttle completely closed. The aircraft is flown to the runway, rotated (raise the nose) slightly to hold it off the runway, the aircraft then loses airspeed and settles onto the runway. The Comanche can't be flown this way. It will not float the same way. Landings are made by flying to the runway using some power, rotate slightly and ease the power off to let the aircraft settle to the runway.

The club was not permitted to practice landings at Wheelus. There was far too much jet fighter activity. We would have to leave the pattern at Wheelus and fly to a civilian airport about 20 miles away. The city and the airport were named for the reining king of Libya, Idrus. Tony, Ray and I would all fly together. Ray in the right seat and either Tony or I in the left seat with the third guy in the back seat. We would occasionally stop on the ramp and Tony and I would change seats. We normally practiced landings at Idrus or did maneuvers in the area. Ray showed us several maneuvers that are not taught in normal flight instruction programs. We also did some cross country flying. Most of it was along the coast of the Mediterranean Sea. The Libyan government was permitting excavation of the ruins of the ancient Roman city of Leptus Magna. Leptus Magna was located along the Mediterranean coast east of Tripoli. Leptus Magna was about 100 miles from Wheelus and right on the Gulf of Sidra. We made several flights to Leptus Magna and observed the excavations from the air. It soon, however, became obvious to both

Tony and I that we would not be able to get 15 hours in the Comanche in the four month tour at Wheelus given the infrequent opportunities to fly.

Bombs in Space

We had arrived at Wheelus on January 5, 1967. On January 17, 1967 I was promoted to the rank of Captain. Promotions to the rank of Captain were based on serving the required time as a First Lieutenant. My date of rank as a Captain was pushed back to December 5, 1966 to incorporate the time I had spent in the spot promotion program as a Captain while at Incirlik in 1965.

Major Wells' crew took the first alert cycle. They were on it for several days without flying then we took over as the alert crew. It wasn't until the 27th of January that the alert horn sounded sending my crew into the air. Each of the crews flew twice more during the first two weeks of February. All were false alarms. The Russians had not made a single attempt and we had nothing to show for the time. On February 16th our crew was on alert when the horn sounded. We rushed to the aircraft and took off. Again, there was no result. We were directed to return to base. As we approached the field, the approach chute was deployed. When Ray ordered the gear to be extended one of the gear lights did not show down and locked. The indicator is a group of four lights. When the system is turned on and the gear is still up, the lights are red. When the gear is extended for landing and it is locked in place the lights turn green. One of our lights, the one for the left outrigger gear was still red. When the pilots see this situation they don't know whether the problem is with the indicator, which means they can land without further incident, or the gear is not locked in place and may collapse when the weight of the aircraft is lowered on it. The later, quite obviously, could result in a damaged or destroyed aircraft with a possible loss of life.

We continued to fly around while the crew communicated with maintenance and operations personnel on the ground to discuss the problem and decide what to do. We continued to fly around for about 45 minutes with the approach chute still deployed. Suddenly the

166

aircraft seemed to lurch forward. The approach chute had sheared its release bolt and departed from the aircraft. The sudden decrease in drag caused the aircraft to lurch forward. The decision was finally made. We would land trying to keep weight off of the outrigger gear as long as possible. The outrigger gear was not one of the main weight bearing points so even if it failed a good soft landing may not result in significant damage to the aircraft. Ray made a very smooth landing and the gear remained in place. We later learned that the problem was in the light and not the gear. It did, however, make for a tense hour or so.

Chapter 15   Trip To Tunis

We had been at Wheelus for about two months. Doug Wells' crew was scheduled to be replaced by another Forbes based Tell-Two crew. There was a planned week overlap after the new crew's arrival and the departure of Doug's crew. This was an opportunity for the crew that was staying, namely ours, to take some time off. We intended to use this opportunity to do some sight seeing and increase our flying time in the Comanche at the same time. We planned a trip from Wheelus to the city of Tunis in Tunisia. The trip was planned to cover three days. We reserved the Comanche for the trip. The Libyan government required departing aircraft to get an exit permit and arriving aircraft to get an entry permit. Ray said that he would file the necessary paperwork. We would have to clear customs upon our arrival in Tunis. The approvals came back prior to our departure date. We were set to go. We would depart about 6 AM.

On the morning we were to depart, Ray told us he would meet us at the aircraft. We weren't sure how he was going to do that since we only had one crew vehicle but we didn't dwell on it. Tony and I arrived at the aircraft with our baggage about 5:30 on the morning of March 3rd. As we drove up, we could see Ray on the other side of the aircraft. As we walked around the aircraft we saw a lady standing beside Ray. We had seen her before and knew who she was. She was an employee of the Base Exchange. Ray had been dating her. She was half Arab and half Italian and carried an Italian passport. We asked Ray what she was doing here. He said "She's going with us". Both Tony and I started to object. Ray must have seen the surprise and concern on our faces, because he quickly told us that it was all very legal. All of the proper paperwork had been filed. He assured us that everything was OK. He finally convinced us but we still had a bad feeling about it.

American military personnel in many of the countries we operated in, at that time, were not required to carry passports. Military orders served the same purpose. The host countries customs were performed on the military installations, often by proxy American military personnel. This meant that we would have been permitted to depart

Wheelus and fly direct to Tunis without clearing through a civilian facility. Ray's girlfriend, however, was a different story. We would now have to fly first to the Idrus airport, clear her through customs and then depart for Tunis. Ray again assured us that there would not be a problem. Our plan was that Tony would fly the leg to Tunis. I was scheduled to fly the return leg. So, Tony was in the left seat. I was in the right seat although aero club rules specified that Ray should have been there. Ray and his girlfriend were in the back seat. We took off from Wheelus and flew to Idrus. When we met the Libyan customs officials they looked concerned and troubled. They could not understand why three American military men had this half-Arab woman with them. At one point it appeared that the trip would have to be canceled. Ray did a lot of talking and explaining. Tony and I kept our mouths shut and left it to Ray. At one point I counted eight different Libyan agents who seemed to be focusing on our party. They were rushing in and out of the room we were placed in. After about two hours they agreed everything was OK and allowed us to depart.

The flight from Idrus to Tunis was smooth and uneventful. The weather was good. The flight followed the coastline most of the route. About halfway to Tunis there is a large island just off shore by the name of Djerba. We flew over that island. As we approached the Tunis airport we could see a large old stone castle in the middle of the harbor. We later learned that this had been an old pirate stronghold in the previous century. We landed at the Tunis airport. Tony made a good landing. We left the airport and took a taxi to a hotel. We found that we had a little trouble communicating. In the majority of the foreign countries I had visited up to that time enough English is spoken that I had little trouble getting around and being understood. English is the second language in most countries and the people are normally quite helpful. In Tunisia, French is the second language. English is seldom spoken. We had to use a lot of hand signals.

Photography was one of my hobbies at that time. I had a good Nikon camera with multiple lenses and took pictures where ever I went. I would have them developed as slides. I had accumulated several boxes of slides in my travels. Because of the trouble in communicating I walked on most of my sightseeing outings. Tony occasionally walked with me. Ray and his girlfriend went their own way. We would meet for dinner in the evening. Tunis is an old dusty city with a lot of stone block construction. The people had a stern look about them as if they had the weight of the world on their shoulders. They would, however, break into a broad smile when you spoke to them. Even thou communication was difficult they were very courteous. I walked to the harbor so I could take pictures of the pirate fort. I specifically recall one picture that I took during my walking tours. I was walking down a street by myself and walked past a stone building. It had open windows and the windows were covered with large prison like vertical bars. The bars were on both the inside and the outside of the window box separated by about 18 inches. In the middle of the window box was a bright eyed child that was clearly under the age of two. His only clothing was a diaper. There was no one else around. The child looked up at me as I took his picture. I called this one "Arab Baby Sitting". On the evening of the second day in Tunis, we met for dinner. Ray informed us he had received a telegram from the detachment commander at Wheelus. Hotel accommodations in Tunis did not include a telephone. The telegram was the only way to reach us. The telegram instructed us to return immediately and return directly to Wheelus without a stop at Idrus. This sounded like a strange order. The part of not stopping at Idrus was repeated for emphasis. We weren't sure of the reason for these odd instructions but we would obviously comply with them.

The next morning we departed Tunis at about 7AM. I was in the left seat and flying the aircraft. Tony was in the right seat and Ray and his girl friend were again in the back. The weather was good but there were low clouds over the Mediterranean Sea that extended onshore as far as the eye could see. We had not been able to get any weather information before departing Tunis. We were a little concerned that this fog extended all the way to Wheelus. We would not be able navigate by map reading as we had done flying to Tunis. The only navigational aid available along the route was a radio beacon (NDB) on Djerba Island. We would be out of range of the facilities at Wheelus for most of the flight. Unfortunately, that beacon

170

was not on the air. We attempted to call Djerba on the radio. Again, to no avail.   The plight of the "Lady Be Good" began to play lightly on our minds. We had been flying on a heading only without any references or navigational clues. We felt that we might end up well out over the Sahara Desert. Tony and I came up with a simple plan, offset our heading so we knew we would be over the waters of the Mediterranean Sea, descend below the stratus and then angle slightly toward the land until we could see the shore. We could then follow the coast line until we were close to Wheelus. Ray could make the instrument approach into Wheelus if necessary. The biggest problem we faced was the accuracy of the altimeter. The instrument is pressure sensitive and since the pressure can be different between two locations it must be adjusted for pressure changes. This adjustment is called an altimeter setting. Failure to make the adjustments could result in the readings being as much as a couple of hundred feet in error. New settings are obtained through radio communication with ground facilities. We had been unable to raise anyone. The altimeter setting for Tunis was set when we departed but hadn't been changed since.

I started to descend the aircraft toward the stratus clouds below. We soon reached the top of the clouds. The altimeter read 700 feet. I told Tony to keep his eyes outside the cockpit and watch for the water. I stayed on instruments and descended very slowly into the fog. A couple of minutes later Tony said he could see the water. Our altimeter read just over 100 feet. I changed the heading about 30 degrees toward the coast. We flew over several small fishing boats. They had sail masts sticking up. We weren't too far above them. Tony said we were close enough to see their wide eyed looks. It must have been an amazing sight for them to see an airplane (probably for the first time) zip over head near mast top level in a dense fog. It was only a few minutes before we saw the coast. I turned to fly along it. It was at this point that Ray decided it was wise for him to get into the right seat, so Tony and Ray traded places. Ray took over flying the aircraft. We followed the coast in that fog to a point that was about 100 miles from Wheelus. Then we broke out of the fog into clear skies. The coastal area was marshy and there were numerous flocks of ducks flying in the area. Ray maneuvered to avoid them.

The air was bumpy after we cleared the fog and became more so as we approached Wheelus. When we approached Wheelus the tower informed us that we had a party waiting for us and directed us to taxi to a specific spot on the ramp. This was a little unusual but everything concerning our instructions to return to Wheelus had been so. Ray felt this might be some VIPs. It was very bumpy coming down final. Ray was concerned about a bouncy landing in front of VIPs so he decided that he should make the landing. The lady in the back seat was having trouble with air sickness. It was quite bumpy. We were about two miles from touch down when she began to vomit from the air sickness. She covered the back of our seats and the area between the front seats. Some of the vomit landed on the outside of my right pant leg. We landed and taxied to the spot the tower had instructed. Waiting there for us were two full Colonels, our detachment commander (whose name I have forgotten) and the base commander as well as a man in a suit and tie who turned out to be a representative from the American Ambassador to Libya's office. They did not look happy. With a lingering smell of vomit, we climbed out of the aircraft and met our greeting party.

Called Before the Commander

Our greeting party talked to Ray for several minutes. They didn't seem to want to talk to Tony or myself. We stood back and kept our mouths shut. Our detachment commander finally told us he wanted to see all three of us in uniform in his office at 1PM the next day. Nobody spoke on the trip back to the BOQ. When we arrived each us went to our rooms. I saw Tony in the break room later in the day but neither of us met or talked to Ray. Tony and I felt that the three of us were in serious trouble. We weren't sure what exactly we had done wrong but the serious demeanor of our commander confirmed for us that we would soon find out. The next day we drove in silence to the operations area, formally posted into the commander's office and stood at attention awaiting our fate. The colonel told us that Ray had admitted his role in the affair, confirmed that he had raised objections and he acknowledged that our finally consenting to the situation may have been influenced by the fact that Ray was our boss. He admonished us for poor judgment and excused Tony and I. Ray received some disciplinary action but I never knew just what type it was. We returned to the BOQ to learn that the new crew had just taken off and we were now on alert status.

The orders to fly directly back to Wheelus bypassing Idrus had come from the office of the American Ambassador to Libya. The Libyan customs agents had released us to fly to Tunis but were still apparently troubled. They had called the base operations at Wheelus trying to find out what this woman was doing on our aircraft. The base commander was uncertain what was going on. There was concern that we would be accused of being smugglers on our return and end up in a Libyan jail. They wanted us back safely at Wheelus until they could determine what was going on. The irony of the situation is that the only rule we had violated was the aero club rule that only members were permitted to ride in club aircraft. The exception, of course, was the young lady with Ray. She was legally required to clear customs back into Libya. She had not. I'm not sure what happened to her. I hope the American consulate helped her since we were acting on their orders.

Paul's Refusal to Fly.

On March 8th the alert alarm sounded. The five of us headed for our vehicle and drove to the flight line. We started the engines and started to taxi for takeoff. About half way to the runway Paul came over the interphone and informed Ray that he could not fly today. Ray asked if he was sick. He said no, he just could not fly today. The aircraft was stopped on the taxiway and the conversation between the pilot (Ray) and the navigator (Paul) continued. Paul re-stated that he could not fly with Ray. He gave some hint that the reason was that Ray's behavior was so reprehensible that he couldn't fly with him. Ray attempted to persuade Paul that even though we have differences we are on duty and our differences should not prevent us from doing that duty. The conversation continued over the interphone for several more minutes. Paul finally stated that he refused to fly with Ray. There was a long pause. Ray finally broke the silence by calling the

173

tower and advising them the aircraft was retuning to the ramp. He then called operations and informed them of the same. The operations officer asked for the reason. Ray asked the operations officer to meet the aircraft and that he would inform him further at that time.

Return to Forbes

During the days that followed the detachment commander talked to each of us. The decision was made to delay Major Wells' crews return and have our crew take their place and return home. We would return to Forbes with the aircraft they were scheduled to take back. Paul agreed to navigate the aircraft back to Forbes. On March 14th we flew the aircraft to Torrejon AFB outside of Madrid, Spain. The following day we flew an eleven and a half hour flight back to Forbes. It would be my final flight in the B-47 aircraft.

Captain Paul was taken off the crew and removed from flight status. He was subsequently removed from the service. I never knew his removal status. I did hear that he returned to Boston and the rumor was that he committed suicide about a year later. I do not know whether that is true but I have a bad feeling that it might be. I have reflected on the incident and Paul several times during the intervening years. I did not know Paul well. I don't think any of us did. I can't help but feel the two incidents, the plunge over the cliff at Shemya and the gear problem at Wheelus played heavily on his mind. Both of us were on both those aircraft and the two incidents were only four months apart. During the time between the Shemya incident and the deployment to Wheelus we did not fly together. I know that the flights I was on during that period I was anxious about a hard landing. Paul may have experienced one or more incidents during that period that added to his burden. I still include him in my prayers.

Air Force Pilot Training

My aspiration, when I first became interested in the Air Force, was to attend pilot training. That goal was still very much alive. Applications to attend Air Force Pilot training came from several sources. The number of applicants always far exceeded the available training slots. The selections to fill those slots were broken down into categories. This process was consistent with what my recruiter had originally explained to me at the time of my entry into the Air Force. The majority of the slots were reserved for recent graduates of the Air Force Academy and the ROTC programs. Each of these programs had an allocation of slots and each had their own selection boards. Applicants from previously rated (primarily navigators) active duty personnel had a smaller allocation that also had its own selection board. This board met once a year. Rated navigators were required to submit an application each year they wished to be considered. A new physical was required for each application. I had submitted an application each year that I had been assigned to Forbes. I submitted the application to the base personnel office. Personnel would send the application to the Wing Commanders office for comment. It was then sent to the selection board. I would receive a copy which included the commander's comments. The commander's comments on each of my applications included the phrase; "This officer is presently serving in a critical skill which requires extensive training. Replacing him would impose a significant burden on this unit's ability to perform its mission." This statement, of course, was available to the members of the selection board. I was not selected during any of the three years that I applied while at Forbes. I'm not sure how these comments by my commander affected my chances but I came to believe that they were the primary reason that I was not being selected. Air Force regulations established a maximum age for submitting an application to pilot training at 26 and a half. Additionally, even if I were selected I would have to start training by the age of 27 and a half. In late 1966 I was 25 and a half. If I remained in the 55th I was certain that I would never be selected. I had to find another way to meet this goal.

I had a lengthy talk with the personnel officer who supervised the section that handled training applications. He informed me that there was an additional category of slots to Air Force Pilot training allocated to the Air Guard. There were generally up to 100 slots a year reserved for them. He advised me that if I was transferred to the Air Force Reserves I could go to any of the Air Guard units around the country and apply to join them. I would then be eligible to apply for one of these slots. I would retain my rank and seniority. He said that the training slots allocated to the Air Guard were filled by their own selection board. By late 1966 I had served my required active duty commitment. I would be eligible to transfer to the reserves or the Air Guard. I started calling the various Air Guard units to explore the possibility of transferring to one of them. The one that sounded the most encouraging to me was the Kentucky Air Guard. They flew the F-101 aircraft, a fighter with the nickname of Voodoo. They were an interceptor unit. The colonel in charge advised me that the F-101 was a single seat aircraft and as a result all of his flying personnel were already pilots. He did have an authorized position for a wing Electronic Warfare Officer which had never been filled. He assured me that if I transferred to the reserves he would pick me up in that slot. He said that since they had operated for years without a wing EWO he would not try to hold me if I were selected to fill one of the slots to pilot training. He made the comment that an officer with dual qualifications would be nice to have. He emphasized to me that this would not guarantee that I would be selected for one of the slots but that given my record the chances were very good. If I was able to attend pilot training I would be returned to the Kentucky unit after graduation and fly the F-101.

The 55th SRW was in a transitional process at that time. The RB-47H aircraft was being phased out. The job of the 55th was being split up. The main body of the wing was to be transferred to Offutt AFB near Omaha, Nebraska. New units were being activated at Eielson AFB near Fairbanks and at Yokota AFB in Japan. Both would have permanently assigned flight crews and would fly a converted version of the C-135B aircraft. The 55th s' crews at Forbes were to be distributed to these new locations. In March of 1967 the transition was still in the planning stage. Very few personnel moves had actually been made. The majority of the personnel moves had been staff and command individuals and not flight crew members.

I had completed all of the leg work in my plan following my return from Shemya and prior to my deployment to Wheelus. I had resolved to apply for transfer to the Air Guard. Upon my return from Wheelus on March 15, 1967 I immediately put my plan to transfer to the Kentucky Air Guard into operation. To the best of my knowledge the 55th s planning for the transition from Forbes had not reached the point of cutting individual orders for crew members. I was concerned that if they had already issued orders to re-assign me to one of the three locations my application for transfer to the reserves would be disapproved. The personnel officer I had talked to had advised me that if I received orders assigning me to an over seas location any application to the reserves, that had not been previously approved, would be put on hold until my overseas assignment was complete. I immediately went to personnel to submit an application to be transferred to the reserves. This was done on March 21st. On March 23, 1967 I received a set of orders reassigning me to Yokota AFB effective April 20th. I confirmed with the personnel officer I had been talking to that this effectively voided my application to transfer to the reserves. I had been foiled again. I vowed that my first action when I reached Yokota would be to submit another application for pilot training. I still had a year of eligibility.

Schweitzer Crew – First Deployment – Brize Norton (Summer 1964)

Capt. Schweitzer (Pilot/AC), Capt. Hoose (Copilot), Capt Bates (Navigator)
Lt. Lesinski (Raven 1), Lt. Perrizo (Raven 2), Lt. Lewis (Raven 3)

Smiley's Flying Circus – Iron Lung Project – Incirlik (Fall 1965)

Back Row: Maj. Smiley (Pilot/AC), Lt. Snyder (Copilot), Maj. Miller (Navigator)
Maj. Rock (Raven 1), Capt. Perrizo (Raven 2), Capt. Cain (Raven 3)
Front Row: Maintenance Personnel (In Uniform), Project personnel (Civilian Clothes)

Morris Crew – Iron Lung Project – Yokota (Winter 1966)

Capt. Pruss (Raven 3), Lt. Perrizo (Raven 2), Capt. Cain (Raven 1), Doug (Project Officer)
Capt. Miller (Navigator), Lt. Snyder (Copilot), Capt. Morris (Pilot/AC)

Project Aircraft (4291) was in the wash rack so the Firefly Project aircraft (4295), which was
also deployed to Yokota, was used as a photo backdrop.

Receiving the Distinguished Flying Cross - (Winter 1965)

Colonel Mixon (55th Wing Commander) is on my left

Chapter 16   Yokota Again

Yokota Air Force Base

The war in Viet Nam was rapidly heating up and Travis Air Force Base in California had become a jump off point for military personnel of all three services to the Far East theatre. Unlike the Second World War where most troops were transported on ships the main method of transfer was now by air. The job was beyond the capacity of existing military transport so the Pentagon used contract commercial carriers to do the job. Several budding air lines got their start under these contracts. World Airways was one of the largest of these new carriers. A family acquaintance from the town where my mother was teaching high school, Norwood, had recently left the Air Force and had gotten a job with Trans Caribbean Airlines as a navigator. Trans Caribbean had re-assigned all of its aircraft to this contract transport role. I met him briefly a year later as he was passing through Kadena on one of these trips. Both of these fledgling airlines flew older DC-8 aircraft.

The first two crew members reassigned from the 55th to Yokota were a Captain Blaine and I. Our reporting dates were the same so our orders had us traveling together. Blaine had been married and divorced but had custody of his three children. He had elected not take his children with him. He left them with his mother. So he was on an unaccompanied tour which meant he would be treated, like me, as a bachelor for the tour of duty. The first leg of our journey began on April 18th . We boarded a military aircraft for a flight to Travis. The next day we boarded a World Airways DC-8 for the flight to Yokota. The majority of the passengers were in Army uniform. They were likely headed to the war zone in South Viet Nam. The flight was full. When we arrived at Yokota Blaine and I located our bags and headed to the housing office. The rest of the passengers would continue on to Viet Nam.

Yokota AFB is about 30 miles north of Tokyo, Japan. It is near the town of Fusa. The base was used largely by the U.S. Air Force. It had a 10,000 foot plus runway and had become a major stopover point for the heavy jet traffic between the west coast of the United States and bases in South East Asia. Several propeller driven aircraft were still being used by the Air Force. Tachikawa AFB, a few miles from

Yokota, was used by them. The war in Viet Nam was rapidly ratcheting up and the volume of materials and the personnel to support the war effort were increasing dramatically. That made both Yokota and Tachikawa very busy terminals. The bases were under the command of Pacific Air Command (PACAF) which had its headquarters in Honolulu, Hawaii. PACAFs span of authority extended to the bases in South East Asia (Viet Nam and Thailand). Yokota was the home of the 5th Air Force which was a subordinate unit to PACAF and controlled the bases in Japan and Okinawa.

The Strategic Air command (SAC) had had a minimal presence in the Pacific prior to America's increased involvement in the war in Viet Nam. The 55th s Operating Location 2 at Yokota had been the rare SAC unit in the Pacific theatre. By 1966 SAC was assuming an increasing larger role in the region as a result of the escalating war. Normally, Air Force assets that were moved to the Pacific region were placed under the authority of PACAF. The SAC units were an exception. SAC insisted on retaining control over its deployed assets. The 3rd Air division was established and placed under the command of Major General Krumm. The 3rd Air Division was headquartered at Anderson AFB on the island of Guam. The new SAC unit that was being activated at Yokota, the one I had joined, was named Detachment 1 of the 3rd Air Division.

I arrived at Yokota AFB in April of 1967. At the time I arrived the detachment had not yet received any of its aircraft and Blaine and I were the first crew members to arrive. The only personnel in place when we arrived were a skeleton headquarters staff. The crews and aircraft were not scheduled to arrive for a couple of months. The staff was surprised to see us. Rightly or wrongly, this convinced me that my orders to Yokota had been expedited to prevent me from transferring to the reserves and eventually to the Kentucky Air Guard. The Detachment 1 staff on hand in April of 1967 was minimal. They were a carryover from the 55th s Operating Location 2 staff. The commander was Colonel John Harvey. Major Ed Kelly was the Operations Officer. Colonel Harvey would be retiring within a couple of months. His replacement, Colonel Gunn, had just arrived. The day to day operation of the Detachment was still much the same as it had been as OL-2. There was a deployed crew from Forbes flying the RB-47H aircraft. The next couple of months would see a continuous stream of incoming staff to support the new mission. By late May the crews and the aircraft were scheduled to start arriving. Major Kelly was a very busy man. He had to cover both the ongoing OL-2 operation as well as gearing up for the new detachment mission. Blaine and I had little to do for the next two months so we were assigned to assist Major Kelly.

Major Kelly was a bear of a man. He had been a varsity football player in college. The Air Force bases in the Western Pacific had established sports competitions between them. Each base had a football team. The team would be drawn from personnel assigned to the base. During football season a significant part of their time was devoted to this endeavor. An informal league had been established. The level of competition was quite high. It compared to that at the small college level. The base commanders took the games quite seriously. Ed Kelly was the coach of the Yokota team. I remember him introducing us to a husky young Second Lieutenant on his football team. The young man had just arrived and was assigned to one of the other base units. During his college days the Lieutenant had been a quarterback for the University of Oklahoma football team. Major Kelly seemed quite enthusiastic about having him on the team.

The first duties assigned to me were as the detachment's security officer. The duties of this position included being responsible for the safes that housed the classified documents used by the detachment. This had been part of Ed Kelly's duties. I knew very little about the Air Force regulations that pertained to security so I spent a lot of time reading them. Several times during the next couple of months I acted as the Mission Monitor for the RB-47H sorties. As explained in an earlier chapter, those missions were flown under radio silence. This was known as a covert posture. The crew would break radio silence at a few predetermined positions on their route to make a position report. While the aircraft was airborne an officer from the detachment's operations staff was required to be in the Operations

Command Post to receive these position reports. That officer was known as the Mission Monitor. The Mission Monitor would use these reports to update the aircraft's progress with concerned agencies such as air traffic control facilities and the detachment staff. If a position report was missed the Mission Monitor would alert the detachment commander and the search and rescue command posts. This task had also been one of Major Kelly's responsibilities.

By the middle of May Major Kelly had expanded my duties to include the Mission Briefing Officer. Each time an operational sortie was launched a pre-mission briefing was held with the staff and crew prior to the crew going to the aircraft. This briefing would review the mission profile, brief the expected weather along the route and answer any questions by the crew, the staff or the commander. The briefing officer conducted the majority of the briefing with the exception of the weather. An officer from the base weather office would conduct this portion. I only acted as the Mission Briefing Officer once. Near the end of the briefing Colonel Gunn (Colonel Harvey had retired) asked me a rather obscure question. I didn't have a clue how to answer him. Major Kelly told me, a couple of days later, that the Colonel did not want me to be the briefing officer again. I was relieved of that duty. Ed confided in me that I was not the problem. Colonel Gunn had been unhappy that Ed was delegating the job and the question was an off the wall one that he knew I could not answer. Ed had been chewed out for not doing the job himself.

Security Officer
When the flight training and certification process had begun my primary duties had changed to being a flight crew member. I did retain, probably because no one else wanted it, the collateral duty of detachment security officer. As the security officer I was responsible to ensure that only authorized personnel had access to the classified documents, to ensure that all authorized personnel were trained and briefed on the proper procedures for handling classified documents while in their possession and that the documents were properly secured in the safe when they were not in use. Being an authorized

181

person meant that an individual had met two general requirements. They must have had the appropriate level of clearance. The three general clearance levels in ascending order were <u>Confidential</u>, <u>Secret</u> and <u>Top Secret</u>. A Top Secret clearance required an extensive back ground investigation which would have been completed before they arrived at Yokota. All of the flight crew members and most of the staff assigned to the detachment held a <u>Top Secret</u> clearance. Secondly, they must have a <u>Need to Know</u> the information to do their job. That means that even if you had a <u>Top Secret</u> clearance, if the document did not pertain to your job you would not be given access to it. When each new individual arrived in the squadron I had to verify with the base Air Police squadron their clearance level and then certify to the Air Police Squadron that they had a <u>Need to Know</u> to do their job. This was done with the exchange of several documents which required my signature several times. Copies of these documents were retained by both the detachment and the Air Police Squadron.

When an Authorized member of the detachment needed to use a classified document they had to adhere to the following procedure;

1-Sign for the document to remove it from the safe.

2-Ensure that only authorized personnel have access to the information while it was in their possession. This would include being aware of an unauthorized person who might be looking over their shoulder while they worked or someone over hearing a discussion of the material.

3-Return the document to the safe when they are finished using it and sign it back in.

During the early summer of 1967 Major Kelly had been reassigned and he had been replaced by a Lt. Colonel Gottschalk. Colonel Gottschalk's previous assignment had been at SAC headquarters at Offutt AFB in Nebraska. In my security officer role I had several direct friendly confrontations with Colonel Gottschalk over the next few months. Colonel Gottschalk was too lax in the second requirement above. In his previous assignment at Offutt AFB he had worked in a secure area. A secure area is one where access to the area is controlled. Anyone entering the area must pass a security check point to gain access. The guards normally check a list of authorized personnel. Everyone in his previous work group had been authorized access to the classified material in their safe so leaving a classified document unattended within the secure area was not a problem. Our detachment building was not considered a secure area. There was no security check point for entering the building. Anyone who had access to the base could walk into the building without being challenged. When documents were taken from the safe they had to be guarded and the user had to be aware of who was around them. Colonel Gottschalk would frequently have classified documents on his desk. His desk was next to an aisle between the operations area and the crew briefing area. It was a relatively busy area. He would occasionally leave his desk for some reason (to get a cup of coffee or talk to another staff member) and leave the document open on the top of his desk. On several occasions I walked by Colonel Gottschalk's desk and saw a TOP SECRET document left unattended on the top of his desk. I would wait by his desk for him to return. When he returned I would advise him that he needed to be more careful. He would be very apologetic but it continued to happen. One day, instead of waiting for his return I took the document and signed it back into the safe. Since I had been on my way to lunch I left the area for lunch before he returned to his desk. When I returned from lunch I learned that Colonel Gottschalk had gone into a panic and searched frantically for the document. He had gone to several staff members in the detachment asking if they had seen the document. None had. Finally, one of them was signing a different document out of the safe and informed the Colonel that his document had been properly returned to the safe. The sign-In log showed that I had signed it back in. I went over to the colonel's desk. He had a sheepish look on his face. He agreed that I had done what I should have done under the circumstances. I sat down and we discussed what he could do to ensure that this didn't happen again. I never caught him leaving a document unattended again.

Inspector General Arrives

In early June the detachment was scheduled for an inspection by a team from the Strategic Air Command's (SAC) Inspector General's office. I had little experience with this type of inspection. Lt. Colonel Lionel, one of the new staff mission briefing officers, must have sensed my concern. He told me that he had been a security officer and had gone through several of this type of inspection. He spent a great deal of time with me in preparation for the event. About a week before the team was due to arrive I received a classified package from the inspection team. It contained a list of the team members, their levels of clearance and what types of documents they could see. Colonel Lionel advised me that there might be some members of the team that I would have to deny access to some documents.

On June 14th a team from the Office of the SAC Inspector General arrived. The office normally had a couple of teams in the field at any point in time. The one inspecting us was just one of them. The office was commanded by a Brigadier General (One Star). The teams were normally commanded by a Lt. Colonel or a full Colonel. The General accompanied his teams in the field only on rare occasions. He had, however, chosen to accompany this team. I suspect that the fact we were located near Tokyo, Japan may have had something to do with his decision. He did not actively participate in the inspection. Colonel Gunn, our detachment commander, welcomed the team and we sat down for the initial briefing which outlined what they would be doing over the next two days. Colonel Gunn wanted all of the staff present including me. During the course of the briefing the General asked about a specific classified document. He wasn't clear about its language so he asked to see it. Colonel Gunn asked me to fetch it. Unfortunately the General's name was not on the access list that had been sent to me the week before and I so advised the Colonel "I'm sorry sir but the General's name is not on the access list." Colonel Gunn gave me a startled look. He stared at me for a couple of seconds and then looked at the General who was now grinning from ear to ear. Everyone at the table relaxed and the briefing proceeded. I'm sure that the General met the requirements for access but due to a last minute decision to join the team his name had been omitted from the official list. Colonel Lionel had briefed me to stand my ground and allow access only to those on the list. It was a typical SAC trick of the Curtis LeMay era. Fortunately I had been fore warned.

The RC-135M

The C-135 aircraft was developed by Boeing to serve as an airborne gas station. The KC-135A was by far the most numerous version of the aircraft and was replacing the KC-97 as SAC's primary tanker aircraft. The air frame was similar to the commercial Boeing 720 and 707 aircraft series. The KC-135A preceded both of those aircraft. The KC-135A was equipped with the J-57 engine, a turbojet engine. The turbojet had been the standard during the early period of jet engine technology. When Boeing later developed the two similar commercial aircraft types, the 720 and the 707, they equipped them with the newer and more advanced turbo fan engines, versions of which, are still in common usage in most jet aircraft. The C-135B was a later version of the tanker that was equipped with turbo fan engines. It was not capable of acting as a tanker but could act as a receiver aircraft. It was intended to be used as a transport and cargo aircraft and was far less numerous than the KC-135A.

All three of the new units that were replacing the Forbes version of the 55th would use a converted version of the C-135B aircraft. The version used by the 55th at Offutt would be designated as the RC-135C. The unit at Yokota, Detachment One of the Third Air Division, would use a version designated as the RC-135M. The unit at Eielson AFB would use a version designated as the RC-135D.

The RC-135M was equipped with the TF-33 turbo fan engines. It was capable of mid-air refueling. The first thing we noted about the aircraft was that it was much roomier than the RB-47H had been, almost palatial by comparison. The forward compartment was occupied by the pilots and the navigators. Each crew had two pilots and two navigators. There was a much larger enclosed rear compartment that housed the equipment and positions of operation for the ravens. The rear compartment extended to a point just in front of the rear access door. The rear of the aircraft had two bunks, the relief facilities and a small galley for warming up our in-flight lunches. We now carried our own Early Warning Platform personnel with us on the aircraft. Their equipment and operating positions were in the same enclosed compartment where the ravens worked. There were several early warning positions. The two Raven positions were located at the rear most part of the enclosure. There was a walkway that ran along the rear enclosed compartment on the left side of the aircraft. It allowed access to both compartments and the facilities in the rear of the aircraft. Initially, each crew had two ravens assigned. This would change later as described in the next chapter. The RC-135M had a distinctive looking long black bulbous type nose. Detachment One of the 3rd Air division (at Yokota) was scheduled to get six of the aircraft.

Certification Training

By late May the air crews had begun to arrive. The first two crews would be the standardization crews. Crew M-01 was commanded by Major Bennie Allen. Crew M-02 was commanded by Captain Paul Martin. I was assigned to crew M-03. Captain Vic Prizlusky was our Aircraft Commander. Captain Dave Frutchey was the Co-pilot. Each crew was to have two navigators. The Navigator One was Captain Max Moore. The Navigator Two was Captain Greg Krossnoff. Captain Willie Mueller was the Raven One and I was the Raven Two. The RC-135M carried its own early warning platform. The early warning crew consisted of about a dozen or so enlisted crew members and had their own supervisor. The front end crew had a compartment at the front of the aircraft similar to the layout on a commercial airliner. The entry door to the forward compartment was not closed and locked as it would be on an airliner. Behind the front compartment there was the rear enclosed compartment. This enclosed compartment, as described above, was where the ravens and the early warning crew worked. Survival kits were lined up in the aisle along the left side of the rear enclosed compartment which left a narrow walkway. Our first crew training mission was on June 1st . We flew five training missions in June. The final one was our certification evaluation. The crew was now certified as a combat ready crew.

Operational Missions

Detachment One's area of responsibility to conduct peripheral reconnaissance missions ran from South East Asia to the southern tip of the Kamchahkta Peninsula. This included Viet Nam and North Korea. Our first operational mission was on July 6, 1967. The sorties from Yokota were normally about 12 hours long and would require a mid-air refueling. Our tasks during the On Watch period were similar in nature to those during the RB-47H operations.

Our first operational sortie turned out to be an exciting one. Upon our return to Yokota we learned that the weather had deteriorated considerably. All airports, military or civil, have established criteria under which a properly equipped aircraft may attempt to land.

This criteria has two basic parameters, the height of the ceiling (the height of the lowest cloud layer above the ground at the airport) and the prevailing visibility. The criteria varies dependant on the accuracy of the type of equipment being used to make the approach to the runway and the terrain features at or near the airport. The idea, again, is to give the pilot sufficient time once he/she visually acquires the runway (exits the cloud layer) to properly align the aircraft with the runway and put the aircraft in the proper attitude to land while clearing all obstacles. This criteria is known as the Minimums. At most civil airports the Minimums will vary from one airport to another. The Air Force had established a common set of Minimums that applied to the majority of Air Force installations, a ceiling of 200 feet and a visibility of a half a mile. The reported weather upon our return to Yokota was below Minimums but it was varying somewhat. The other option was to proceed to another airport, a planned Alternate that was above Minimums. Sorties were planned so that you would have sufficient fuel remaining to make the planned Alternate. Our planned Alternate on this flight was Iwakuni MCAS in Southern Japan. Since conditions seemed to vary, Major Prizlusky (he had been promoted in mid June) had decided to remain in the area to see if the

187

weather would come above our <u>Minimums</u>. In a half hour or so, we reached the point where our fuel supply forced us to choose between our planned <u>Alternate</u> at Iwakuni or be committed to land at Yokota.

Vic finally decided to try landing at Yokota. When we finally started our approach to landing we were down to the point where we had only enough fuel to make a single attempt at landing. If we were not able to land we would run out of fuel. The reported weather was still slightly below our Minimums. The procedures for a blind approach (still in the clouds) are as follows;

1-The aircraft flaps are extended to 30 degrees. Flaps provide greater low speed lift and allow the aircraft to approach the runway at a slower speed.

2-The pilot flying the aircraft keeps his attention inside the cockpit monitoring the flight instruments.

3-The pilot not flying the aircraft keeps his attention outside the aircraft looking for the runway.

4-Once the non flying pilot sights the runway he calls "Runway In Sight".

5-The pilot flying the aircraft transitions his attention from the instruments to a visual view of the runway.

6-When they had the runway visually in sight they could then extend the flaps to 50 degrees.

7-The landing is completed. If a go-around is required (generally because the runway never becomes visible) the throttles are advanced and if the flaps had been extended to 50 degrees they are retracted to 30 degrees for the go-around.

Our descent was continued below <u>Minimums</u>. Dave called "Runway in Sight" Vic called "50 flaps". I felt the aircraft bank right for a couple of seconds and then level. As soon as the aircraft leveled we contacted the runway. We had landed. The final turn to align with the runway had been done very close to ground.

Our third operational mission was on July 27th. We had been flying for several hours and were flying over South Korea, monitoring activity in North Korea, when the front cockpit started to fill with an acrid smoke. It was quickly determined that the source was just under the floorboard of the front compartment. The backup battery system was located there. The navigators went to the circuit breaker panel and pulled the breaker for the battery. Within several minutes the smoke started to thin out. The mission was aborted and we returned to Yokota. The problem had shortened out scheduled flight by only two hours.

Some Free Time

When Major Kelly left the detachment my level of administrative duties diminished significantly. Additional staff members had been arriving weekly so my assistance was no longer needed. This coincided with the start of my crew's flight training which meant my primary focus had shifted as well. Most of our duty time was spent planning and flying training sorties and later operational reconnaissance sorties. The net result was that I had more free time. I spent many of these free days golfing. The Japanese town of Fusa is located adjacent to the base. Not far from Fusa was a rather exclusive golf course. It was open to members only but in order to maintain a good relationship with the numerous American military bases the club reserved a block of membership slots for American military personnel. I believe the intent was for these slots to be filled by higher ranking officers. The membership fee was reduced for these slots and was quite reasonable by American standards. Captain Leo Johnson, the copilot on the incident at Shemya, had been assigned to the detachment. He and I inquired about these slots at the club office. We were told there were several available so we joined the club. The week ends were very busy and the colonels and generals had priority. Leo and I played during the week. Week days were slow enough that we generally played as a twosome. We were able to play at least twice a week for the entire summer. My game gradually improved. My average score for a round of golf dropped to about 90. One day everything seemed to go well. I had birded the 10th hole. Leo was marking the score card and commented "You know that you are one under par through 10 holes." The realization must have unnerved me because things started to go awry. I finished the round with a score of

189

84. This meant that I had played the first 10 holes at one stroke under par and the final 8 holes at 13 strokes over par. I had gone from par golf to double bogey golf. It was still, however, my personal best round. That summer would also be the last time I was able to play more often than once a month.

Sumo Wrestling

The bachelor housing at Yokota was in individual four bedroom units. Each unit was a separate building. The unit consisted of four bedrooms that surrounded a large general room. There were no provisions for cooking. Each bachelor had a bedroom and shared the large general area. Blaine and I had been assigned to the same unit. One of the other officers in our housing unit was a new Second Lieutenant from the island of Maui in Hawaii. His name was Corrie Tokunagawa. He worked in base personnel. Corrie had been a high school class mate of a man by the name of Jesse Kuhaulua. Jesse was a huge man that had come to Japan to join the Grand Sumo Association. He was one of the early non-Japanese to be permitted to join. Jesse was six foot three inches in height and weighted about 360 pounds. Corrie had re-established contact with his high school friend and spent a great deal of his weekends in Tokyo with him. Each sumo wrestler (known in Japanese as a "Rikkishi") assumed a sumo name (like a stage name). Jesse's sumo name was Takamiyama. At that time there were between 800 and 1000 wrestlers in the association. They were divided into six different hierarchical divisions. New members started in the lowest division and could progress upward by continually posting winning records. When they reached the top of a lower division they could move to the bottom of the next higher division. It was structured much like our professional baseball leagues. The top two divisions had about 40 Rikkishi each. So when you reached the second highest division known as Juryo you were in the top ten percent of the rankings. The top division known as the Makuuchi division could be equated to our Major Leagues in baseball. Jesse joined the association in the summer of 1964 following his graduation from high school. In the summer of 1967 he had advanced to the top of the second highest division (Juryo). In the fall of the year he advanced to the top division and stayed there for the next 15 years. Takamiyama became one of the most successful Rikkishi in sumo history. He set several records for wins and durability for the top division. Some of those records still stand today. I was able to attend one days matches with Corrie. It was a very enjoyable trip. I was not, however, able to meet Takamiyama in person.

Chapter 17　　　Okinawa

The Gulf of Tonkin incident occurred in August of 1964. North Vietnamese patrol boats had reportedly fired on an American ship in the Gulf of Tonkin. President Johnson responded by authorizing an air strike by naval aircraft on targets in North Viet Nam. This was the opening American salvo of the Viet Nam war. The United States would soon commit ground troops in South Viet Nam. All major branches of the military, the Air Force, the Army, the Navy and the Marines would have forces involved. Air strikes against targets in North Viet Nam would become routine. The air strikes by Air Force units over the North were launched from Thailand and Naval air strikes were launched from carrier based aircraft in the Gulf of Tonkin. The conflict was escalating month by month. By late summer of 1967 the mission of Detachment 1 of the 3rd Air Division would be affected by the escalating war in Viet Nam. We learned that we would begin flying missions in the Gulf of Tonkin in direct support of the bombing campaign against North Viet Nam. The new mission would be named Combat Apple. Combat Apple aircraft would set up an orbit about fifteen miles off the coast of North Viet Nam. We were to keep a twenty four hour a day, seven day a week vigil, a demanding requirement for an organization with only six aircraft assigned. We would use the same RC-135M equipment configuration that we had used at Yokota. Our base of operation would also change. The unit was being moved to Kadena AFB in Okinawa. The move to Kadena was to begin in September.

Bombers at Kadena

During the decade of the 1950s the United States lost it's monopoly on the capability to deliver a nuclear bomb. As the Soviet Union approached parity with us in the capacity to deliver these weapons our focus changed to the development of a second strike capability. A second strike capability means the ability to strike back after absorbing a destructive first strike from the Soviet Union. Both countries now possessed a sufficient first strike capability to completely destroy the other. The key to a second strike capability was to have enough strike resources that would survive the first strike and be able to completely destroy the enemy with these surviving resources. Only then could a second strike capability deter the Soviets from launching a first strike. The second strike capability was the corner stone of the <u>Mutually Assured Destruction</u> (MAD) concept that constituted our national policy from this point forward. MAD was considered the key to preventing either side from initiating a first strike.

This second strike capability by the U.S. took the form of a triad of nuclear delivery systems. The triad consisted of, a manned bomber force, a strategic missile force and the Trident submarine fleet. The first two systems were assigned to the Air Force, specifically the Strategic Air Command (SAC). The latter was assigned to the Navy. The bomber force would survive the first strike by becoming airborne prior to the arrival of the Soviet missiles and flying far enough away to avoid destruction from the attack. The missile force was placed in underground silos that were hardened to survive the most powerful nuclear bomb except for a direct hit. They could be launched after the Soviets missiles arrived. The Trident submarine force was deployed to the open seas and placed in a covert posture to mask their locations. The crews that manned both of the systems under the Strategic Air Command maintained an alert posture which enabled them to be launched in a minimum interval of time in response to a nuclear attack by the Soviet Union. This minimum interval of time was calculated based on the theoretical time it would take for the Soviet ICBMs to reach their targets in the United States once their launch was detected. In theory this interval was less than 30 minutes. To ensure survivability of our bomber force a response time of 15 minutes was established. To guarantee that the bomber force could be airborne in this short time interval SAC initiated the <u>Alert Force</u> concept. The <u>Alert Force</u> concept required that a portion of the aircraft assigned to each bomb wing would be readied for immediate launch. The aircraft would have been pre-flighted and the carts used to start the engines would be in place and connected for immediate use. A portion of the crews would be housed in a special facility on the flight line adjacent to those aircraft. The crews assigned to the wing would rotate duty periods in alert status. SAC required wings to train personnel in alert status to have the entire <u>Alert Force</u> airborne in 15 minutes from the time they were notified. Notification would be made using a speaker system to broadcast a loud horn like noise. The speaker system was known as the klaxon.

Initially, in the late 1940s and the very early 1950s the B-36 and the B-29 aircraft were the primary delivery vehicles used by the manned bomber force. They were replaced by the B-47 aircraft which began to reach operational units by the early 1950s. The B-52 was developed a few years later. It began replacing the B-47 in the late 1950s and the early 1960s. By the mid 1960s most of the B-47 aircraft used as bombers had been retired. The B-52 aircraft, in its several different models ranging from the B-52A to the B-52H, were used solely in this nuclear delivery role. As the newer models of the B-52 became available they replaced the older models in most of SAC's bomb wings. The older models were retired and ended up at Davis Monthan AFB, the Air Force's aircraft graveyard, in Arizona. By the mid 1960s, the B-52D was being replaced and phased out. The Air Force command decided not to retire the model but to convert it to a conventional bombing role. The war in South Viet Nam had escalated to the point where Air Force commanders saw the need for a heavier bombing campaign. The B-52D would fill this new role. The 3rd Air Division was activated at Anderson AFB in Guam and would be in charge of all B-52D units in the Pacific. SAC set up a base of operations for this new role at three locations. The bases were at Anderson AFB on the island of Guam, Utapuo AFB near Bangkok, Thailand and at Kadena AFB in Okinawa. Each base was equipped with B-52D bomber and KC-135A tanker aircraft. Bombing missions over South Viet Nam were launched from each of these bases.

The 4252nd Bomb Wing was established at Kadena. It reported directly to The Third Air Division commander at Anderson AFB. The Third Air Division controlled all SAC resources in the Orient. The wing (the 4252nd) was commanded by a Brigadier General. When a relevant target area had been identified a group of bombers and tankers were launched from Kadena. On some days additional groups were launched. Each group typically consisted of ten bombers and a like number of tankers. The aircraft in the group would take off one after another in rapid succession. As one aircraft rolled down the runway the next would taxi into position on the runway. When the aircraft ahead of them lifted off the next aircraft would start it's takeoff roll. This continued until all twenty aircraft were airborne.

Both the B-52D and the KC-135A used the J57 engine. The J57 engines, like the J-47 engine used on the B-47 aircraft, augmented its thrust during the takeoff roll using a water/alcohol mixture. The use of water/alcohol generated large clouds of dense black smoke. As you might expect after a few aircraft had taken off a thick cloud of black smoke shrouded the runway area. I had a pilot from the 4252nd tell me that if you were one of the last in the group to take off visibility would be somewhat limited and the air that had been stirred up by the preceding aircraft would be quite turbulent. It made for an exciting takeoff. The tankers would accompany the bombers as far as their fuel load would permit, re-fuel the bombers and return to Kadena. The bombers then continued to their targets.

The aircraft were permanently assigned to the 4252nd Wing. The flight crews were temporarily deployed from B-52 and KC-135 equipped wings in the states. The crews were at Kadena on 179 day Temporary Duty (TDY) deployments. A deployment of 180 days or more, by Air Force regulation, would have required a permanent re-assignment, so the temporary deployments were limited to 179 days. As time dragged on these crews would endure a second and often a third temporary deployment. One group told me that they had spent more time at Kadena over the preceding two year period than they had at their permanently assigned base where their families remained.

The B-52D bombing missions were restricted to targets in South Viet Nam. Their bombing raids were not extended to targets in North Viet Nam until the 1970s. Each B-52 carried a huge bomb load. The bombs were mostly 500 pound and 1000 pound bombs. Several 500 pound bombs were carried on pylons on the wings but the majority of the bomb load was carried in the bomb bay in the fuselage. The rain of explosions from a group of ten bombers had a devastating affect on the enemy troops. The concussion from the explosions could be felt at considerable distances. The ground would literally seem to shake like a major earthquake for miles.   The <u>Military Assistance Command Viet Nam</u> or MACV, located in Saigon, had operational control over all U.S. Forces in Viet Nam. In 1967 the MACV commander was General William Westmoreland. MACV was subordinate to Pacific Command located at Pearl Harbor in Hawaii. Admiral McCain was its commander. MACV did not, however, exercise direct control over the B-52s. SAC insisted on complete control over the use of the B-52s. The Third Air division at Anderson AFB decided how and when the B-52s would be used. The 3rd Air Division was under the command of Major General Krumm and reported directly to SAC headquarters at Offutt AFB in Omaha.

The resultant coordination chain in the use of B-52 bombing strikes was complicated. The rumors that we were hearing indicated that most of their bombing raids were ineffective, in part because of this parallel command structure. A strict procedure had to be followed. It went something like this; Requests from field units on the ground for bombing raids could not be made directly to the B-52 unit commanders. They had to go up the command structure to MACV headquarters. MACV would forward the requests to the SAC-Far East Command Center at Anderson AFB. The SAC Far East Command Center would decide to send a strike force. The strike force would be tasked and launched from one of the three SAC operating bases. The strike group would then fly to the target and drop their bombs. Each of the B-52 bases was located some distance from the war zone. For example, the flight from Kadena to target areas in South Viet Nam would take about three hours. The elapsed time from the request for a raid until its application could be as much as a full day. The targets during the early years were generally Viet Cong ground forces operating in rural or forested areas. The Viet Cong units were smaller indigenous guerrilla units that stayed on the move. Often as not by the time the B-52 bombing raids were run the Viet Cong were long gone. The devastating bombs would often obliterate an unoccupied stand of trees. True or not this was the widely expressed view of the B-52 bombing raids. The B-52 crews were tagged with the uncomplimentary moniker <u>Monkey Killers</u> by the ground units because, in their view, the only casualties were often the native monkeys that occupied the forests The psychological affect on the Viet Cong forces, however, was significant. Captured enemy soldiers stated that the bombing raids were frightening events even when their units had left the immediate area of the bombing.

The pressure on aircraft and crews of the 4252nd was high. One could see from casual observation that there was a shortage of parts to keep the operation going. Several of the B-52s had obviously been cannibalized for parts and were not usable. I remember one that was missing its vertical stabilizer (tail) for several months. Fortunately, given the pressures of the mission, there were few accidents or incidents. One in particular, however, is noteworthy. The B-52, similar to the B-47, required very long runways. They were very heavy and slightly under powered. They could not be accelerated to near take off speed, abort the takeoff run and stop the aircraft on the existing runway. An acceleration speed check was used similar to that used on the B-47 as described earlier. If a problem occurred after the acceleration check the aircraft was committed to continue the takeoff. On this particular evening one of the B-52 aircraft had accelerated to near decision speed (acceleration check) and decided to abort the takeoff. They were not able to stop on the remaining runway. The aircraft ran off the end of the runway, the landing gear collapsed and the aircraft was severally damaged. It was on fire. The aircraft was heavily loaded with fuel and had a full load of bombs. The crew evacuated the aircraft. Some of their exit points from the aircraft were too far above the ground to jump so they used the ropes provided to exit. The gunner's position on the B-52D is located in the tail area of the aircraft. He operates the guns directly. Later versions of the B-52 aircraft moved the gunner's position up to the front crew compartment and he operated the guns remotely. The gunner's exit from the rear compartment also used a rope to descend from the aircraft to the ground. There was a large earthen berm near the crash site. All the crew members ran to the berm and hid behind it. Two of the crew members had run through burning fuel to reach the berm. The gunner was one of these two. Both received severe burns. Both of the burned crew members were eventually evacuated to the Air Force burn center located at Brooks AFB near San Antonio, Texas. The gunner later died from his burns.

As the aircraft burned the fire eventually reached the bombs. The first to explode were the ones on pylons on the wing. They went off one at a time. When the fire reached the bomb bay in the fuselage, it ignited all the bombs at once. The resulting explosion hurled pieces of the aircraft several miles away. The town of Kadena was a small Okinawan village not far from the crash site. The base had been named after this small village. The   residents of the village thought that World War Three had started and the town was completely evacuated. I was in my room in the BOQ at the time which was located about two to three miles from the crash site. I heard the first bombs, the ones on the wing pylons, explode. There was a boom followed by a delay of several seconds and then another boom. When the bomb bay went there was a tremendous boom and I noticed the window in my room flex back and forth from the shock wave.

Transfer to Kadena

Our unit from Yokota would be re-named as the 82nd Strategic Reconnaissance Squadron (SRS) and was assigned to the 4252nd Bomb wing. When we arrived in early September of 1967, Kadena was a very busy base. The bombers and tanker crews were flying daily. There was a second reconnaissance unit under the 4252nd. It used the SR-71 aircraft. The SR-71 flew photo reconnaissance at altitudes well above all other classes of aircraft. It was capable of flying at Mach 3. The SR-71s based at Kadena flew missions over both South and North Viet Nam. They came to be known by the nick name Habu. The Habu is a black poisonous snake indigenous to Okinawa. The 82nd SRS would be added to this complex mix of aircraft and missions.

I made the transfer from Yokota to Kadena on September 10, 1967. Since I, as a bachelor, had very few personal belongings to take with me, I was able to pack everything in a couple of bags. I loaded them on one of our aircraft that was being ferried from Yokota to

Kadena and made the transfer to Kadena on one of our aircraft.

The 82nd SRS

The 82nd Strategic Reconnaissance Squadron (SRS) was given office space in the 4252nd Building. The new squadron commander was Lt. Colonel Marvin Morss. The deputy commander was Lt. Colonel Warren Alysworth. Colonel Alysworth had been a long time member of the 55th SRW and already knew several of the 82nd crew members from his days at Forbes. Both had arrived at Kadena shortly before I arrived in September. Aside from the two commanders there was very little administrative staff assigned to the squadron. None of the staff members of Detachment One at Yokota were transferred to Kadena. This meant that many of the squadron's administrative tasks were assigned to crew members as collateral duties. Since I had served in the capacity at Yokota, by default, I retained the collateral duty as the squadron security officer. The crews that had been assigned to Detachment One at Yokota were all transferred to the 82nd. The crews that had completed the certification process at Yokota were not required to re-certify at Kadena. New crew members were, of course, required to go through a certification process. The unit's flying workload was projected to increase significantly. As a result several additional crews were developed and staffed by newly assigned personnel. During the fall of 1967 there was a steady influx of arriving personnel. The On Watch period had also increased significantly. With two Ravens on each crew and two Raven positions to staff during the entire twelve and one half hours of On Watch, the need for an additional Raven on each crew soon became apparent. Within the first couple of months a third Raven was added to each crew.

Each new arrival that had not been assigned to Detachment One at Yokota had to complete the required verification of their security clearances as part of their in-processing. This required several documents that needed to be sent back and forth between my office and the Air Police Squadron at Kadena. To complete the processing my signature was required nine different times on various documents. Since I had a fairly heavy flying load and was frequently not available during normal duty hours, Colonel Morss appointed two additional security officers. The two new security officers were new at the job and not familiar with the procedures so I developed an instructional guide that gave them a step by step checklist to follow. The checklist included examples of each of the documents and the routing requirements. Both Colonel Morss and Colonel Alysworth would be promoted from Lt. Colonel to full Colonel while at Kadena.

Combat Apple

The first Combat Apple mission was flown on September 13, 1967. A single mission was flown each day for the first few days. Each of the flights would be about nineteen and one half hours in duration. The trip from Kadena to the Gulf of Tonkin took about three hours. The aircraft would enter an orbit just off the North Vietnamese coast. The orbit would be maintained for the next twelve and one half hours. The return trip back to Kadena took another three hours for a total of nineteen and one half hours. After the first few days we increased to two flights a day. The two flights a day ensured continuous coverage. Each flight would spend twelve hours on station and overlap with their replacement for a half hour. The aircraft would complete at least one mid-air refueling during the twelve hour orbit period. If the refueling could not be completed the aircraft would not be able to return to Kadena. They would have to continue to a base in Thailand and land while a replacement aircraft would be launched from Kadena. This, however, proved to be a rare situation.

The orbit area was about 15 miles from the North Vietnamese coast. On most days, the view from the cockpit afforded a panoramic view of North Viet Nam's coastal sections. The harbors at Haiphong were clearly visible. Haiphong was a routine port of call for the Soviet ships re-supplying the North Vietnamese. We could see numerous ships in the Gulf of Tonkin and we assumed that most were U.S. Navy ships but were aware that some were Russian. There was no effort by the Navy to interdict the Russian vessels since the Gulf of Tonkin was considered international waters. A U.S. aircraft carrier maintained a position in the Gulf of Tonkin. Its location was known as Yankee Station. The carrier had an air traffic control unit that

200

provided air traffic control services to all U.S. aircraft in the Gulf. The call sign of the control unit was Red Crown. We remained in radio contact and under the control of Red Crown during the entire twelve and one half hours of our orbit. Red Crown also controlled all of the naval strike missions that flew over North Viet Nam. Our Combat Apple missions were not flown under a Covert posture like most of the other reconnaissance operations we had previously been involved in. The Navy provided us with a fighter escort while we were in the Gulf. The escort normally consisted of two F-4s whose job included defending us in the event of an enemy aircraft attack.

My crew, S-03M, would be flying the second Combat Apple mission. The first mission was flown by Major Ben Allen's crew, S-01M. Major Prizlusky, our crew commander, and Captain Willie Mueller, our Raven One, were also aboard the first mission to familiarize themselves with the operation. The Combat Apple mission required the two Raven positions to be On Watch for the entire twelve and one half hours. Each of the crews was augmented, as mentioned earlier, with an extra Raven. The three Ravens covered the two positions. This allowed for breaks for the Ravens. One Raven would be on break at all times. Breaks were rotated. For the front end crew, while in our orbit, one navigator and one pilot could handle their duties. The aircraft would be on autopilot so the pilot's workload was not too demanding while we were in orbit. One pilot was required to be in his seat at all times. The pilots and the navigators could also take breaks.

When I was on break I often went to the front compartment which provided a better view. Occasionally, while one of the pilots was on break, I sat in the vacant pilot seat during my break period. Both pilots on the crew were aware of my aspirations to go to pilot training and my private flying. They occasionally allowed me to make the scheduled turns in the orbit using the autopilot controls. On one occasion Captain Dave Frutchey, the Co-pilot, disconnected the autopilot and let me hand fly the aircraft. I tried to use only very small movements of the control column but I had trouble maintaining the assigned altitude. Even with the small movements I was over

201

controlling. The altitude was varying by several hundred feet. Apparently, the up and down changes were making the crew in the back end uncomfortable. They complained to Dave and our experiment ended.

Typhoons

Typhoons were a regular seasonal feature in the area of the Pacific Ocean which Okinawa occupied. They, obviously, would restrict our ability to maintain the 24 hour a day coverage in the Gulf of Tonkin that the <u>Combat Apple</u> operations order required. So whenever the path of a typhoon was forecast to be close to Okinawa we would deploy several aircraft and crews to Clark AFB in the Philippine Islands. We flew our missions from Clark until the danger had passed and then we returned to Kadena. These deployments were often done on short notice. This meant that the men with families on Okinawa would leave with their aircraft and the families would have to prepare for the typhoon on their own. The squadron responded to this situation by forming an assistance committee of those crew members who did not deploy to assist the families of those that did. One or two members of the assistance committee would visit each family and help them prepare for the typhoon. Preparation meant boarding up the windows, ensuring sufficient food stocks etc. I was on the deployed group and the assistance committee several times during my 15 months at Kadena.

Crossing Paths with Don Williams

As mentioned earlier, the majority of the B-52D aircraft had been scheduled for replacement and retirement. Instead of retirement, however, they had been converted from their nuclear delivery role to a conventional bombing platform and used in the air war in South Viet Nam. One of the units, the bomb wing at Glasgow AFB near Glasgow, Montana, was the lone exception. They had retained their B-52Ds configured for the nuclear delivery role. Captain Don Williams, who had been my neighbor at Mather AFB, had been assigned to that unit. One day, in March of 1968, I had gone to the club for lunch. I ran into Don. My initial assumption was that he was on one of the deployed crews in the 4252nd flying conventional bombing raids over South Viet Nam. We had lunch together and during our conversation he indicated that he was not on one of the regular deployed crews but on a special mission. He could not give me any further information. Don was at Kadena only about a week. He seemed to have a lot of free time. Finally Don told me that they had been ordered back to Glasgow. The mission had been elevated up the chain of command and was disapproved. The only parting comment Don made was "We came to level Wonsan". I didn't ask any questions and he didn't offer any further information. Both of us knew better than to talk about it further. It did however leave a lot of unanswered questions.

Those of us in the reconnaissance business were accustomed to being involved in highly sensitive projects and being told only enough information to do our part. It often left us with many unanswered questions. Normally, however, we had enough information that combined with our experience we could make a good educated guess. In this case the first obvious piece of puzzle was clear. A U.S. naval reconnaissance vessel, the Pueblo, had been recently boarded and captured by the North Koreans. The capture had occurred just off   shore from the city of Wonsan in North Korea. The fact that the city of Wonsan had been the focus of their planned special mission likely meant that theirs was to be a retaliatory raid for the actions of the North Koreans. A mission of this sort, a raid on a country that we were not presently at war with, would have required approval at a very high level, likely all the way up to the President. Someone at a much lower level had probably planned the raid and moved the resources into place awaiting approval to execute the plan. It was no surprise that such a mission would be disapproved. It would very likely have been viewed by both the Russians and the Chinese as an affront and opened the proverbial Pandora's Box. The second question, "Was the planned raid to use conventional bombs?" If that were the case it would have been logical to use the aircraft and crews already in place at Kadena instead of bringing in a crew from Glasgow AFB. Don never indicated whether they had bought one of their own aircraft, one that was equipped to deliver a nuclear weapon, with them from Glasgow. If they had, it would have blended in with unknown but very serious consequences. Again, it would be no surprise if such a mission would be disapproved.

Chapter 18   Twenty Four/Seven

Combat Apple Mission

The Combat Apple mission was a twenty four hour a day and seven day a week operation. The 82nd SRS had six RC-135M aircraft. Keeping the aircraft operational and in the air given this limited number placed a heavy burden on the maintenance personnel of the unit. It required two aircraft each day and a third one ready to replace one of the first two in the event one of them had to abort and return. The length of the sorties pushed the crews to their limit. The nineteen and a half hour missions were considerably longer than we had flown in the past. One of the sorties for each day would depart Kadena shortly after mid night and land back at Kadena the following early evening. The other sortie would depart shortly after noon and return during the early morning of the following day. The longest flight that I had been on prior to the Combat Apple project had been thirteen hours and twenty minutes. Seven to eight hour flights had been closer to the norm. We built up our flight time totals very rapidly over the next couple of years. My average monthly flight time up to that time had been around 25 to 30 hours. My busiest month had been 56 flight hours. The Air Force had several rules in place that governed the limits that a crew member could be used. The maximum allowable monthly limit on flight time was 120 hours in the air. The maximum allowable flight time in any three month period was 330 hours. I was to push those limits several times during the next year or so.

My first Combat Apple sortie was flown on September 14, 1967. The first sortie of the program had been flown the day before by Major Allen's crew. We flew the second one. I would eventually fly 71 Combat Apple missions while a member of the 82nd. I would fly another 13 missions into the Gulf of Tonkin during a later temporary duty tour at Kadena under a different project for a total of 84 sorties in the theatre. The first sortie was typical of most of them. We took three hours to fly from Kadena to a point off the South Vietnamese coast near the Demilitarized Zone (DMZ). We then turned about 90 degrees to the right and entered the Gulf Of Tonkin. The first part of the flight was over the ocean and we were under the control of the

Hong Kong Oceanic Air Traffic Control facility. That flight corridor was a busy one. It was used by the B-52 aircraft on bombing raids to South Viet Nam as well as the transport activity to support the <u>Military Assistance Command-Viet Nam</u> (MACV) war effort. The air corridor was often near the saturation point. We would spend the next twelve and a half hours in a race track orbit off the coast of North Viet Nam. We broke out of the orbit after several hours to complete a mid-air refueling and then returned to the orbit. When our relief arrived we would stay another half an hour in the area and then depart for home.

There was an additional seat in the front cockpit called the jump seat. It was a retractable seat that could be snapped into place just behind the pilot's seats and centered in the space between them. It would be stowed when it was not in use. The jump seat afforded a clear view of the entire instrument panels of both pilots. The jump seat was not normally used. The only time it was normally used was when an extra pilot was on board. Extra pilots were added when an instructor pilot was added to provide pilot training or when an evaluator was on board to conduct an evaluation on one of the pilots. Both of the pilots on my crew were well aware of my frustrated desire to get into Air Force pilot training and the private flying that I had been doing. The crew had three Ravens but only two Raven positions. The spare Raven would generally occupy one of the seats in the break area near the rear part of the aircraft during takeoff and landing. The pilots on my crew allowed me to ride the jump seat during takeoff and landing. They also allowed me to sit in the unoccupied pilot's seat during my break periods when one of them was also on break. I occupied the jump seat for takeoff and landing during most of the crew's sorties.

On the return trip from the Gulf we often were assigned a very high altitude (41,000 to 45,000 feet) by Hong Kong control in order to separate us from the volume of opposite direction traffic. These altitudes were near our maximum altitude. It placed us close to what is often referred to as "Coffin Corner". Each aircraft has an airspeed at which it will stall. A stalled condition causes an aircraft to start falling out of the sky. The condition occurs when the air is not moving over the wing area fast enough to provide the necessary lift to keep the aircraft flying at that altitude. A stall condition often produces a sudden break which pitches the nose of the aircraft down several degrees. The sudden break is normally preceded by a mild bouncing action known as the stall buffet. Many aircraft are designed to produce that stall buffet to alert the pilot to the impending stall and take corrective action in time to prevent it. Recovery from a stall condition in a heavy aircraft normally results in a very substantial loss of altitude (providing, of course, you have the altitude to lose). The thinner the air at the time the stall occurs the more altitude it takes to recover. To be entirely correct in our terminology this is actually called a low speed stall. This is to differentiate it from another type of stalled condition known as a high speed stall. The causes of a high speed stall are complicated. A simple explanation is that the air is flowing over the wing so fast that a sudden disruption causes the air stream to break away from the wing resulting in a sudden lose of lift and a stall. The aircraft has a speed where it would experience a low speed stall and another faster speed where it would experience a high speed stall. Both will vary depending on the weight of the aircraft. They actually vary significantly on the same flight due to the difference in weight at takeoff and the weight at landing. As an aircraft increases its altitude these two different stall speeds get closer together. When the altitude approaches the aircraft's maximum altitude (for that weight) these two speeds are only a few knots apart (knots are nearly equivalent to miles per hour). Any sudden movement can induce a stall and the aircraft will nose over and start to fall. This area where the two stall speeds are converging is known as "Coffin Corner". Our greatest concern on these return trips were thunderstorms. Thunderstorms often occur over these ocean areas and they can reach above 50,000 feet. When flying at an altitude near the "Coffin Corner" the turbulence from a neighboring thunderstorm could induce one these stalled conditions.

Combat Apple Mission Profile

Once we entered the Gulf of Tonkin we were under the control of Red Crown, the air traffic control unit on board a U. S. aircraft carrier at Yankee Station. We would enter a race track orbit about 15 to 20 miles off the coast of North Viet Nam. The orbit was flown between a point that was off shore from the town of Vinh which is a about a third of the way up North Viet Nam from the DMZ to a point that was off shore from the port of Haiphong which was not far from the Chinese and Vietnamese border. It took us right over an island in the gulf known as Ile Bach Long. Ile Bach Long was North Vietnamese territory. We flew over this island for about a year before someone in our command hierarchy realized it and we were forbidden from over flying it anymore. They felt the North Vietnamese could place a SAM or AAA gun there to shoot us down. In practice this was not realistic. The island was very small and had been continuously used by the U. S. Navies' carrier based strike aircraft as a bomb dump. Whenever an aircraft had been unable to drop all of their bombs on their raids over North Viet Nam they would drop them on Ile Bach Long so they didn't have to land on the carrier with live bombs. We felt that the only thing that could still be living on Ile Bach Long would be a few insects if that. It was not a real threat but we complied with the directive.

Each of the Ravens had specific search assignments. One of the primary tasks during the months that I flew the missions was to find an arming signal used by the Surface-To-Air missiles (The Russian SA-2 system). We now knew a great deal about this missile system. We knew the system had a search type radar which NATO had named the <u>Fan Song</u>. This radar was used to locate and track potential targets. Once the missile was launched we knew that it was radar controlled. The guidance radar went by the NATO name of <u>BG-06</u>. When the missile was nearing its target it used a self-contained radar homing system to zero in on its target. This had been the profile for the system. Recent photo reconnaissance flights had discovered a small square box on the top of the radar vehicle that had not been there before. The speculation was that this was an arming signal device. The missile system was being widely used by the North Vietnamese to combat the bombing raids by U. S. aircraft. The problem for the North Vietnamese, according to the speculation, was that once the missile was armed, if it was launched and missed its target it would fall back to earth over their territory and explode when it hit the ground with the potential for killing some of their own citizens and causing property damage. The speculation was that this new box had been added to control the arming or possible disarming of the missile. We were tasked to search for this signal. If we could find it then it might be possible to jam it before the missile was armed. This could render it useless. Unfortunately, we never found the signal if in fact it existed.

The Navy provided a continuous escort for us while we were in the Gulf of Tonkin. The escort normally consisted of two F-4 fighters from a carrier that was based in the Gulf. We seldom actually saw our escort. We had to assume they were keeping a close eye on us. Theoretically, if an enemy fighter had attempted to attack us they could easily make a quick dash in our direction, launch a missile and quickly retreat back over land. It would have been fairly easy. We were a pretty fat and slow target and flying fairly close to the shore. Fortunately, the North Vietnamese pilots were very cautious about engaging any of our aircraft unless they had a clear advantage. We had clear air superiority over the area. Our fighter and bomber aircraft were penetrating their air space to conduct daily bombing raids and our escort would have shown no hesitation in pursuing any of their aircraft that had the audacity to venture into the Gulf. The Navy considered the Gulf its arena.

The enemy fighters were closely watched and controlled by their controllers on the ground. They were directed to engage our aircraft only when their ground personnel felt they had a clear advantage. They closely followed these precautions even deep in their own territory. The waters of the Gulf were our domain. Any venture into that arena would have evoked a massive response by our Navy. I think the North Vietnamese pilots were well aware of this. An incident that I will describe later in this chapter clearly illustrates this.

The Combat Apple operations order did have a procedure for us to follow in the event they decided to go after our aircraft. We would receive a code word from Red Crown control (SALVO SOUTH). We were to turn immediately away from the coast line and retreat as rapidly as possible. This happened only once while I was flying in the Gulf. The lone incident is described in more detail later in this chapter.

We normally maintained an altitude of between 30,000 and 35,000 feet while on our orbit. This provided us with a panoramic view from the cockpit. We could see the ships on the waters below but could seldom see other aircraft. Most of the Navy aircraft conducting the bombing raids would have been at a much lower altitude as they operated from the carriers. We could, however, eavesdrop on their radio communications. We had to stay tuned to the assigned Red Crown frequency but could use another radio to monitor the chatter that went on between aircraft. One day a pair of Air Force F-4s had flown out over the Gulf. This was a bit unusual because the Air Force bombing and air cover raids were launched from bases in Thailand and seldom got as far east as the Gulf. One of these F-4s had been damaged over North Viet Nam and was not able to return to his base in Thailand. He could not land on a carrier deck as the Navy aircraft could. So the closest place for him to land would be south to the Da Nang Air Field in South Viet Nam. His wing mate was accompanying him. The chatter on the radio indicated that the wing mate was tucked in close and trying to assess the damage to his partner's aircraft. The conversation was well controlled and very calm. It continued for several minutes. It appeared that they were getting close to the DMZ which would have put them near the airfield at Da Nang. Suddenly the wing man was screaming over the radio "Jesus Christ, get out of there. You're on fire". Both men in the wounded F-4 then had apparently ejected from the aircraft. The pilots in the other aircraft kept up a running commentary of what was happening. They described both parachutes as opening. One of the chutes, however, had opened as what is called a <u>Roman Candle</u>. This means that the chute canopy was twisted around itself much like when you twist a towel that you are attempting to ring the water out of it. The chute had not deployed and filled with air. The poor guy was apparently not successful in breaking the <u>Roman Candle</u> and disappeared from the view of the pilot on the radio. The second crewman landed on a small island slightly northeast of the DMZ known as Tiger Island. They saw him standing on the ground. The island unfortunately also had a few North Vietnamese troops. The Marines at Da Nang were alerted and they responded with several ground attack aircraft. They made several firing passes attempting to keep the North Vietnamese from reaching the pilot until a rescue helicopter could reach him. They were not successful. The man was captured. The whole affair over the radio had taken about 40 minutes.

On April 19, 1968 we were had just completed our mid-air refueling and returned to our orbit. Vic, the pilot, had gone on break and Dave was in his seat. I was on break so I went up to the front cockpit and sat down in Vic's seat. Dave and I had chatted for a while when he noticed a contrail high above our altitude. Contrails occur rather infrequently and when they do they are not present at all altitudes. They are the result of moisture condensing in the exhaust of an aircraft when it hits the colder air. They occur only when the air at that altitude has a high enough moisture content. When they do occur they paint a vivid picture of aircraft flights across the sky. This contrail was still well over the land but headed straight out toward the Gulf. We were not pulling contrails at our altitude. The contrail we were watching was the only one in the sky. As we watched it we saw, while it was still over the land, a second contrail coming straight up toward it. The second contrail did not reach the altitude of the first. It looped over and fell toward the ground. It was obviously a North Vietnamese SAM missile that had been fired at an intruder but could not get high enough. We were not concerned. We felt that it was likely a U. S. aircraft, possibly an SR-71. We knew the SR-71 flew out of Kadena and made flights over North Vietnam. A few minutes later Red Crown called us with the code word SALVO SOUTH. We turned and headed out into the Gulf. Red Crown's frequencies came alive. They were launching aircraft off of the carriers as rapidly as possible. Soon we could see contrails from two aircraft that had broken the contrail level, which was well above our altitude, as they climbed toward the contrail we were watching. They were climbing almost vertically. I suspect these contrails were from our escort fighters. They would have already been near our altitude and could respond faster than the ones coming off the carriers. As the lead aircraft closed on the target you could see the contrail of the missile he fired. It went straight to the first contrail we were watching. The first contrail began to tumble. It tumbled down until it no longer was pulling contrails. About the same time four more aircraft started pulling contrails, obviously the ones that had been launched from the carrier as they climbed toward the target.

We landed back at Kadena in the early evening. The news on Armed Forces television that night said that a Mig-21 had been shot down over the Gulf of Tonkin earlier that day. It was several days before the true facts in the incident became clear. The aircraft that had been shot down turned out not to be a Mig-21 at all. In fact it did not even belong to the North Vietnamese. It was an American reconnaissance drone (a small unmanned photo reconnaissance aircraft). It had been launched from an airborne C130 aircraft. It was pre-programmed to fly a high altitude reconnaissance (near 60,000 feet) flight over North Vietnam. The plan was for the drone to fly out over the Gulf and deploy a parachute. Once it had descended down to the C-130s altitude it would be snatched in mid-air by the C-130. This C-130 was specially configured for this mission. It had booms extending from the front of the aircraft which extended across the front of the aircraft's engines. The booms would prevent the parachute canopy from getting tangled in the C130's props as it snatched it in mid-air. That seemed like a very tricky operation, to say the least. The pilots on the C-130 had been yelling over the radio to leave their drone alone, but in the excitement of the moment, apparently, no one had heard them. I wonder if that would qualify as a friendly fire incident.

The North Vietnamese fighters had not been ineffective. One of the reasons for their cautious tactics was that they had a limited number of aircraft and were badly outnumbered by ours. Many of their pilots were actually quite good. They had shot down numerous U. S. strike aircraft. I had heard that about three or four of the North Vietnamese pilots had shot down five or more of our aircraft which made them combat aces. The most famous of these aces was a Colonel Toon who flew the older Mig-17 aircraft. His final engagement with U. S. forces was against one of the U. S. Navy's aces of the Viet Nam war, Lt. Randy Cunningham. That particular air battle has been the subject of a recent program about air combat on the Military Channel on cable television. During the summer of 1968 another of their combat aces was the bait for an elaborate combined Air Force and Navy trap. Communications between the ground units and the Vietnamese pilots was constantly monitored by U. S. communications specialists. They were often able to recognize the pilot by his voice. In the case of this particular pilot they had established a pattern to the way he operated. This allowed our planners to predict his actions and a plan was developed to gang up on him. The plan was executed successfully and the guy was hit with several missiles from our aircraft. His aircraft blew up.

The Demands of Combat Apple

The constant twenty four/seven operation of the Combat Apple program placed a heavy burden on the aircraft, the crews and the maintenance personnel of the 82nd. Military forces in the time of war have always had to make do with the resources they had on hand at the time and to continue to work to effectively accomplish their assigned mission. They really have little choice. This has been true of the U. S. Military in each of our wars and it was true of the personnel of the 82nd during the Combat Apple operation. Some of the incidents that occur during war time are frightening, some are funny and some actually result in someone paying the ultimate price. To my knowledge no one involved in the Combat Apple program was ever required to pay that ultimate price as had been the case with the 55th's RB-47s. There were, however, several incidents that went beyond the routine.

The demands of the program forced the crews of the 82nd to dramatically increase the number of hours they spent in the air. Each of the sorties was nineteen and a half hours in length and we were averaging five or six sorties each month. The air in the pressurized cabin is quite dry which is easily tolerated in a short flight but takes a larger toll during a long flight. The takeoff time for one of the sorties was shortly after midnight. This meant that we would be up all night and most of the next day. The other takeoff time was shortly after noon. We routinely switched back and forth. The constant changes obviously affected sleeping patterns. Most of the men had families that had accompanied them to Okinawa. Those of you who have small children know that they follow their own routine and can be quite noisy while they are awake. Sleep by crew members had to be fitted into all of these circumstances. Occasionally when the takeoff was after mid night we may have been able to get only a few hours of sleep but depending on the family activities, maybe not. So it was often the case on the flight that took off after mid night that by the time we landed we had been up for better part of two days with maybe a couple hours of sleep. I recall a couple of instances where I had to fill in for a Raven on another crew because he was sick and not able make his scheduled flight. On one of these I was notified a few hours before the scheduled mid night take off and had not been able to get any sleep.

Crew Fatigue

One of the incidents to which I attribute this accumulated stress and fatigue occurred on October 20, 1968. We were approaching Kadena to land at the end of another sortie. As a crew we were approaching the maximum flight time limits for any three consecutive months that had been established by the Air Force. The crew had flown 108 hours and 10 minutes in August, 100 hours and 35 minutes in September and had already logged 92 hours and 5 minutes in October. We would finish the month with a total of 319 hours and 25 minutes for the three month period. I had flown one extra sortie with

214

another crew in September. My totals for September were 119 hours and 25 minutes, just under the monthly limit. I had logged 338 hours and 55 minutes for the three month period. This was above the 330 hour limit and as such violated the regulations. On this day we had departed Kadena shortly after noon and were returning around 8 AM the following morning. To explain what happened next requires me to digress a little.

Kadena was a very busy air field. When an aircraft neared the airport to land they would be passed to the approach controller. The approach controller would guide the aircraft during its descent from its en-route altitude to its entry to the final approach phase. The normal descent profile was to progressively drop from its en-route altitude to its final approach altitude in a series of steps. Each step would be at a different altitude. At each of these steps the aircraft would be leveled and remain at that step until instructed to drop to the next step. When traffic was heavy the controller would likely have an aircraft assigned to each of the altitude steps. When the lowest step was cleared he would descent each aircraft to the next lower step. He would do so in a sequence starting at the lowest step and working to the highest step. This would continue until the aircraft reached its final approach altitude. The final approach sequence began at a point called the Initial Approach Point or IAP. The IAP altitude was the lowest step in the process. The step down procedure was not always necessary particularly under light traffic conditions. The procedure was, however, a routine procedure and tended to be used under all traffic conditions.

When an aircraft nears the IAP it would already be sequenced in the landing stream and instructed to report over the IAP. The IAP at Kadena on this approach was a specific point over the water at an altitude of 2100 feet. At the IAP control of the aircraft would be passed to the final approach controller. At civil airports in the United States the final approach controller is known as the Local controller. He/she authorizes the aircraft to land. The aircraft uses an onboard instrument which follows a ground based electronic signal known as the Instrument Landing System or ILS to guide it to the runway threshold. In the 1960s the military used a system known as a Ground Controlled Approach or GCA for guidance to the runway threshold instead of the ILS. GCA approaches were used at all military installations world wide. The final approach controller was known as the GCA controller. The GCA controller tracked the aircraft on his radar and provided verbal instructions on course and descent rate which guided the aircraft to a landing.

Following a long flight such as ours Vic wanted to get down as quickly as possible. He did not like the step down procedure after a long flight. He would make a special request when initial contact was established with the approach controller. He would ask to be cleared to the IAP with "descend at pilot's discretion". This means that he wanted to skip the step down procedure and was requesting the authority to delay the start of his descent until the last minute and then descend as fast as possible leveling out just before he reached the IAP. He didn't always get approval but occasionally did. When he received approval the only concern was that he had to ensure that he was at the IAP altitude by the time he reached that point. When he received approval he would wait until the last minute to start the descent. Then, he would extend the speed brakes to their full travel and reduce the throttles to idle and descend as fast as he could. This rapid descent meant that the aircraft skin did not have time to warm up as the aircraft descended. It would still be very cold when we landed. The result was a great deal of condensation on the skin of the aircraft. It would actually drip almost like light rain or drizzle on to the ramp below. The speed brakes were a large door like panel on the top of each wing that could be deflected as much as 60 degrees upward. It would hold the aircraft speed down in a rapid descent. It would also create a great deal of extra drag. On this particular day I was in the jump seat for landing. Vic made his regular request which was granted. The speed brakes were extended to their maximum of 60 degrees and the throttles were pulled back to idle. The aircraft came hurtling down out of the sky.

216

We arrived at a point just before the IAP at 2100 feet. The aircraft was leveled out and the engines throttles advanced. The aircraft, however, continued to sink. Vic continued to advance the throttles which slowed the sink rate but did not stop it. The throttles were almost at full power. The descent rate was slowed considerably but had not been stopped. The pilots were looking around to try to determine what the problem was. I spotted the speed break handle and started to yell, "Speed Brakes". Before I got it out Dave's hand as on the lever and he retracted them. He had realized the problem a split second before I had. The aircraft leveled out. We were down to about 1000 feet, at least 1000 feet below where we should have been. Fortunately, we were landing from the ocean end of the runway and were over the water the entire time. The GCA controller had issued several warnings about our being too low without any acknowledgment from the pilots. They were too busy. They advised him they had found the problem and were able to continue the approach. We landed normally. It was a much flatter approach that it should have been.

The pilots had checklists that they were to follow for each phase of flight. Checklists are designed to prevent them from omitting a critical factor. The pilots on this approach had performed the Final Approach checklist and checked all of the items on it. There is no item on the check list concerning the speed brakes. They are not normally used on the final approach to landing.

Equipment Problems

Several incidents were attributable to the strain on the aircraft, its equipment, and the maintenance crews. The mission success rate remained, however, very high. The 82nd lost very little time on station in the Gulf of Tonkin. We often had to use an aircraft that still had some problems but those problems were not critical to the safety of the aircraft and crew. These problems would have kept the aircraft on the ground in a normal peace time situation. Some of these problems were obvious before we took off. Others would appear while we were in flight. I will cover only those incidents that happened to a flight that I was on. Obviously this number can be multiplied several times when those incidents that happened to other crews are included.

On October 15, 1967 my crew was scheduled to fly the late night flight that took off shortly after mid night. Major Ben Allen, the Standboard chief was scheduled to go with us. He was doing an evaluation on our pilots. He rode the jump seat for takeoff and landing. When we started our takeoff roll we were very heavy which was normal. The acceleration speed check would be required. We started the roll and accelerated normally. Just before we reached the time for the speed check I heard a loud boom coming from the left side of the aircraft. I was riding in one of the Raven seats which were located somewhat aft of the engines. The boom came from the direction of the engines. The sound of the engines went to idle and the aircraft was stopped. We had used almost all of the 11,200 feet of the runway. The problem was with the number one engine on the left wing and it was quickly shut down. The aircraft was returned to the ramp using the remaining three engines. A maintenance truck was quickly dispatched. The cowling on the number one engine was missing. It had blown off the engine and was retrieved the next day some distance from the runway. The crew transferred to the backup aircraft and we took off again. Our second take off was about an hour late.

On December 2, 1967 we had taken off on the midnight mission. We were a little over two hours into the flight and would soon be entering the Gulf. I had remained in the jump seat after takeoff. The flight had been routine to that point. One of the pilots noticed an abnormally high fuel flow on the left out board engine. The fuel flow gage normally reads about 2000 pounds an hour in normal cruise. The gage on the number one engine was reading 6000 pounds an hour. An abnormal reading on a gauge can mean one of two things. The first is that it is indicating some kind of a problem. The second is that the gauge itself is malfunctioning. Crews are never certain until it can be checked out. Vic asked me to go back to the mid part of the aircraft in the aisle along the left side of the rear crew compartment and take a look at the engine. There was an interphone jack located behind the wing area where I could plug into and talk to the pilots while I observed the rear part of the wing and the engines. It was a moonless night so the pilots had turned the landing lights on. The landing lights are mounted on the front of the wings but they provided a little illumination over the rear part of the engines. I could see a large white stream coming out of the underside of the wing just inside the out board engine. It appeared to be about two to three feet wide. The aircraft was obviously streaming raw fuel. The stream extended back behind the aircraft as far as I could see which on that moonless night was not very far. I advised Vic about what I was seeing. He told me they were going to close the fuel cut off value to the number one engine. This would stop the flow of fuel to that engine. A moment later the entire stream of fuel suddenly ignited. The fire stream lite up the sky almost like it was day light. The forward end of the flash had begun just inside the rear end of the engine itself. The flash was gone in an instant and the white stream had disappeared. I must confess that my heart was in my throat at what I had just seen. Vic came over the interphone asking, "What happened". His voice had an excited edge to it. He had obviously seen a flash of light. I tried to answer him but found I wasn't able to right away.   He asked the same question again. I finally said "I'll explain to you when I get back up front." I unplugged from the interphone and returned to the cockpit. I explained to the pilots what I had seen. My explanation was followed by a long period of silence. We started to discuss what had just happened. One of the pilots speculated that we were lucky that the explosion had not damaged the engine or the wing. That could have potentially been catastrophic at the speed we were flying. The mission was aborted at that point and we returned to Kadena. We landed at Kadena five hours after we had departed. The crew transferred to the backup aircraft and took off in it. The second flight was completed as planned but was only thirteen hours in length.

On March 17, 1968 my crew was scheduled to fly the noon

departure slot. We pre-flighted the aircraft and determined that the Liquid Oxygen Converter (LOX) was not working. Each crew position on the aircraft had an oxygen supply panel. We were required to wear our helmets whenever the aircraft was in the air. The helmets were equipped with an oxygen mask which was strapped to one side on the front side of the helmet. When we occupied a crew position we plugged into the supply panel at that position. This would have enabled us to quickly go on oxygen if the situation demanded by clipping the other side of the mask into the helmet and turning the supply switch on. The main supply source of oxygen was stored in liquid form. This liquid form would be converted to a gaseous form as it was supplied to the position supply panels. When the converter was not working there would be no oxygen available at a crew member's supply panel. This lack of oxygen would not ordinarily be a problem. The aircraft cabin was pressurized so a supplemental source of oxygen was not necessary unless we lost cabin pressurization. The only alternative source of oxygen was the small emergency walk around bottle. These bottles were good for only about a 10 minute supply. The emergency procedure in the case of a loss of cabin pressure is to descend the aircraft to 10,000 feet as rapidly as possible where the air pressure in an unpressurized cabin would provide a sufficient amount of oxygen. The lower altitude would dramatically increase the fuel consumption rate of the aircraft. If this situation occurred during our transit back from the Gulf it could put us a significant distance from any usable runway and our on board fuel level would be at its lowest level during the flight. Under peace time conditions this condition would ordinarily mean that we could not use this aircraft. The backup aircraft, however, had a serious engine problem so it could not be used. The demands of a war time situation meant that we would use this aircraft which is what we did. The flight was completed without difficulty.

Life on Okinawa
   Okinawa is the largest island in a long chain of islands extending from just south of Kyushu, the southern-most of Japan's main islands,

to just east of Taiwan. The island chain is known as the Ryukyu Islands. During the age of exploration (15th & 16th centuries), the Dutch and English sailors referred to the islands as the great Loo Choo. The Japanese pronunciation of the letters RYU sounded like Loo and KYU sounded like Choo to them. The entire chain of islands is a present day Japanese prefecture. The United States had captured the island of Okinawa near the end of WWII and in the latter part of the 1960s still retained administrative control over it. Administrative control of the island was not returned to Japan until 1972. Okinawa had its own government structure but it had to acquiesce to the U. S. Military command in matters of mutual or conflicting interest. The island of Okinawa is approximately 60 miles in length oriented in a NNE by SSW direction. It varies in width from about three miles to twelve miles. Toward the northern part of the island there is a large peninsula, the Motobu Peninsula, which extends about 15 miles toward the WNW. The entire island consists of approximately 877 square miles. In the decades following WWII a significant portion of the island had been converted to U. S. military bases. There were more than six major U. S. Military installations on the island and each of the services had at least one. The importance to the U. S. of the bases on Okinawa increased as the war in Viet Nam intensified. In the late 1960s there were approximately 100,000 American servicemen and their dependents on the island which had a total population of about one million people. The majority of the U. S. Military presence was in the southern half of the island where the majority of the Okinawan population also lived. The island would have been fairly densely populated even without the presence of our military personnel. The northern part of the island is predominately rural in nature. It is more mountainous than the southern half with less land suitable for cultivation. Agriculture and fishing are the primary livelihoods. Nago is the only city of any size in the northern half of the island.

The U. S. military had gobbled up a significant amount of the land area on Okinawa to build its military installations which included much of the most cultivatable land on the island. Most of that land had been privately owned by Okinawans farmers. The department of defense was compensating the people whose land had been confiscated. For example, the Futema MCAS, near Ginowan City, sits on land that was owned by about 1500 Okinawan farmers. I got to know one of families who were receiving compensation. They were receiving monthly lease payments which have now continued for several decades. Some of those families that gave up their land were happy with this arrangement while others wanted their land back.

There must have been several types of arrangements. One in particular I found to be unusual. The flight line was an area of restricted access. When we were scheduled to fly we would gather at our operations building and be bused to the aircraft. To gain access to the flight line we would have to pass through a security check point. We would be dressed in our flight suits but the guards would still check each of our security badges. They would board the bus and check each of us individually. On a couple of occasions I remember, while we were being checked, seeing a local Okinawan farmer approach the check point pushing a wheel barrel type push cart. He was waved right on through by the guards. I learned that they were farming the land inside the restricted area. The land had belonged to them before the base was there and the Air Force was allowing them to continue to farm it even though it was inside the restricted area. It was an ironic scene to see a modern aircraft, such as the SR-71, rolling down the runway and within several hundred yards a local farmer working the land in the centuries old traditional manner.

The people of Okinawa were a gentle, friendly people and there seemed to be little outward resentment and unrest among the population of the island even given the pervasive presence and disruptive influence of the American military. There were infrequent public marches or demonstrations both in favor of and against the U. S. Military presence. They were always peaceful. They seemed more like rallies than protests. Several of the local people that I got to know told me they had marched in both types. They were paid $5 by each group that sponsored the rally. We were able to move freely about the island without concern. I spent many of my off duty hours exploring the island, looking for the sights where the WWII battles had been fought and meeting the local people. Toward the latter part of my tour on Okinawa I had met and was dating an Okinawan girl whom I subsequently would marry. She was from the northern part of the island so I started spending a great deal of time in that part of the island. This was an area away from the military bases where I was often the only non-Okinawan in the gatherings we were part of. I was able to get a better feel for the traditional culture and customs of the people of Okinawa. English was widely spoken by the Okinawans in the southern half of the island but not as much in the northern half. My Japanese was not good but was improving. There was a native Okinawan language which was similar in structure to Japanese. It was still widely spoken in the northern part of the island particularly by the older people. Japanese was being taught in the schools. The school children were actually being discouraged from using the Okinawan language. Sadly, many of the younger people were not learning their native language.

The majority of the U. S. military personnel on the island were on accompanied tours of duty. That means they were able to bring their families with them. The Marines were the only exception. They were required to leave their families back in the states. There was a significant amount of available housing on the bases. Some families were forced to find temporary housing in the surrounding communities when they first arrived but most were able to eventually move into base furnished housing. Bachelors and unaccompanied married personnel were housed in barracks or Bachelor Officers Quarters (BOQ) on the base. My BOQ quarters were a single room with a semi-private bath.

Typhoons were frequent visitors to Okinawa so the military built their buildings to cope with them. Our building had an outer wall which shielded us from the fury of the typhoons. The children of the military personnel were not required to attend Okinawan schools. The department of defense had funded a school system for them complete with American teachers. The schools were complete from elementary through high school. The teachers were U. S. certified teachers who were on annual contracts with the Department of Defense. They were required to have a minimum of two years of experience teaching in American schools to apply. They were provided with on base housing as part of their contract. Most of the teachers were single or unaccompanied and they were housed in the BOQ. There was a single high school that served the entire island, Kubasaki High school, located half way between the two major cities in the southern part of the island, Naha and Koza. College level classes were also available to military personnel. The college classes were provided by the University of Maryland Far East Division and the majority of the classes were held at Kubasaki High School in the evenings. The University of Maryland did not use its regular faculty but hired contract instructors specifically for the Far East Division. I used this opportunity to continue my college education. I was able to complete 20 credit hours while assigned to Kadena.

There was a military aero club on the island. It was based at the Yomitan air field located about half way up the length of the island. Yomitan had a large paved runway that had been built by the United States military. It was originally built as an emergency field for military use shortly after the end of WWII and was large enough to accommodate propeller driven aircraft such as the C-130 but not jet aircraft. By the mid-1960s, the few propeller driven aircraft that flew into Okinawa used the Naha air field at the south end of the island. During my time in Okinawa, Yomitan Field was being used exclusively by the aero club. The aero club had about 10 to 15 aircraft. All were small single engine types. There were five Cessna 150s which were used primarily for flight instruction. The club used a scheduling book, and due to the heavy instructional usage of these aircraft one had to reserve them as much as a week in advance. Fortunately, the club also had several older types with a tail wheel that were not routinely used for instruction. Since I already had a private license I normally flew one of the older types. I found that one of these would be available most of the time. I did not have to reserve them in advance.

The aero club aircraft were only permitted to fly from Yomitan toward the northern part of the island and on the west side of the island where there were no military installations. Only U. S. Military or DOD civilian personnel were allowed to fly them. The Okinawans were not permitted to use their own air space. There were a few Okinawan mechanics that maintained the club's aircraft. They were permitted to make maintenance test flights near the Yomitan airport but could not venture away from it. The student pilots receiving instruction would use an area over the water just north of Yomitan. I tried to avoid this area because of the traffic. There was a small air field a few miles from the northern end of the island called Okuma. It was part of a military rest and recuperation area. Adjacent to the runway were cabins and picnicking areas. The cabins could be rented by military personnel. The runway was on a small piece of land that jutted out toward the water. It had a three foot sea wall at either end. I frequently flew to Okuma and spent the time doing touch and go landings there. The short runway and the sea walls made it an interesting place to land. To get to Okuma from Yomitan I had to fly over the peninsula (the Motobu Peninsula) that extended toward the west. I had read that the Japanese army had built several small air fields on the peninsula during WWII. They had long since been abandoned. One day I decided to fly over the peninsula to see if I could find evidence of any of them. The area was mostly covered in small farms with a few widely spaced houses. There were a few stands of trees. I was flying about 500 feet above the ground but was not able to make out anything that looked like it had been a runway. I decided to go down to take a closer look and descended to about 100 feet above the ground. I purposely avoided flying over any of the houses. I still couldn't discern anything. The only thing I was able see was a poor elderly lady that had likely been working in her field who seemed to be running in a panic toward her house. I realized that I was being very careless and probably scaring her. I abandoned my search and climbed back up to altitude.

Stress and Alcohol

Alcohol consumption has been viewed in the popular culture and in war movies as a common way for soldiers and airman to relieve the stress of the strict discipline, combat fatigue and family separation that are an integral part of military life. There is a measure of truth to that view. It was, however, more prevalent when the average soldier was a young single man serving for only a few years in a time of national need. The military services, of the 1960s and in the intervening years up to the present, particularly the Air Force, has increasingly become a career occupation by married personnel, both male and female. This trend has had a strong moderating influence on the reality of that popular view mentioned above. The consumption of alcohol was and is still a part of the military culture but generally not significantly more pronounced than the society at large. And like the wider culture there were some military personnel who had a drinking problem. Personnel in the Strategic Air Command (SAC) were subject to closer scrutiny than those in other commands. This scrutiny was a direct result of the fact that the personnel of SAC handled nuclear weapons. SAC had established the Human Reliability program for those that had close contact with nuclear weapons as part of their job. Any abnormal behavior that could theoretically be interpreted as jeopardizing your reliability could result in losing your job and being transferred to a position that was not covered by the program. Alcohol consumption could and occasionally was a reason for such removals. This also served as a moderating influence.

Over-seas assignments for many military personnel served as yet another form of stress. These locations offered few familiar surroundings and pursuits. Add to this the fact that alcohol beverages were very cheap (no taxation) at overseas bases. The level of alcohol consumption tended to increase. Captain Blaine, who had accompanied me in the transfer from Forbes to Yokota, had also transferred to Okinawa. We were not on the same crew and our paths did not cross frequently at work but his room in the BOQ at Kadena was only three doors down from mine. We occasionally went out on the town together on our days off. Several months after we arrived at

Kadena it was becoming obvious to me that he was developing a serious drinking problem. One evening, after spending several hours in my room studying for an upcoming college exam, I decided to take a short break and go for a walk. It was about 10:00 o'clock in the evening. As I walked down the hall I encountered Blaine who was just returning from down town. He had a distinct smell of alcohol and appeared slightly inebriated. He said he had come home early because he had to fly that evening. I asked him if he meant the midnight takeoff time. He said yes. I was surprised. I told him that he couldn't fly in his present condition. He said he was alright. I persisted and finally convinced him to call in sick and tell his boss that I would take his place on the flight. I dressed in my flight clothes and headed for the squadron assembly area.

On November 16, 1967 a typhoon was headed in Okinawa's direction. My crew ferried one of our aircraft to Clark AFB in the Philippine Islands. The Combat Apple missions were also recovered at Clark. We flew the mission that departed after midnight on the 17th of November and returned to Clark at the end of the sortie. The 82nd now had four of its aircraft at Clark. Blaine's crew was one of the crews at Clark. On the night of the 18th a group of us gathered at the Officers club and started to down Tequilas. I left early but apparently Blaine did not. The next morning all of the aircraft were scheduled to return to Kadena. The typhoon took an unexpected turn back toward Okinawa so our departures were delayed. We waited on the ramp for the orders to depart. Blaine was badly hung over and apparently, unbeknownst to anyone, had decided to board one of the aircraft and lay down for a nap. It was well into the afternoon before we received the all clear to return to Kadena. One of the aircraft would remain at Clark and take the next Combat Apple mission from there. The rest of us were to return to Kadena. Blaine's crew was to take the first aircraft home but no one could find him. His boss, Major Curzon, came to me and asked if I knew where he was at. I told him that I had seen Blaine on the ramp several hours ago but didn't know where he had gone. His crew took off without him. My crew departed an hour later. The third crew found Blaine when they boarded the aircraft and

227

woke him up. He returned to Kadena with them. He received an admonishment for not returning with his own crew.

Apparently, Blaine had not learned his lesson from the first time I had replaced him because it occurred again. He showed up to fly in much the same slightly inebriated condition. I was not in my room that night to intercept him. His boss would not let him fly. They tried to reach me but I was not in my room. They eventually found a replacement and sent Blaine home. This incident combined with the one at Clark forced the commander to take some action. Blaine was taken off his crew and transferred to the 4252nd as a mission briefing officer. This was a non-flying job. Before each of the B-52/KC-135 gaggles launched, the crews assembled in a large briefing room to receive the details of their sorties. To conduct these briefings was now Blaine's job. The job was a day job and he did quite well at it.

Return to the States

In the fall of 1968 my 18 month overseas tour was coming to an end. I had inquired about extending it another year. I enjoyed living and working on Okinawa and, of course, wasn't ready to leave my girl friend behind. I was told that an extension was not possible. My last Combat Apple sortie was on December 2, 1968. I received orders that transferred me back to the 55th which was now located at Offutt AFB. Captain Blaine and I would again be traveling together. His return date was the same as mine. On December 7, 1968 we boarded another World airways flight from Kadena to Travis AFB in California. We had decided to take some leave at Travis and travel on our own by train to Omaha. It was a leisurely trip. We had been advised at Travis not to wear our uniforms during the trip. The Democratic convention in Chicago a few months earlier had been one of the most contemptuous in our history and much of the confrontation had been over the country's involvement in the war in Viet Nam. Men in uniform were very unpopular and often the target for harassment in December of 1968. We made the trip in civilian clothes and didn't experience any problem. Our short haircuts apparently didn't give us away. We arrived in Omaha on the 12th.

Chapter 19   Return to the 55th

Offutt AFB

Strategic Air Command (SAC) headquarters is located at Offutt AFB. It is a large complex that is the dominant feature on the base. SAC is commanded by a four star General. General Curtis LeMay was one of the early commanders and the principle architect of it's mode of operation. A large replica of an ICBM missile is displayed in front of the complex. Some of the command's working area is located underground and is hardened to enable it to survive a Soviet first strike. Security within the complex is very tight. The operations of the 55th , while it was located at Forbes, were geared to support the planners of the Strategic Air Command at Offutt. The processing of the mission materials (recordings, logs, etc) from the 55th 's sorties was done by the 544th squadron which was located inside of SAC headquarters. A courier had been needed to transport the mission materials from Forbes or one of the forward Operating Locations (OLs), where the data was gathered, to the 544th for processing. The move of the 55th to Offutt integrated the entire operation at a single location. The general mode of operation had also changed. The operational sorties flown by the crews at Offutt would depart from Offutt instead of a forward operating location and often land back at Offutt once the sortie was complete. Those sorties that landed at a forward location would return to Offutt within a few days. This eliminated the need for couriers to transport the mission materials. With the 55th now located at Offutt a representative from the 544th could meet the sorties upon their return.

The 55th's buildings were located close to SAC headquarters. The 55th at Offutt had two squadrons assigned to it. The reconnaissance crews were assigned to the 343rd Strategic Reconnaissance Squadron (SRS), the same squadron number that had been used at Forbes. The crews of the 343rd SRS flew the RC-135C aircraft which, as described earlier, was a modified version of the C-135B aircraft. The second squadron was the 38th. This number had also been used at Forbes but it no longer had any reconnaissance crews assigned. The mission of the 38th was known by the project name <u>Looking Glass</u>. They also flew a modified version of the C-135B aircraft. The 55th was the only major flying unit on the base.

Living Quarters

Much as we had at Forbes the bachelors in the 55th often rented and shared a house. When I arrived at Offutt one of the bachelor ravens assigned to the 55th , Rex Lawson, had bought a four bedroom house in Bellevue. Bellevue was the suburb of Omaha that was adjacent to the base where the majority of the personnel of the 55th lived. He was renting two of the bedrooms to other members of the 55th. The other two bachelors were Captain Bill Browning, who was a pilot and crew commander of a 343rd squadron reconnaissance crew and Captain Rick Ramirez, a navigator on a 38th squadron Looking Glass crew. The fourth bedroom was in the basement and was not being used. Rex agreed to rent it to me. I lived at that location for 12 of the 15 months that I spent at Offutt. It enabled me to keep abreast of the activities of both of the squadrons of the 55th. Rex became engaged to a girl from the Omaha area. When he married, the rest of us had to find another place to live. I spent the final three months sharing a trailer house with another raven from the wing.

Looking Glass

The mission of the Looking Glass project was to act as a back up to the National Command Authority in the event of a first strike by the Soviet Union. The master plan to activate the nuclear triad (bombers, missiles, and Trident submarines) was outlined in the Single Integrated Operations Plan or SIOP. Under the SIOP when an incoming Russian Inter-Continental Ballistic Missile (ICBM) launch was detected by our long range radars, the bomber alert force would be launched and fly to their Fail Safe points. Their Fail Safe points were a pre-determined point along their route, well clear of the destruction from a Soviet first strike, where they were expected to orbit until they received an order to continue on to their assigned targets. The order to launch a nuclear attack on the Soviet Union was reserved for the President of the United States to make. Once the President (or   his legally authorized representative if he were killed or incapacitated) decided to send a second strike force to destroy the Soviet Union he would inform the SAC command structure at Offutt and the command structure controlling the Trident Submarine fleet of his decision. The decision would be relayed to the bombers holding at their Fail Safe points and the alert crews manning our ICBM missile sites. The bomber and missile crews would be informed by transmitting a secret code (the GO code) telling the bombers holding at their Fail Safe points to continue on to their targets and the missile crews to launch their missiles. There were several safe guards in place to guard against any individual co-opting the system as was depicted in the 1960s movies "Dr. Strangelove" and "Seven Days in May". One of these safe guards was to require an action by more than one individual at each step in the process before it advanced to the next step. This duality of persons was required for any action at each step. For example, in each bomber, when a message to GO was transmitted to each bomber crew holding at it's Fail Safe point, the sealed (GO CODE) package would be broken open and two members of the crew would have to separately authenticate the message and would have separate keys to enable their on board bomb delivery systems.

If the Soviet first strike destroyed the nation's Capital and wiped out the National Command Authority before a decision could be made and communicated, the SAC command structure could make the decision to GO. If the SAC command structure had been destroyed by the Soviet first strike, the personnel on board the Looking Glass aircraft could send the bombers to their targets and give the missile crews the order to launch their ICBMs. The Looking Glass aircraft was the final backup authority that could ensure a second strike was launched in the event the ground based authorities were specifically targeted and eliminated. In concept, to effectively act as a deterrent under the Mutually Assured Destruction (MAD) theory, this back up was necessary to prevent the Soviets from directing a sneak attack focusing on our command authority.

One of the Looking Glass aircraft would be in the air at all times. They varied their routes so that their location in the air was not predicable. There was always an Air Force officer of General rank on board who was in charge of the <u>Looking Glass</u> operation in the air. He was the one with the authority to send the second strike toward the Soviet Union in the event that all higher command authority was wiped out. All of the General officers who manned the <u>Looking Glass</u> were SAC personnel. They would take turns doing a tour of duty at Offutt for a week or so. A special suite of rooms were reserved for them at the Offutt Inn, a part of the BOQ housing facilities on the base. Each <u>Looking Glass</u> flight was scheduled to be eight and a half hours long. They could not land until their replacement was airborne. If their replacement was delayed they had to continue beyond their scheduled time. If the extended time was lengthy, they would do a mid-air refueling in order to stay in the air. This continued 24/7 until President George H. W. Bush gave the order to end the alert posture in the early 1990s.

Each of the <u>Looking Glass</u> crews had an instructor pilot as the crew commander. They were advertised as some of the best pilots in SAC. The reason for this requirement was that all of the Generals in SAC had, at one time, been an active pilot. When they, the Generals, were assigned to a <u>Looking Glass</u> flight, they almost always insisted on making the takeoff and landings. The problem was that very few of them had any experience in flying jet aircraft. Their experience was in WWII and Korean War vintage propeller driven aircraft. Most of them had done little actual flying for many years. So it is safe to say that most of them were in over their head when they flew the C-135. It was a delicate job for the instructor pilot. He was technically in command of the aircraft but for a Major to take control of the aircraft from a two star General was a tough decision. A confidential log book with individual profiles on the Generals was kept in the 38th orderly room and maintained by the <u>Looking Glass</u> instructor pilots. It contained information on each general's flying skills, their habits, and their personality traits. At the conclusion of each flight, the instructor pilot on the flight would add any information he felt pertinent to the log. The instructor pilot always reviewed this log book prior to each flight to be prepared for the

General with whom he would be flying. From a Raven's Perch Captain Ramirez had several interesting stories to tell about the generals he had flown with. He said one General had insisted that they shut down both of the outboard engines when they had the runway in sight for landing. This had apparently been an often used procedure on the B-29. Even at the lighter weight at landing the two remaining engines on the C-135 would not have been sufficient to make a safe go-around if it became necessary. Another story concerned a General who was a back slapper. This General was quite a large man. He would greet a member of the crew by saying "How're you doing son", and wallop them on the back. He often hit hard enough to nearly knock the wind out of the unfortunate fellow he greeted. Another incident that Rick described involved a general who was reluctant to apply any braking to the aircraft on the roll out after landing. He also had a tendency to land long (well down the runway at touch down). One of the instructor pilots, Major Culver, had to take control of the aircraft, away from this particular General. On this particular landing, the General had landed well down the runway. Major Culver waited for the General to use the brakes, which he did not. A subtle suggestion was made to use the brakes. It was ignored. When it was clear that the aircraft might not be able to stop on the remaining runway, Major Culver took control. The General reacted angrily. As a result, Major Culver was transferred to the 343rd squadron and ended up as the Second Aircraft Commander (a position discussed later) on my crew.

Rick said that the one star Generals were the hardest to deal with. They tended to be pushy and very aware of their rank. The three star Generals were more relaxed. SACs four star General (there was only one) did not fly on Looking Glass sorties. Most of the Generals that flew the Looking Glass flights were one or two star Generals. Occasionally a three star General would be on board. One in particular flew often, General Martin. He was the commander of 15th Air Force located at March AFB in the Los Angles area. Rick said that he was a real gentleman and also quite a good pilot.

The 343rd Squadron

The reconnaissance operations of the 55th were the responsibility of the crews of the 343rd Squadron. As discussed in an earlier chapter, the 55th s mission responsibilities at Forbes had been broken up and distributed. The main body of the 55th had been transferred to Offutt. Two new units had been activated, one at Yokota AFB in Japan, and a second at Eielson AFB in Alaska. The forward Operating Location (OL) concept, that had been the center piece of the operation at Forbes, had depended on extended deployments. This concept was discontinued. The new units assumed responsibility for specific areas and extended deployments became a thing of the past for most crews. Detachment 1 of the 3rd Air division at Yokota had taken over what had been the responsibility of OL-2. The unit at Eielson took over what had been the responsibility of OL-3. The 55th at Offutt took responsibility for the remainder of the areas. The 55th would retain and use a single forward location at Upper Heyford AFB in England. That was the original plan. The Viet Nam War had forced the operation at Yokota to move to Okinawa and change its mission to directly support the war effort in Viet Nam. The operation at Offutt had to assume responsibility for the area that had been assigned to the Yokota operation. By the time of my arrival at Offutt, there were two distinct formats for the sorties flown from Offutt. The first type would depart from Offutt, fly to its assigned area, complete its specific reconnaissance activity (the ON WATCH segment), return and land back at Offutt. These sorties would be quite lengthy and required one or more mid-air refuelings. They could be as long as 24 hours in length. There was talk around the squadron that headquarters was considering extending some flights to as long as 36 hours. Fortunately, the flight surgeons' office was able to convince the commanders that 36 hour sorties would seriously impact safety and was a bad idea. The second type would depart form Offutt, complete its specific reconnaissance activity and land at one of three forward locations. The forward locations included Kadena AFB in Okinawa, Eielson AFB, in Alaska and Upper Heyford AFB in England. A few days later they would depart from the forward location, complete their assigned mission, and land back at Offutt. These sorties would be from 15 to 18 hours in length. Occasionally, a third, shorter sortie, would be flown sandwiched between the two back and forth trips. There were no lengthy deployments. The round robin trips were no longer than a week in length. Due to the length of the sorties an extra pilot was added to the crews. The extra pilot was referred to as the Second AC (Aircraft Commander). He would be fully qualified as a crew commander and often substituted for a crew commander on shorter flights that did not require all three pilots. The Second AC would fly with the crew on the longer sorties. An operational scheduling office had been established. Their job was to schedule crews to cover the operational sorties. The scheduling officers had a good deal more flexibility than had been possible in the operation at Forbes. At Forbes a crew was deployed and they would fly all of the assigned sorties. Strict crew integrity was maintained. If one member of the crew was not able to fly it would affect the availability of the entire crew. At Offutt crew integrity was not as strict. Each scheduled assignment applied to a single or a pair of sorties and thus it was easier to substitute as the need arose. Substitutions were quite common. On the long sorties all three pilots would be scheduled. On the shorter sorties one of the aircraft commander qualified pilots would be dropped. Lengthy deployments were a thing of the past for the majority of 55th 's crews.

The only special project that the 55th had in the spring of 1969, that I was aware of, was the Iron Lung project. It was a continuation of the project at Forbes that I had been a part of. The mission profiles were similar. The project had two crews assigned and a single aircraft. Lengthy deployments were still required for the Iron Lung crews for any project activity. The Iron Lung crews were required to certify on the standard RC-135C configuration. Again, the special project was an additional certification. The Iron Lung crews were utilized in the standard operations scheduling when they were not specifically involved in the special project activity. A couple of months after I arrived at Offutt I would again be assigned to one of the Iron Lung crews.

The aircraft used for the Iron Lung project was an older C-135A model. It had the J-57 engines rather than the newer fan jet engines. Lockheed was still the prime contractor for any airframe modifications. E-Systems in Greenville, Texas was now the contractor for the Ravens' electronic equipment. The project continued for several more years. The name of the project was changed to <u>Briar Patch</u> at a later date. Each crew, when we were deployed on a project activity, had two pilots, two navigators and three Ravens.

The RC-135C Aircraft

Like most of the aircraft involved in reconnaissance, the RC-135C aircraft had its own distinctive look. It had a long rectangular bulge on either side toward the front of the aircraft. They looked like large cheeks. These were radoms which housed many of the antennas used by the ravens' equipment. There were three raven positions. Much of the reconnaissance on the aircraft was automated. It required monitoring but not continuous actions by one of the ravens. The Raven One and the Raven Two positions contained several automated systems. The Raven Three position was completely manual. I was certified as a Raven Three. I did not have much involvement with the jobs of the other two raven positions so my knowledge of their operations is quite limited. There was an additional crew member added for each operational sortie. This position was known as the <u>Airborne Maintenance Technician</u> or AMT. The AMT was not assigned to the 343rd but was a member of one of the maintenance squadrons. Their scheduling was done by their squadron personnel. The job of the AMT was to keep the equipment used by the Raven One and the Raven Two working throughout the entire flight. The AMT was normally a senior sergeant. My younger brother Mike became an AMT in the 55th. We did not serve in the 55th at the same time. His tour with the wing was well after I had left the unit.

An aisle ran along the left side of the aircraft from the forward cockpit area to the rear of the aircraft. There was not a lot of room in the mid part of the aircraft. The Raven One, Raven Two and AMT positions were located there. Their areas were somewhat restricted in space but nothing to compare to the cramped quarters in the RB-47H. The Raven Three's position was near the rear of the aircraft; just forward of the bunks, the galley area and the relief facilities in the extreme rear of the aircraft. The Raven Three's area was much more open and roomy. It was located adjacent to the rear entry door. The rear entry door had a window, so for the first time in my time on a reconnaissance crew I could see outside of the aircraft while I sat at my position. The Raven Three position had the normal complement of receivers, analyzers and recorders. In addition, it had two camera systems which added a pictorial view of the signals being processed in addition to the electronic recordings and logs. One of the camera systems was a large movie camera system that was very similar to the one used by the Hollywood film industry at that point in time. The second was a special high speed camera. The film cartridge for the high speed camera was about 24 inches in diameter which housed a large amount of film. The camera ran at such a high speed that if it were run continuously the film would be exhausted in about 90 seconds. We used this camera sparingly. We only ran a short burst for each intercept we processed. The camera was quite noisy when it was running. We only occasionally carried a second cartridge of high speed film. The cartridge was metal, quite heavy and a task to change in-flight.

Accidents and Incidents

During the time that I flew on the RC-135C and RC-135M aircraft (from June of 1967 through March of 1970) they had a much better safety record than had been the case with the RB-47H. During the 16 months that I flew on the RC-135M from Yokota and Kadena, there were no incidents that resulted in serious injury or death to a crew member nor any that resulted in serious structural damage to an aircraft. There was a single incident that rose to this level at Offutt involving an RC-135C and another that involved an RC-135W assigned to the unit at Eielson AFB.

The accident at Offutt occurred on a training flight during takeoff.

237

There were three pilots and two navigators aboard but no ravens. The purpose, as I understood it, was for pilot and navigator training. The pilot in the left seat, in command of the flight, was an instructor pilot. The third pilot, new to the crew, was in the right seat. The second pilot, a qualified aircraft commander (Second AC), was seated in the stowable jump seat just behind the pilot seats. The second Navigator was in a jump seat toward the rear of the forward compartment directly behind the left pilot seat. An equipment rack covered part of the area directly in front of the navigator in the jump seat. Major Jimmie Reinhardt was riding the jump seat and a Lt. Kennedy was in the right pilot's seat. I have no recollection nor do my records show the names of any of the other members of the crew on this flight. Lt. Kennedy was making the takeoff under the watchful eye of the instructor pilot. On takeoff an aircraft is accelerated down the runway until it reaches take off speed. The nose is then raised (rotated) and the aircraft would become airborne. On this day Lt. Kennedy rotated the aircraft for takeoff but over rotated it. The procedure for rotating any of the versions of the C-135 aircraft is similar to that used on the Boeing 707 commercial aircraft. The nose is raised to break ground and allowed to initially rise to about 8 degrees nose up. As the aircraft gains speed the nose is allowed to slowly rise to about 15 degrees nose up and the 15 degree angle is maintained during climb out. If the nose is raised to a higher angle (described as the angle of attack) too early it could easily put the aircraft in a condition described as being behind the power curve. In short, this means that the aircraft does not have enough power (lift which is a factor of the speed) at that angle of attack to climb or even maintain its altitude and will likely sink back toward the ground. Whenever the nose is raised additional drag is created. If the nose is raised too far too early the drag created is too great for the aircraft to climb. The aircraft would need to gain additional speed to counter act the excessive drag created by rotating too far too early. Until it attains that additional speed it will slowly sink back toward the ground. If the pilot reacts by lowering the nose at this point, in an effort to decrease the drag and there by increasing the rate of acceleration, it would immediately increase the sink rate until the aircraft gains enough speed to arrest the sink rate. Unfortunately, when the aircraft is that close to the ground a crash is the most likely outcome. On this flight the instructor pilot took control of the aircraft and attempted to recover from the situation. He was unable to do so and the aircraft crashed off the end of the runway. The aircraft was on fire. The two pilots in the front seats exited the aircraft by opening the windows beside each pilot seat. The jump seat that the extra navigator occupied had broken loose on impact and slammed him into the equipment rack in front of him. The impact had killed him. Major Reinhardt's seat also broke loose and he ended up draped over the throttle quadrant between the pilot seats. The navigator and Major Reinhardt also left the aircraft through the pilot's window. They carried the body of the extra navigator with them. He was the only fatality. There were several injuries and some burns to the surviving crew members but none was life threatening.

Lisa Anne

The unit at Eielson had established a detachment at Shemya. It kept flight crews and maintenance personnel there to support the operation. All of the personnel were assigned to Eielson and their tours at Shemya were done in temporary duty status. Both the flight crews and the maintenance personnel were rotated at intervals. A special project aircraft operated from Shemya. This may have been a replacement for the Tell-Two project. I never knew the exact nature of their mission. Shemya was near the recovery end of the Russian's missile test range so it would be logical that this may have been their mission. The project name was Lisa Anne. The project had a single RC-135W aircraft. It was a modified version of the C-135B aircraft. The standard configuration aircraft used by the Eielson unit was the RC-135D. The RC-135W was a one of a kind special project aircraft. The aircraft was used to fly the operational sorties from Shemya as well as ferrying personnel back and forth between Shemya and Eielson. On this fateful day the aircraft was flying from Shemya ferrying operations and maintenance personnel back to Eielson. The Aircraft Commander for the flight was a Major Michaud. He had been a crew commander in the 55th at Forbes. While they were still over the waters between Shemya and the Alaskan mainland Air Traffic Control received an emergency call from the aircraft. The call stated that the aircraft was experiencing a severe vibration and was difficult to control. That was the final transmission from the aircraft. It was not heard from again and never arrived at its destination. The unit at Eielson immediately initiated a search operation. Several crews from the 55th would join in the search. One of the 55th s crews that participated in the search was commanded by Captain Bill Browning who lived in the same house as I did in Bellevue. The search was continued for several days. Bill said that no trace of the aircraft or crew was found. Several months later a single main landing gear from an aircraft washed up on shore on one of the islands in the Aleutian chain. They suspected that it was from the Lisa Anne aircraft but were unable to confirm it.

Operational Sorties

The operational reconnaissance sorties flown from Offutt served much the same purpose as they had at Forbes. The raven's job was to monitor, analyze, and record electronic emissions from enemy countries to maintain SACs strategic data bases. The sorties that originated at Offutt had much longer commutes to the On Watch segment of the sorties, where the ravens were monitoring enemy electronic emissions, than had been the case while operating from the forward locations that were typical while the wing was at Forbes. All of the operational sorties required at least one mid-air refueling to extend its range to complete the long missions. A typical operational sortie would depart from Offutt with less than a full fuel load. The runway at Offutt was about 10,000 feet in length and a little short for a maximum gross weight take off. A mid-air refueling would be completed about three to four hours after departure. If the sortie was scheduled to be 24 hours in length a second mid-air refueling would be required.

Sorties to the Orient would refuel over Alaska. The On Watch portion of the flight could focus on the Kamchahkta Peninsula, the

Kurile Island chain, the Sea of Okhotsk, or Sakhalin Island. Occasionally North Korea would be included. The flights would normally land at Kadena. The return flight would focus on the same areas as the trip from Offutt. These flights varied from 15 to 18 hours in duration. Often a third flight would be sandwiched between the two back and forth flights. It would be shorter in length, normally six to eight hours in duration. The focus on the shorter sortie would normally be on North Korea, Communist China or South East Asia.

Sorties flown from Offutt would also augment the Eielson operation. These flights would be flown along the polar side of the Soviet Union as far as the east side as Novaya Zemlya Island. They often landed at Eielson. Flights to the east would cover the area from the west side of Novaya Zemlya Island to the east end of the Mediterranean Sea. These flights would land at either Upper Heyford AFB in England or would return to Offutt. The flights landing in England were 16 to 18 hours long. The ones returning to Offutt could be long as 24 hours in duration.

Certification

Captain Blaine and I had arrived in Omaha on December 12, 1969. I took leave over the holidays and did not start my certification training until the start of the new year. The first two training sorties were flown with Major Reinhardt's crew. The first training flight was on January 20th and the second flight on January 24th. I was certified on the second flight. Following certification I was not immediately assigned to a crew but used as a fill in reserve. The 55th was still flying Common Cause sorties around Cuba. I flew a Common Cause sortie on February 4th and another one on February 13th. Both of these were with Major Jim Jones' crew. His was one of the Iron Lung special project crews. On the 15th of February I was formally assigned to his crew and was again part of the Iron Lung project.

Chapter 20　　　　Iron Lung Again

The <u>Iron Lung</u> project used an older version of the C-135 aircraft. As mentioned earlier, it was a modified version of the KC-135A aircraft whose original mission had been airborne refueling. The refueling boom had been removed. Several antennas had been added. A system to allow the aircraft to be the receiver in a mid-air refueling was added. In all other respects it was nearly identical to its original configuration. Its designation was the RC-135R. The project mode of operation was similar to that which had been used in the <u>Iron Lung</u> project at Forbes. The aircraft would be reconfigured prior to each deployment much the same as had been done at Forbes. Reconfigurations meant changes in the equipment operated by the Ravens and different antenna arrangements. The Lockheed Company was still the prime contractor and responsible for airframe modifications. The configuration of the Raven's equipment was sub-contracted to E-Systems located at Greenville, Texas. Funding and over sight for the project was also the same as it had been at Forbes. Operational sorties would be flown as a part of lengthy deployments.

Lockheed had a major plant in the Fort Worth area. In preparation for each deployment the aircraft would be flown to Carswell AFB which is located just outside of Ft. Worth for updating and left in the hands of the Lockheed engineers. The aircraft would remain at Carswell during modifications. When the modifications were complete a crew would be sent back to Carswell to retrieve the aircraft. The raven's task was to concentrate on a particular radar system. They would conduct an in-depth analysis of the system focusing on power measurements. The next Iron Lung project was scheduled for a deployment to Kadena later in the spring.

RC-135R

The RC-135R used the older J57 engines, required water/alcohol augmentation for takeoff and was much more sluggish on takeoff than the RC-135C or the RC-135M. There was a whole series of antennas along the top of the aircraft. It looked a little like a porcupine. On this modification the engineers had removed all of the aircraft insulation in order to get to the interior roof area to install the antennas. They had failed to replace all of the insulation so the noise level inside the cabin was extremely high. We were not able to hear one another without the aid of the headsets inside our helmets. I have had some hearing loss since my active duty period and I felt that this deployment in the RC-135R had a lot to do with it.

The aircraft had been flown to Carswell prior to my being assigned to the crew and by late February it was ready to be returned to Offutt. Prior to returning several test flights were scheduled from Carswell. One of the crews would go to Carswell to fly the test flights and return to Offutt with the aircraft. Major Jones, the crew commander (AC) would not go with us. Major Butts, the Second AC on the crew would fly the test flights at Carswell with us. Major Dan Mateik was the Raven One and in charge of the rear end crew (the ravens). Captain Duke Armstrong was the Raven Two and I was the Raven Three. All three ravens would make the trip to Carswell. We flew to Ft. Worth via commercial carrier. The first test flight was on February 27th. There were additional test flights. We discovered a couple of minor problems that needed to be fixed so we returned to Offutt via commercial carrier on March 8th. As a result of the items that needed to be fixed the deployment was delayed until May. Major Jones and the front end part of the crew would retrieve the aircraft when the corrections were complete. The aircraft was returned to Offutt a couple of weeks later and the scheduled deployment date for the project set for the 28th of May. The sorties, during the deployment, were scheduled to last between 7 and 9 hours. The augmented RC-135C crew, which included three pilots, would not be needed because of the shorter flight times. We were to deploy with three ravens, two navigators and two pilots. The crew's second AC would stay home.

In the interim I was used as a spare on operational sorties and training flights. I flew several training flights and a single Common Cause sortie in March and early April. On April 16th I flew an operational sortie with Major Clark's crew. The On Watch area was off the polar side of Russia between Alaska and the East side of

Novaya Zemlya Island. The flight landed at Eielson AFB near Fairbanks. The return flight to Offutt was on April 20th. This flight went the opposite direction. It went over the polar area and along the west side of Novaya Zemlya and the Kola Peninsula. We landed back at Offutt after 18 hours and 35 minutes in the air. On April 24th I flew an operational sortie with Major Nunn's crew. The On Watch area was near the Eastern European countries and landed at Upper Heyford AFB in England. The return trip again visited the area west of Novaya Zemlya and landed back at Offutt. Both of the flights on this trip were around 16 hours in length.

The Iron Lung project was still being tasked by the CIA and they were providing partial funding. Most of the agency's personnel that were involved in the project had never actually seen the aircraft so we were asked to fly it to Andrews AFB near the Washington DC so they could tour the aircraft. The flight to Andrews was on May 13th. Major Culver, the Instructor Pilot who had angered the General on the Looking Glass flight mentioned above, had become the second AC on our crew. He was the AC for the trip to Andrews AFB. We spent most of the afternoon of May 13th setting up and standing by the aircraft to explain our operation and answer any questions. The display period lasted about three hours with a steady stream of people touring the aircraft. It seemed obvious to me that there were many more who took the tour than could have had any direct involvement with the project. We returned to Offutt the following day.

In May I got my first taste of the 24 hour long operational flights. They departed from and returned to Offutt. The first was on May 7th with Major Nunn's crew. The second was on May 22nd with Captain Irwin's Crew. Ironically, both flights lasted exactly 24 hours. After flying 70 plus sorties of 19 and a half hours I thought that 24 hours would not be much different. They did, however, seem to be much longer. Following the second 24 hour sortie my crew started its preparation for our scheduled deployment with the Iron Lung project. I would be returning to Okinawa for at least a couple of months.

The purpose of this deployment was to assess a new communications system that the Communist Chinese had installed.

244

They had acquired it from the East Germans. The system supposedly consisted of a series of towers that used a highly directional signal to minimize eaves dropping. The locations of a couple of the towers were known to us. The speculation was that the signal was a very narrow beam between pairs of towers. The signal would obviously continue beyond the second tower and extend beyond the country boundaries. We would be able to intercept the extension of the signal by flying off shore over international waters. Our job was to determine the location of the various towers and to analyze and record the signal for later detailed analysis. The plan was to keep our routes along and parallel to the coast. As we flew along the coast we would pass though several of the narrow beams. This would enable us to plot a point of intercept as well as determine the actual width of the beam. By flying routes at different distances from the coast we could use the points of intercept to extrapolate the alignment of the various towers. Several of these lines would allow us to pin point locations. An example will illustrate. A flight along the coast 15 miles off shore would yield a point of intercept. Another flight 30 miles off shore would yield another intercept point. Connecting these two points and extending the line would give us a <u>Line Of Position</u> (LOP) on the transmitter. The same procedure in a different area, intercepting the same signal, would give us a second LOP. The interception of the two LOPs would determine the location of the transmitter. The deployment was to be divided into two segments. Each of the two <u>Iron Lung</u> crews would handle one of the segments. Our crew was scheduled to handle the first segment. The early sorties in the deployment focused on locating the various transmitting sights. Once the sights were pinpointed the task was to conduct further analysis including power measurements and determine beam widths. Many of the sorties would take us into the Gulf of Tonkin focusing on the southern half of China and North Viet Nam. In the months that followed the project we learned that the East German system was much less sophisticated than had been expected. The technology was well behind our own and the beam was actually not very narrow.

Return to Okinawa

On May 28th we departed Offutt with aircraft 5-3121, an RC-135R, bound for Kadena. The purpose of this flight was solely to ferry the aircraft to Kadena. Major Jim Jones was the Aircraft Commander. The crew consisted of two pilots, two navigators and three ravens. Major Dan Matiek was the Raven One. The flight lasted 16 hours and 20 minutes. On this flight my total accumulated Air Force flight time passed the 3000 hour mark. As I alluded to earlier, the noise level inside the aircraft was considerably higher than any we had previously experienced. We did not learn until somewhat later the reason for the higher noise level. The engineers at Lockheed had removed part of the aircraft's insulation, to make their antenna installations, and had failed to replace all of it. It was impossible to hold a conversation, particularly in the rear of the aircraft where the ravens worked, even if you shouted. The only way we could communicate was via the interphone. We wore flight helmets whenever we were airborne which helped shield us from some of the noise. I generally rode the retraceable jump seat between the pilots for take offs and landings. The noise level was much lower in the front cockpit.

Our first flight from Kadena was on June 11th. It was a short orientation and familiarization flight of two hours and 30 minutes. The first five operational sorties were into the Gulf of Tonkin. Each of the flights was about nine hours in length. Given the fact that it took about three hours to fly from Kadena to the Gulf and a like number of hours to return our On Watch period was fairly short, about three hours. Any flight into the Gulf was considered, by the Air Force, to be a combat mission. We were not, however, directly supporting the war effort in Viet Nam. Our focus on these sorties was the southern part of China as well as Hainan Island. The task was to determine the deployment of this new communications system in China and ascertain if it extended into North Viet Nam. There were four operational flights into the Gulf of Tonkin in June and another on July 3rd. All of these flights were from eight to nine hours in length and did not need a mid-air refueling. We were the only 55th based aircraft and crew that was operating continuously from Kadena during the next several months but the back and forth sorties between Offutt and Kadena by the RC-135C meant that often two 55th based aircraft and crews were at Kadena for short periods. We used the 82nd SRS facilities and support while at Kadena. As was normal, the RC-135C crews would often sandwich a shorter, in theatre, sortie while at Kadena. Since the Iron Lung crew members were still qualified and current on the RC-135C we could fill in on these in theatre sorties as the need arose. On July 5th I filled in on Captain Heller's crew on a sortie into the Gulf of Tonkin.

Starting on July 6th the attention of the project shifted to other parts of China. We flew six more operational sorties during July. On the 25th of July we returned, with the aircraft, to Offutt. The first phase of the project deployment was complete. The other Iron Lung crew, commanded by Major Regis Urschler, would handle the second phase of the deployment. The second half of the project would focus more on power measurements and beam width. It was determined that there was a need for an additional Raven during the second half of the project. I was assigned as that additional Raven and was temporarily assigned to Major Urschler's crew. I would be returning to Kadena on August 2nd.

We flew six Iron Lung sorties from Kadena in August, five in September, and three in October. The final sortie was flown on October 10th. In addition to the Iron Lung project activity the second deployment included two trips to Clark AFB in the Philippines to avoid an approaching typhoon and two sorties as a fill in on RC-135C flights. The first of these was with Major Tobias's crew on the 18th of August and the second was with Major McCoid's crew on the 13th of October. The project was completed and we returned to Offutt on October 16th.

Urschler Crew – Iron Lung Project – Kadena (Fall 1969)

Crew picture with their aircraft superimposed behind them

Back Row: Lt. Col. Urschler (Pilot/AC), Capt. King (Copilot), Capt. Melton (Navigator 1),
Capt. Shackelford (Navigator 2)
Front Row: Capt. Alsbaugh (Raven 1), Capt. Thomas (Raven 2), Capt. Johnson 9Raven 3),
Capt. Perrizo (Extra Raven)

Chapter 21   Final Months

When an individual joins one of the military services they commit themselves to a specific term of duty. This is referred to as an enlistment. The length of the enlistment varies from one branch of the service to another. When this term is completed they must re-enlist for an additional term to continue. Those wishing to make the military their career must re-commit themselves as each term of enlistment expires. The services often offer a monetary bonus to entice them to re-enlist. The minimum time served to be eligible for retirement is twenty years which would require several re-enlistments. The normal length of the term for those enlisting in the Air Force is four years. This process does not, however, apply to all military personnel but only to a specific range of military ranks which are aptly referred to as the enlisted ranks. The ranks included range from the entry level rank (Private, Airman Basic or Seaman Basic) to the highest sergeant rank (Chief Master Sergeant, Chief Petty Officer, etc.). The officer ranks use an entirely different process. Officers receive a commission which places them in active duty career status. This means their term of duty is indefinite. This term of active duty career status ends only when they apply for and are granted relief from it. The ranks covered by this process range from the initial commissioning rank (Second Lieutenant or Ensign) to the highest ranking General or Admiral and are referred to as the commissioned ranks.

When an officer receives his or her commission they are required to serve a minimum length of time before they can apply to be relieved from active duty career status. The length of the commitment varies depending first on the source of their commission. For example, the length of the commitment for graduates of the Air Force Academy is longer than a graduate of an ROTC program. Additional years may be added as a result of attending some of the more expensive training programs. All of the flight training programs add years to the length of this commitment. Once this commitment was completed, an officer could apply to be relieved of his or her career status. Relief could come from application for retirement, transfer to the reserves, or to resign their commission. These applications are normally approved. There are, however, exceptions. Exceptions are often the result of specific service level needs. The Stop Loss program in 2008 is an example. It was focused on specific skills that were critically needed for the war in Iraq.

On September 22, 1969 I submitted an application to be relieved from career status and transferred to the reserves. The reasons listed on the application were a desire to continue my education and to pursue a career on the civilian economy. This seriously understated my reasons for taking the action. I had initially joined the Air Force because I had run out of money to continue my college studies. My intent was to spend a few years in the service to qualify for the GI bill and use it to continue my education. I had not considered a military career to be a viable option. This attitude had gradually changed during my years of military duty. I had identified with the importance of the job I was doing. I enjoyed working with the men in the units I served in. I enjoyed the opportunity to travel to numerous countries and learn about their cultures. I had come to look upon the military as a career. Had it not been for the frustrations of not getting into pilot training and pessimism about my potential for advancement I would have likely stayed on active duty. I'm sure that my frustration with not getting to pilot training is clear to the reader given the attention I've devoted to the subject in the preceding chapters. I understand the reasons behind the actions of my superiors in my unit and the Air Force selection boards but that did not relieve my frustrations. I have come to feel, in the intervening years, that had it not been for needs of the war in Viet Nam I would probably have been successful in my ambition.

During the decades of the 1940s and 1950s the majority of officers in the Air Force had received their training and their commissions from the Aviation Cadet program. The Aviation Cadet program was an in-service, flying training program. Entry into the program required two years of college. A significant segment of the officers during that period were not college graduates. A college degree was not an important factor in consideration for promotion. I had used this

249

route to become an officer but I had done so in the waning years of the program. The <u>Aviation Cadet</u> program ended during the mid-part of the 1960s. The Air Force was shifting to commissioning programs that required a college degree. A degree was also increasingly becoming an important factor to promotion boards. I was aware of this situation and as a result had made every effort to continue my pursuit of a degree. It had become very obvious to me that given the extensive travel that my job required I stood little chance of completing a degree which, rightly or wrongly, in my mind seriously diminished my promotional potential. It was clear, at least in my mind, that I had to look at alternatives. I had spent the final year of active duty service researching possible alternatives.

My intention was to join an Air Force reserve or an Air Guard unit. It would be a supplemental source of income. I would be able to spend the majority of my time in pursuit of a college degree using the GI bill. I hoped the two sources of income would be sufficient. I had located an Air Guard unit in Portland, Oregon that flew the F-89 aircraft. The F-89 is a two seat jet aircraft. In this unit a pilot occupied the front seat and a Radar Intercept Officer occupied the rear seat. A Radar Intercept Officer was another form of an Electronic Warfare Officer, my specialty. Portland had several good universities. This would be a good fit for me. I left active duty in March of 1970. I immediately went to Okinawa to get married. My wife and I returned to Portland in the middle of May. Upon my arrival in Portland I contacted the Portland Air Guard and advised the commander of my qualifications and intentions. He told me that the unit was scheduled to transition to the F-102 aircraft in less than a year. The F-102 was a single place aircraft that required only a pilot. They were not training any new Radar Intercept Officers so they didn't have a place for me. This turned out to be just another of my grand plans that came to naught.

In late October of 1969 I had returned from the last extended TDY tour to Okinawa as part of the Iron Lung project. I remained on Colonel Jones' crew. Both he and Major Urschler had been promoted to Lt. Colonel at the end of October. Since there was no Iron Lung

250

project activity scheduled for several months, we reverted to the normal routine of the crews of the 55[th.]. These included training sorties and operational missions in the RC-135C aircraft. As mentioned earlier, operational reconnaissance missions in the RC-135C normally departed from Offutt AFB and often landed at one of the forward operating locations with a subsequent return sortie back to Offutt. I was interested in as many of these to Kadena as I could get. I had applied to be transferred to the reserves effective March of 1970. I had become engaged to an Okinawan girl. The wedding was planned for April of 1970. Each trip would be a chance to see her again. I made my wishes known to the schedulers. I volunteered to fly on as many operational sorties as I could to Okinawa. It was in both of our interests. I was able to make four trips to Okinawa during the four and a half months that I remained in the unit.

Colonels Dogs

Kadena AFB had a good quantity of base housing for military personnel. Bachelors would be assigned a room in the barracks or the Bachelor Officers Quarters (BOQ). Married personnel could be assigned to on-base facilities ranging from a town house to a 3 to 4 bed room house with all the facilities that a house in the United States would have (carport/garage, washer/dryer, refrigerator and air conditioning). The factors that determined which of these you would be assigned depended on rank, marital status and the number of dependents. When married personnel arrived on base with their dependents they initially would have to find housing off the base. They could, however, place their name on the waiting list for lodging on base. Accompanied tours were normally 3 years in length. Most married personnel would get into a base house at some point in their tour of duty. Many of the families, both on the base or off the base, had an Okinawan maid. These maids occasionally became like a nanny to their children. I often heard military families speak in glowing terms about their maid. They became like members of the family. Pets were also common for many families. Few of the pets were bought to Okinawa with the families when they arrived. They

251

were generally acquired on Okinawa. As with families everywhere, they often became very attached to their pets and wanted to keep them when they were re-assigned back to the States. It was possible to do so, but it was quite an elaborate process. It required a period of quarantine and shots. The big expense, however, was the actual transporting of the pet back to the States. It had to be done on a commercial airline and was expensive. The Air Force covered the cost of moves but that did not include the cost of transporting a pet. This latter factor was most likely the reason that I ended up helping to transport several dogs back to the states.

The first of the four trips to Okinawa started on November 7th with Major Reinhardt's crew. We departed Offutt, made a mid-air refueling over Alaska and completed our operational segment off the Soviet coast. The flight was 16 hours and 20 minutes long with a landing at Kadena. While at Kadena we were scheduled to fly a local operational mission along the Chinese coast on the 10th of the month. This mission would depart and recover at Kadena. The flight started normally, but about two hours into the flight the aircraft developed some mechanical problems and we had to return to Kadena. The mission was re-scheduled for the 12th. It had to be a short one because we were scheduled for the long trip home on the 13th.

When the crew arrived at the aircraft on the 13th, we started our pre-flight inspection of the aircraft systems. While engaged in this task, a full colonel, whom I did not recognize, approached the aircraft. He was accompanied by a member of the 82nd staff. They talked to Major Reinhardt for several minutes. Then they called me over to join the discussion. It seems that the colonel was being transferred back to SAC headquarters at Offutt. He had a large dog and wanted to get it back to the states. He informed us that the dog had completed his shots and period of quarantine. He had asked our commander if we could take the dog back on our return flight. It had been discussed with Major Reinhardt and he had consented. It seemed very strange to me. This was not a cargo flight, it was an operational reconnaissance mission along the periphery of enemy territory with all the attendant risks. The doubt on my face must have been obvious.

I was advised that this was not a new procedure. Our returning aircraft had done this sort of thing before.

Most of the operating positions on the aircraft were quite cramped. The dog could not be in the cockpit. This would be a safety issue. The only area that had some open space was near the Raven Three's position just in front of the relief facilities and the bunks at the rear of the aircraft. Someone had to watch the dog. I was the Raven Three so that task fell to me. The dog would be delivered to me in a wire cage. He would be sedated and remain in the cage throughout the flight. A party would meet the aircraft upon arrival at Offutt and take the dog from me. The sedation was advertised to last about 10 hours. Return flights from Okinawa often lasted 18 hours. I would have a strange, un-sedated dog, fortunately in a cage, for about half of the flight. I hoped it would be a quiet one but I was expecting the worst. The colonel left to get the dog. It turned out to be a Doberman in a very large wire cage. The bottom of the cage was solid but the top and all the sides were made of heavy wire. It looked very professional and was likely a commercially available product. They placed the cage a couple of feet to the left of my position. The colonel gave me the name and telephone number of the party that would meet us. The dog remained quiet after the colonel left the aircraft.

The engines on the RC-135C are mounted under the wings. The Raven Three position is toward the rear of the aircraft. It is some 20 to 30 feet behind the engines. This is one of the worst places on the aircraft in terms of engine noise, especially during the takeoff run. There are a number of high pitched noises which the engines emit at high RPMs such as during the takeoff roll and climb out.

The ground crew closed the doors and we were ready to taxi to the runway. The dog remained quiet when the engine noise increased for taxing. When the engines spooled up for takeoff roll, however; the dog, still heavily sedated, started a long low howl similar to the call of a coyote. It wasn't loud but a bit disturbing. He continued this for about five minutes and then went quiet. He laid his head down but kept his sorrowful looking eyes glued on me. The dog did not sleep throughout the entire flight. After about 12 hours the sedation appeared to wear off. He shifted his position in the cage easily but was well behaved through the entire flight. He would become restive whenever another member of the crew, on their way to the relief facilities or the galley area, stopped to talk to him. He was calm around me. He had been through an ordeal and apparently considered me a friend. I didn't feed him but did fill his water dish several times. The return flight lasted 19 hours and 10 minutes. When we arrived at Offutt, the people who were to claim the dog were waiting. The whole affair had gone much better than I had expected. I did not, however, want to do it again.

The second trip to Okinawa started on December 5th . I joined Captain Murphy's crew for this trip. The trip to Kadena was similar to the first but a bit longer. We landed at Kadena after 23 hours and 10 minutes in the air. Again, we flew a shorter mission from Kadena before the flight home. The return flight home was on December 11th and was a bit shorter than the flight over. It lasted 18 hours and 40 minutes.

The third trip started on January 27, 1970. It was with Major Irwin's crew. This trip involved only two sorties, one over and the other returning. The trip to Okinawa took 16 hours and 20 Minutes. On the return I was informed that Major Irwin had consented to transport another colonel's dog. This one was smaller, a dachshund. He arrived in a makeshift cage. It was made of chicken wire. The dog had not yet been sedated when it arrived. The owner attempted several times to get the dog to take the pill. The dog would spit it out. We finally told him to just thrust it down the dog's throat. He did and it finally stayed down. The task had taken about 10 minutes. The colonel had to leave the aircraft in a hurry. We were getting ready to depart. The dog was very restless and barked often. The sedation had not yet taken hold. When the engines spooled up for takeoff the dog started barking incessantly. It took about half an hour before he settled down. Then he went to sleep. The sedation eventually wore off. The dog had periods during the remainder of the flight where he would bark and quickly shift his position in the small cage. I wasn't able to quiet him. Several other crew members tried to help but to no avail. The flight was 19 hours and 50 minutes long. I was very happy that it was over. The people that were to pick up the dog were late. I had to wait about 30 minutes for them to arrive. I again vowed I would not do that again but the bottom line is that I probably would not have Choice.

The Return of Malcom

My final operational trip started on March 6th. It was with my own crew under Lt. Colonel Jones. My final day of active duty would be the 23rd of March. The flight from Offutt to Kadena lasted 16 hours and 40 minutes. It followed the normal profile for RC-135C sorties. A mid-air refueling over Alaska, reconnaissance along the Kamchahkta Peninsula, the Kurile islands and Sakhalin Island with a landing at Kadena. On March 11th we flew a mission from Kadena into the Gulf of Tonkin to monitor activity in North Viet Nam returning to land at Kadena. The return flight to Offutt would be on March 13th. As luck would have it, I would be transporting another dog home but this would not be a colonel's dog. This would be a dog I knew.

Captain John Freeman and his wife Patsy were completing their tour on Okinawa. John had been a close friend from our days at Forbes AFB. I had spent some time at their residence during my tour on Okinawa and visited them during the trips back from Offutt. They had a mixed breed dog by the name of Malcom. Malcom was medium sized and about 3 to 4 years old. He was a very calm dog. I had spent enough time at the Freeman house that I knew Malcom quite well. John was being transferred back to Offutt. Both he and Patsy wanted to take Malcom back with them. I told John that I was an old hand at this and I would talk to Colonel Jones about it. Colonel Jones approved the idea and Malcom would return with me. I would leave him with a couple in Omaha that we both knew and Malcom would stay with them until the Freeman's transfer.

On the day of the flight John bought Malcom to the aircraft. The cage was a make shift affair. John had constructed it himself. It consisted of two slabs of plywood for sides and plywood for a floor. Chicken wire was nailed around the ends and served to join the sides

255

together. A makeshift door was near the bottom of the cage. The cage was about 3 feet high and 18 inches wide and stood upright. We both considered it adequate for the trip. I helped John sedate Malcom and we put him in the cage. He was very quite and well behaved. We bid John goodbye.

I expected a much easier time with Malcom than the dogs on the previous trips. I knew this dog and he was very calm and laid back. Things went fine until take off. As the engines spooled up to full power Malcom went berserk. He bit down on the chicken wire in an attempt to get out of the cage. His mouth was bleeding badly. I could do nothing until we broke ground, then I immediately unbuckled from my harness and opened the cage door to get him out. I had him lay down beside my position. He was pressed hard against my left leg and was shaking violently. It was about 20 minutes before the shaking abated to a trembling. Apparently the high pitched sounds had been reverberating between those two slabs of plywood and created an intolerable situation for him. He had not barked through the entire ordeal. The flight lasted 20 hours. I left him out of the cage the entire time. I did not have to use the leash. Malcom stayed pressed against my leg the entire trip. The physical contact seemed to calm him and he maintained it through the entire 20 hours. Whenever I got up to move around the aircraft he followed me. He did not bark the entire flight and except for the take off period he was very well behaved.

When we arrived at Offutt I put him on the leash. I took Malcom home with me and called the people who would be keeping him for the Freemans. I arranged to meet them in a park close to my house. I wanted to give Malcom a chance to run a little. He seemed to be getting back to normal. When the couple arrived to take him he seemed reluctant to go with them. It took some gentle persuasion on my part before he got into their car. I was sad to see him go. We had bonded over the preceding hours.

CEG Evaluation

All crew members on Strategic Air Command's (SAC) combat

ready crews received periodic individual evaluations to ensure that their job performance was up to standards. These evaluations were normally done by specially designated personnel from within the wing and performed on an annual basis. Occasionally personnel from outside the wing would do spot evaluations. These evaluations would focus on an entire crew. An <u>Operational Readiness Inspection</u> (ORI) performed by SAC headquarters personnel was an example. ORIs were comprehensive no notice evaluations of all aspects of a wing's activities and several combat ready crews were evaluated. The evaluation team would arrive unannounced and begin the evaluation. The crew evaluations focused on the crews that were presently on alert. The 55th did not have an alert force at Offutt so we did not receive an ORI, at least while I was a member of the unit. SAC had three major subordinate organizations. They were referred to as numbered Air Forces. Each of the numbered Air Forces was commanded by a three star General. The SAC wings in the western third of the continental United States were assigned to the 15th Air Force with headquarters at March AFB in the Los Angeles area. The SAC wings in the central part of the country were assigned to the 8th Air Force with headquarters at Barksdale AFB near Baton Rouge, Louisiana. The SAC wings in the eastern third of the country were assigned to the 2nd Air Force with headquarters at Westover AFB near Boston. The 55th SRW was assigned to the 8th Air Force. The numbered Air Forces also conducted spot evaluations on combat ready crews. Each had a unit called the <u>Combat Evaluation Group</u> (CEG). They would do spot evaluations on a single crew. The crew to be evaluated would be selected by CEG. The wing would be notified ahead of time of the date and time as well as the crew that was selected. There would be time to prepare. The selected crew would normally have one or two training flights to hone their procedures in preparation. In the latter part of January of 1970 the wing was advised that the 8th Air Force CEG would arrive on base on February 25th to conduct an evaluation on Lt. Colonel Jones' crew. This was my crew. My initial reaction was that I would be replaced on the crew prior to the CEG evaluation because I already had a separation date of March

23rd , a mere month after the scheduled evaluation. It was also a very busy time for me. I was preparing for my wedding in Okinawa following my separation as well as preparing to move from the Omaha area to Portland, Oregon. Failure of the selected crew to pass the CEG evaluation would reflect poorly on the wing. It seemed to me that the wing's leadership would consider it a bad idea to depend on an individual who was mentally absorbed in leaving. It would detract from one's ability to focus on the important task at hand. I was wrong. I was to remain on the crew.   I guess I should have considered it a vote of confidence. I would, therefore, give it my best effort. The crew flew two training flights in preparation. The first was on February 6th, two days after I had returned from a trip to Okinawa. The second was on February 19th. The CEG evaluation took place on February 26th. The crew, including myself, passed with flying colors.

Chapter 22   **Final Thoughts**

During my youth there was a popular song that one occasionally heard on the radio entitled "Old Soldiers Never Die. They Just Fade Away." I don't know much about the origin of the song. I had the impression that it started after the First World War. At the time I found it to be a catchy tune and nothing more. The words had little meaning for me. Some fifty five years later I find it more thought provoking.

Every 18 months the 55th Wing association; an organization of current and former members of the 55th SRW, the 82nd SRS and various other Air Force units that were involved in airborne reconnaissance; hold a reunion. The site of the reunion rotates to various cities around the country. They had been held at regular intervals since the early 1980s. I have attended a few of them over the last 10 years. Most of the attendees, of the last few reunions, are men in their 60s, 70s and 80s. At each of these two or three of the regular attendees are missing. They have passed away. They did in fact die and did not just fade away. What is fading away is the record of their experiences and accomplishments. Most of these experiences are kept in the minds of these old soldiers and in the stories they could tell. These fade into obscurity as they pass on.

A few of the old soldiers who participated in the Second World War, that are still with us, are in their 90s and disappearing rapidly. The families of many of these WWII veterans will tell you that they would not talk about their war experiences. The opportunity to record these experiences is disappearing with them. As I indicated in the Preface I felt that it was important to record the personal experiences of minor players in major events to have a realistic historical record. It was a major factor in my undertaking the effort to write this book.

I began writing this book in 2004 after I retired. At first progress was quite slow. It stopped entirely in 2006 because I went back to work at a full time job. I retired again in 2010 and have devoted more of my effort to it since then. It has been a satisfying endeavor. It forced me to reflect on the activities that I was a part of. Even to the point of considering the "WHY" of our activities. Societies often find that what seems to be imperative at a given point in time diminishes in importance with the passage of time. People who were adversaries become friends. Countries that were hostile to ours become friendly and vice versa. This phenomenon has been repeated frequently throughout recorded history and will likely continue to be so into the future. The adversarial relationship between the United States and the Soviet Union in the first two decades following the Second World War was intense and dangerous. Both possessed weapons of unimaginable destructive power. The confrontation almost resulted in the unthinkable in 1962 during the Cuban Missile Crisis. The concept of Détente and the SALT treaties seemed inconceivable at the time. The period just after the Cuban Missile Crisis marked my entry into the reconnaissance field and is the period that this book focuses on.

The importance of good and accurate intelligence is difficult to overstate. It is used for a variety of purposes, many of which are vital to the wellbeing of a country and its people. It is important for a variety of reasons, among them:

-To decide how much of the country's scarce resources to devote to its military capability. This is often dictated by the capabilities of a potential adversary.

-To learn the intentions of potential adversaries. Diplomatic efforts to prevent military actions must often be proactive. Countries often seek intelligence on the capabilities of friendly countries as well as adversaries. A case in point is the man arrested by the FBI during the 1990s for spying on the United States on behalf of Israel. Israel is an ally and a friend that still saw the need to clandestinely gather intelligence on us.

-The lack of good intelligence is a recipe for overreaction. This may well be the most important aspect for maintaining a peaceful environment. Historically, many an ill-advised military adventure is the result of this over reaction. It is not hard to find a critic in this country that would tell you that our involvement in Iraq in 2003 would fit in to this category.

The closed nature of the Soviet Union's society and the existence of the "Iron Curtain" severely limited the United States' Intelligence communities' ability to collect good intelligence during this dangerous period. We did know that the Soviet Union's capabilities were expanding rapidly and were being increasingly deployed to their remote Eastern provinces which were very close to U.S. Territory in Alaska. The presence of their ICBMs in those Eastern provinces put most of our major cities and military assets well within range. Their intentions, however, were not difficult to gage. Soviet Premier Khrushchev clearly stated their intentions -- Quote: "We will bury you." End Quote --.

We had limited options in our collection methods. During that time frame aerial reconnaissance was the best and most productive of these options. The 55th SRW was a center piece of the aerial reconnaissance activity. The risks seemed well justified to our intelligence community as well as in the minds of the flight crews that were involved. We did not see ourselves as particularly heroic but fully appreciated the importance of what we were doing.

As the events and the participants of this period fade into history contemporary observers may judge these activities to be unnecessarily provocative and bellicose. It is often difficult to appreciate in hind sight what seemed crucial and imperative at the time. It is important to remember, however, that history is full of examples of attempts to placate an aggressive power broker which ultimately resulted in their worst fears being realized. Neville Chamberlain's handling of Adolf Hitler in the late 1930's is a good example. Each new weapon system, once developed, becomes a part of the military equations. It can't be ignored or wished away. Nuclear weapons and their unbelievable destructive power are a reality. The world witnessed a near catastrophic nuclear confrontation during the Cuban Missile Crisis. Joseph Stalin and his successor's ambitions were not that different from those of Adolf Hitler and the Kaiser, both of which resulted in an all out conflict that consumed much of the world's military forces and resulted in death and destruction of unprecedented proportions. Even the most critical observer must acknowledge that the Mutually Assured Destruction concept, as insane as it might appear to them, that drove U. S and Soviet policies for decades, did act as a deterrent. Had the United States, during that period, attempted to placate the Soviet Union by unilateral disarmament or ignored their developing destructive capacity it likely would have adversely changed the history of that period as we know it.

Events are often embellished with the passage of time, particularly those that involve some form of confrontation. It seems to be a common human tendency. I have related a number of events that I was witness to during my years of active military service. I have tried to resist the urge to embellish them. Some of my contemporaries during this period may find some inaccuracies in my story. I would repeat to them that I have related the events from my own recollection and perspective without pleading for their absolute accuracy. It is interesting to me, however, to see the degree of hyperbole that exists in many of the renditions of the period in our present age of the Internet and the Blogosphere. On a recent browser query on the internet I found the following quote by a blogger; -- Quote: "North Vietnamese aircraft often attempted to attack the Combat Apple aircraft without success." End Quote. -- I was involved in the first 16 months of that operation and as stated in an earlier chapter found just the opposite to be true. The North Vietnamese were reluctant to venture into the Gulf of Tonkin. They were badly out numbered. Any attempt by them may have had a good chance of being successful but they were well aware that they would have had little chance of making it home after the attack. It would likely have been suicidal. The United States resources in the gulf were overwhelming.

Finally, I want to comment on the bond that military people develop and carry with them for the rest of their lives. This bond is often developed over a short period of time, perhaps only a year or two during their active military service. It remains with them, however, into their 80s and 90s and is frequently displayed on the hats and jackets they wear. There is a strong inter service rivalry that is apparent among those still on active military duty. As the years pass I have observed that this rivalry is continued in their rhetoric while at the same time the bond grows stronger irrespective of their branch of service. I feel this bond when I'm among friends who served time in the military and at each of the Air Force reunions that I attend.

Appendix A
Airborne Navigation as Taught at James Connally AFB.

Airborne navigation is based on a concept called <u>Dead Reckoning</u> (DR). <u>Dead Reckoning</u> is a process used to predict the position of an aircraft at a future time using presently known factors. These factors include the speed of the aircraft, the direction the aircraft is traveling and the effects of outside influences (such as the wind). The speed and direction of travel of the aircraft can be controlled by the operator but to ensure arrival at a pre-determined point the effects of the outside influences must be assessed and compensated for. The projected position of an aircraft at the selected time in the future is known as the <u>Dead Reckoning</u> or <u>DR</u> (in navigational language) position. The effect of the outside influences used to compute a DR position is based on past or forecast information. When the time of the projected position is reached the navigator determines the actual position (a <u>Fix</u> in navigational language). Using the actual position to update the effects of those outside influences a new DR position is computed for a new future time. The Dead Reckoning process is used in all forms of navigation. The method used to determine the actual position (Fix) will vary. Each phase of the curriculum at James Connally was entitled <u>Dead Reckoning</u> aided by the method used to fix the actual position of the aircraft. Each of those phases is briefly described below.

Dead Reckoning aided by Double Drift and Groundspeed by Timing

An aircraft that wants to fly from point A to point B would follow a heading (direction) along a straight line between the two points. The effect of a wind from the side will push it off this line. The angular difference between the heading and the course (the actual line flown) is called the drift angle. The aircraft flies at a constant speed (airspeed) between the points. If the wind is on the tail or the nose of the aircraft it will either slow the aircraft's movement over the ground or increase it. The progress over the ground will be different than the airspeed. This is called the aircraft's groundspeed.

This technique measures the drift angle and the groundspeed by observing the path and the speed of objects on the ground that pass under the aircraft. The T-29 aircraft had a window in the bottom of the aircraft to allow the student to observe these objects. This technique requires the navigator to look through the window in the bottom of the aircraft. The window has a movable grid superimposed on it. The flow of terrain features below the aircraft is observed. The lines of the movable grid are aligned with the flow of objects passing under the aircraft. This provides the actual drift angle (using an associated device known as the Drift Meter) between the aircraft's heading and its ground track. The objects are then timed using a stop watch. The timing starts when the selected object reaches the front of the grid and stops when it reaches the rear. The aircraft's altitude above these objects must be factored in. A device known as the Radio Altimeter is used to determine the aircraft's Absolute Altitude (above the ground). The aircraft heading is offset twice (to the left then to right of the normal heading) each for a short period of time. Then the heading is returned to normal. The navigator (cadet student) would use these drift angles, the absolute altitude and the timed run to calculate the effect of the wind. The calculated effect of the wind is then applied to the dead reckoning position to determine the actual position (Fix) of the aircraft. This method was widely used during WW2 but not as much by the 1960s.

Dead Reckoning aided by Map Reading

A Sectional topographic chart is used to determine the aircraft's actual (Fix) position. The Dead Reckoning position is plotted on a topographical chart (Map) specific to the area. This gets the navigator in the vicinity. He then tries to match the observed features to those on his chart. When positive identification is made, the distance and direction from the aircraft is determined. The distance is plotted on the chart in the opposite direction. This is the actual aircraft position.

Dead Reckoning aided by Pressure Patterns

I don't recall enough of about this technique to describe it in detail. I do recall that its use was restricted to over water flights. It was not used when flying over land masses. The concept is based on the following factors. Lines of constant pressure can be plotted if they could be comprehensively measured. The closer the lines of constant pressure the stronger the resultant wind. The wind direction flows along the lines. For example, if we measure the pressure at two positions separated by a time lapse and we find no change in the pressure. We are flying along the wind. It is either on our nose or on our tail. If the pressure changes over time, we are flying across lines of pressure. The rate of the changes in pressure when combined with other data can be used to compute the effect of the wind on the heading of the aircraft (drift angle). If the pressure is falling it indicates a drift to one side. If the pressure is rising it indicates drift in the opposite direction.

Celestial Navigation

There were two separate phases of celestial navigation training, entitled <u>Dead Reckoning Aided by Day Celestial</u> and <u>Dead Reckoning Aided by Night Celestial</u>. Each method is based on a common set of concepts and procedures. The following is a brief explanation of those concepts and procedures. To avoid confusion I'll start with a general explanation using one type of celestial body, a star. Any variances will be covered later.

Each celestial body (a star) has a specific location in what is called the <u>Celestial Sphere</u>. The <u>Celestial Sphere</u> is described as a three dimensional spherical view of the sky that surrounds the entire earth. A star's position in the <u>Celestial Sphere</u> remains constant. Our view of the heavens (the <u>Celestial Sphere</u>) is limited. We can only see about half of it. The remainder is hidden from our view below the horizon. Our partial view is called our <u>Celestial Dome</u>. Our <u>Celestial Dome</u> is described as our view of the sky from horizon to horizon from our position on the surface of the earth (or in the air just above the earth) at a specific instant in time. Since the <u>Celestial Sphere</u> appears to us, from our position on earth, to rotate from east to west (the earth is actually doing the rotating) our <u>Celestial Dome</u> (our view of the heavens) is constantly changing. Therefore, while the position of a celestial body remains constant in the <u>Celestial Sphere</u> it is changing constantly in our <u>Celestial Dome</u>. The good news is that since the rotation rate of the earth is known these changes are predictable.

Celestial bodies (I'm confining the discussion to stars for the time being) that are visible have a location within our Celestial Dome that is used to determine our position on earth. As discussed above, the position of a body in our Celestial Dome changes with time. In addition it varies depending on our position on earth (our point of observation). For example, if we were 100 miles further west, our view of the sky would be slightly different and thus so would the predictable position of a celestial body in our Celestial Dome. The exact time and our position on earth are the determinants that govern where a specific celestial body will appear in our Celestial Dome. To predict (calculate) the position of a specific celestial body in our Celestial Dome, we must start from a known position. So we are faced with the dilemma that we are using celestial navigation to determine our present position but to do the calculations to find our present position we must already know it. We can solve this dilemma by using an Assumed Position based on our Dead Reckoning. Using our Assumed Position we can make the calculations. Then we measure the parameters and compare them with our calculations. This allows us to compute corrections from our Assumed Position to locate our actual position.

When we speak of a celestial body's location within our Celestial Dome, what we mean is the direction to the body from our position on earth and its height above the horizon from our point of observation. To make this concept clearer, visualize a cone with its point on the subject star and its' base on the surface of the earth. The base of the cone, where it contacts the earth, would describe a circle. The angle of the sides of the cone would be the same around the complete circle on the surface of the earth. By changing the angle of the cone we could change the size of the circle. There would be an almost unlimited number of possible sizes with the maximum equal to the circumference of the earth and the minimum a single point. We are interested in the one which passes through our position on earth. The circle would move across our Celestial Dome in concert with the subject star. The direction of the star from our assumed position would be to the nearest degree. We refer to this direction as the Azimuth or Zn. Next, imagine a horizontal line (the horizon) through our assumed position. The angle between this horizon line and the side of the cone would be the height of the star above our horizon within our Celestial Dome. We calculate and measure the height above the horizon in terms of its angular elevation. The height is determined to the nearest minute of arc (60 minutes of arc equals one degree). The angular elevation that we calculate from our assumed position is called the Calculated Height or HC. The angular elevation we measure with the sextant is called the Observed Height or HO. The necessary parameters we need to make our calculations are the exact time and our Assumed Position on earth.

Again, the direction is determined to the nearest degree. The largest possible circle would be equal to the circumference of the earth which is about 24,000 miles. Divide this by 360 degrees and we find that we are accurate to about the nearest 67 miles. This would give us a series of points along a line (part of the circle) up to 67 miles long. We refer to this as a Line Of Position or LOP. If the angular elevation of the celestial body were increased the size of the circle would be smaller and as a result the length of the LOP would be shorter. However, the celestial body would have to be nearly straight overhead to yield an LOP short enough to use as a position. So, for practical purposes, we have to settle for only an LOP. A single celestial body will not give us our position. We would need to use a second celestial body whose LOP intersects the first one to give us our actual position.

Now imagine a friend of yours viewing the same celestial body from a position 100 miles away from your position in the direction opposite the Azimuth to the subject celestial body. His imaginary cone would have a larger circle as its base and as a result the angle of the sides of the cone would be less. Conversely, imagine another friend 100 miles away along the Azimuth toward the subject body. The size of his imaginary circle would be smaller and the angle of the sides of the cone would be greater. A difference of one minute of arc in elevation is equal to one nautical mile on the surface of the earth, accurate enough for aerial navigation on an aircraft traveling at seven miles every minute of elapsed time.

- In the language of the navigator we call these calculations our pre-computations or PRECOMPs. Prior to the age of computers (which was the case in 1962) doing these calculations was done by hand and was very time consuming. Navigators normally did their PRECOMPing during mission planning before the flight took off (often the preceding day) and based them on a scheduled take off time. When the flight was delayed all of the PRECOMP work was useless and would have to be re-done in the air. It made for a very unhappy navigator. In the present age of computers the calculations are done by the computer.

To find (PRECOMP) the position of our subject celestial body in our Celestial Dome, we must first determine the apparent progression (remember, the earth is actually doing the rotating) of the Celestial Sphere for an exact moment in time. To do so we use two arbitrary points of reference, one in the Celestial Sphere (the star Aires) and the other at a point on earth (Greenwich, England). Their positions relative to one another will help us to determine our Celestial Dome. Since the apparent progression of the Celestial Sphere is from East to West the earthly reference point is actually a longitude (meridian). The Greenwich Meridian (the zero longitude) passes through Greenwich, England and is our earthly point of reference. This angular difference between the longitude which the star Aires is over and the Greenwich Meridian is called the Greenwich Hour Angle or GHA. We use a publication called the Air Almanac, which is updated monthly, to determine the position of the star Aires for the selected time.

Next we determine the angular difference from the Greenwich Meridian to our Assumed Position (longitude on earth). This gives us the Longitudinal Hour Angle or LHA of our Assumed Position. When we add these two together (GHA + LHA) we get the Sidereal Hour Angle or SHA.

The SHA is used to make our calculations (PRECOMPs). It is used in both Day and Night celestial computations. The stars (that we use at night) occupy a constant position in the Celestial Sphere. Their position would vary in our <u>Celestial Dome</u> for the same SHA depending on the latitude of our <u>Assumed Position</u>. This fact gives us the concept that is central to celestial positioning.

At the same latitude for a given SHA the position of a subject star in our <u>Celestial Dome</u> would be the same from day to day.

Let's look at his concept from a different perspective. If we observed the position of a particular star in our <u>Celestial Dome</u> at the exact same time each day from exactly the same location on earth, the star would appear in a slightly different position each succeeding day. The difference would be approximately one degree of arc from its position on the preceding day (The change over the course of a year would be 360 degrees. There are 365 days in a year so the change is approximately a degree a day). We would also find that our SHA for that exact time each day would also change approximately a degree each day. That is just another way of stating the concept in bold above. This fact enables the construction of a set of tables that can be used for our computations. These tables were entitled the <u>HO-249</u> tables and were used (by Air Force navigators) for PRECOMPing stars. The SHA and the <u>Assumed Position</u>'s latitude are the operative parameters for using the tables.

The sun, moon and planets, however, do not occupy a constant position in the <u>Celestial Sphere</u> and thus their position in our <u>Celestial Dome</u> will vary from day to day for the same latitude for a given SHA. A factor known as <u>Declination</u> is used in place of latitude. The <u>Air Almanac</u>, which is published monthly, is used in computations on the sun, moon and planets.

Using the SHA, for the exact time of our proposed celestial observation, and the <u>Assumed Position</u>'s latitude or declination we determine (calculate) the subject celestial bodies' position in our <u>Celestial Dome</u> in terms of its azimuth (ZN) and calculated (HC) angular height above the horizon. Next, we measure the elevation of the celestial body above the horizon with a sextant (at the exact time we used in the PRECOMP) which gives us the angular observed height (HO) above the horizon. Now we compare the results (HO) to the elevation we computed (HC) for the <u>Assumed Position</u>. The difference gives us the correction to apply to the <u>Assumed Position</u>. The resulting elevation is in the form of an angle (in degrees and minutes of arc). A variation of a minute of arc (there are 60 minutes in each degree) translates to a nautical mile (slightly longer than the statute mile that we use in the United States) difference in our position on earth. The sextant when used in aerial navigation and in the hands of a good navigator yields positions accurate to within a mile or two. On board ships with gyro stabilized sextants elevation measurements can be made down to the second of arc (there are 60 seconds of arc for each minute). Jet aircraft travel approximately 7 miles a minute so an accuracy of a mile or two is acceptable.

The difference between the HO and the HC is applied along the Azimuth (ZN). As indicated above, the correction will give us only a <u>Line of Position</u> (LOP). If the Observed elevation (HO) is less than the computed elevation (HC) it means we are farther away (the cone's circle is larger) from the celestial body (along the Azimuth) than our <u>Assumed Position</u> placed us. We would plot a point one nautical mile away from the <u>Assumed Position</u> along the azimuth for each minute of arc difference. Our <u>Line of Position</u> is drawn through that point and perpendicular to the Azimuth. . We are somewhere along that line. If the Observed elevation (HO) is more than the computed elevation (HC) it means we are closer (the cone's circle is smaller) to the body (along the Azimuth) than our <u>Assumed Position</u> placed us. The correction is applied in the opposite direction. Again, we get a single <u>Line of Position</u>. A second <u>Line of Position</u> from another celestial body which intersects the first one gives us our actual position.

Obviously we can only take one celestial measurement with the sextant at a time. So our <u>Lines of Position</u> (LOPs) from different stars would be for slightly different times. We would advance or retard each LOP using our heading and airspeed to a common time to obtain a position (Fix).

Dead Reckoning aided by Day Celestial

Day celestial navigation uses celestial bodies that are visible during the day (the sun and maybe the moon). These bodies do not occupy a constant position in the Celestial Sphere but SHA is still used. A factor known as Declination is used instead of latitude. Another section of the Airmen's Almanac is used in place of the HO-249 tables. The result is still a single Line of Position (LOP) for the celestial body. The sun is often the only visible celestial body. This would limit us to a single LOP. To find the actual (Fix) position it must be combined with other forms of navigation. Navigators often refer to these single LOPs as speed lines or course lines depending on how they are oriented to the direction of flight.

Dead Reckoning aided by Night Celestial

Night celestial navigation uses celestial bodies that are visible at night as references. Each Celestial body still gives us only a single Line Of Position (LOP). Several stars (and possibly a planet or two) are generally visible in our Celestial Dome at any point in time. Thus, we are normally able to determine the actual (Fix) position of the aircraft using only night celestial techniques.

We extract the subject stars' parameters from a book of tables known as the HO-249. The tables in the HO-249 were compiled using trigometric calculations for each possible SHA at each degree graduation in latitude. The navigator uses the latitude of the Assumed Position and extrapolates between the graduations listed in the tables. Ironically, during the age of exploration sailors (like Sir Francis Drake or Ferdinand Magellan) did not have tables to work with. They had to make the trigometric calculations themselves. This yields the azimuth (ZN) and the calculated height (HC) above the horizon for the selected star at the selected time at the Assumed Position.

Dead Reckoning aided by Grid Navigation

Grid navigation is the form of navigational reference used in high latitudes (north or south). Most charts used in navigation are laid out using True bearings. This means that the lines of longitude run from the actual (True) North Pole to the actual (True) South Pole. Aircraft, however, are flown using a magnetic compass. The magnetic poles are displaced from the actual true poles by several hundred miles. As a result there are two types of headings (True and Magnetic). The navigator tracks the aircraft using <u>True</u> directions. The pilots control the aircraft heading in reference to a magnetic compass and thus are using <u>Magnetic</u> directions. When the navigator directs the pilot to turn to a new heading he must first convert his <u>True</u> heading to a <u>Magnetic one</u>. When converting from one to the other a correction factor know as <u>Variation</u> is applied. Lines of constant <u>Variation</u> are plotted on all aerial navigation charts. This works well at lower and mid latitudes.

Longitudinal lines converge as they move toward either of the <u>True</u> poles. The closer the longitudinal lines the faster the change in <u>Variation</u>. Lines of longitude have their maximum physical separation at the equator. As they progress either north or south they close the distance until they merge at the poles. As indicated above this converging effect (and the resultant change in <u>Variation</u>) is not problematic at lower and mid latitudes, but becomes so at high latitudes. When an aircraft attempts to fly a straight line across the longitudes, the heading would need to be changed so frequently as to be impracticable. These factors make the jobs of both pilots and navigators very demanding and imprecise when flying in high latitudes. The solution is to use a type of navigation known as <u>Grid Navigation</u>. <u>Grid Navigation</u> uses special charts and uses a gyro stabilized compass rather than a magnetic one. Special charts are used with a grid pattern laid out on the chart. The headings are known as <u>Grid</u> headings. Now both the navigator and the pilot are using the same compass and no corrections are needed.

Dead Reckoning Aided By Loran

Loran A navigation was used in the off shore areas by ships and aircraft. It consisted of pairs of transmitters located along the coasts. The Loran A system has been replaced by the Loran C system in recent years. Loran A was usable only over water and was limited to a couple of hundred miles off shore (<u>Line of Sight</u> distances). Loran

C can now be used anywhere in the world including over land. During the 1960s only Loran A was available.

One of the Loran A transmitters was called the Primary while the other was called the Slave. They were located up to 100 miles apart. The primary site transmitted a signal. The signal radiated in all directions. When the signal from the Primary transmitter was received at the Slave site it automatically triggers the transmission of a signal by the Slave sight on a pre-determined paired frequency. This signal also radiates in all directions. Ships or aircraft that were within line-of-sight range of both receive both signals. The difference in the arrival time between the signals varied depending on your position relative to the two transmitter sights. There were multiple positions that would have the same time difference in the arrival of the two signals. These positions formed a line. This, then, became a <u>Line of Position</u>. These lines of equal time difference for each specific pair of transmitters were pre-drawn on special Loran charts. The charts color coded the lines associated with different pairs of transmitting sites. The navigator was able to fix his position using the LOPs from two or more paired transmitting units.

Waco, Texas does not have a coastline. It is located several hundred miles inland. Loran A navigation could only be done off shore. A cross country trip from James Connally AFB to Kindley AFB in Bermuda was used for the flight training portion of this phase. It included a stop over at Homestead AFB in Florida.

Dead Reckoning Aided By Radar

The final phase was the radar phase. The onboard radar system emits a highly directional signal that radiates along a specific bearing from the aircraft. The brief (in millionth of a second) period of transmission is followed by a much longer period of listening. The radiated signal strikes objects along that bearing and is reflected. The signal is reflected in many directions depending on the shape of the object it strikes. Some of this reflected signal is returned to the aircraft and detected during this longer period of listening. The difference between the time of transmission and the time of return depends on the distance of the object which reflected the signal. This gives us the direction to and the distance of the object. That information is sufficient to display it as a position on the radar scope. Each period of transmission followed by a period of listening is known as a radar cycle. Following each completed radar cycle the antenna is moved and the cycle is repeated at different bearings progressively around the compass rose. The amount of signal that is reflected depends on several factors. The major factors are the composition of the object and the flatness (shape) of the surface perpendicular to the path of the signal. When the sensitivity (gain) of the receiver is set too high, everything reflects the signal and is displayed. This is called ground clutter. The navigator learns to adjust the gain so that only prominent terrain features are displayed. These returns are compared to a topographical chart to find similar objects. This allows the navigator to position (Fix) the aircraft.

Appendix B   The B-47 Aircraft

Aircraft Design and Development

The B-47 was a revolutionary aircraft when it was initially developed and test flown. Jet powered aircraft were a new technology in the mid-1940s. The XB-47 aircraft's first test flight was in 1947. The engineers at Boeing faced several problems that had to be overcome. The B-47s wings were thin and swept back. The engineers felt that the thin wings were necessary to attain the higher speeds they wanted. This led to the first problem. The thin wings could not support the heavy loads required of the main weight bearing gear. This meant that the main gear had to be placed in the fuselage, arranged in tandem, rather than abreast on each of the wings. The tandem gear, a solution to the first problem, created the second problem. To rotate an aircraft for takeoff the aircraft's elevator (located on the tail of the aircraft) forces the tail down which raises the nose for takeoff. The pivot point (the fulcrum in physics) was the rear main gear which was located much closer to the rear than the nose of the aircraft and well aft of the aircraft's center of lift. As a result the force needed to raise the nose was excessive. To illustrate why this is a problem visualize a teeter totter with one end twice the distance from the pivot point as the other. If one tried to raise a person on the long end of the teeter totter by pushing down on the short end it would take a lot more force than if the same was tried by pushing down on the long end with the person on the short end. The Boeing engineer's solution was to attach the wings to the fuselage with a positive angle of attack as the aircraft sat on the ground. The angle of attack means the orientation of the wings to the air flow passing over them. The act of raising the nose in most aircraft increases the angle of attack (to positive) which forces the aircraft to takeoff. With the B-47s wings in a positive angle of attack (as it sat on the ground as well as when it charged down the runway for takeoff) the aircraft could takeoff without the need for the pilot to significantly raise the nose.

Appendix B

The B-47 was also a very clean aircraft. By clean I mean that it offers less resistance (less drag) to the air while in flight than most aircraft in its class. This was an important factor in establishing its reputation during the early 1950s as the fastest bomber in the world. It was as fast as any aircraft in the world including fighters for a decade after its development. It was said that no fighter in the world, at that time, could attempt a tail attack and expect to close with the B-47. The clean nature of the aircraft (less drag) made it more difficult to slow down when that was desired

The maximum gross weight of the original design models was significantly increased in the versions that went into production. Air Force operational needs further increased the weight of the aircraft. The result was that the aircraft was considered to be somewhat under powered. The J-47 engines on the "H" model produced about 6,000 pounds of thrust each. This gave the aircraft a total of about 36,000 pounds of thrust. By comparison, the center engine alone on the L1011 aircraft produced 53,000 pounds of thrust. To compensate for this situation the designers of the B-47 added a water/alcohol system which increased the thrust another 1,200 pounds per engine. This gave the RB-47H a total of 43,200 pounds of thrust for takeoff.

The next problem was related to the increased weight to the original design. The original design maximum takeoff weight of the XB-47 was 125,000 pounds. The weight of the aircraft increased dramatically as it went into production and with each new version. The RB-47H generally had a takeoff weight greater than 170,000 pounds. The B47E models, on alert duty, often weighted more than 200,000 pounds. All of the B-47s as well as their eventual replacement, the B-52, required very long take off rolls.

The landing rolls were also a problem due to the clean aircraft profile and the heavier weight (which required a higher speed at touch down). Boeing engineers addressed this problem by adding a brake chute. The brake chute was a large chute to help slow the aircraft after landing. It was deployed after touch down and jettisoned after the aircraft was slowed to a near stop.

Jet engine technology was new but improving rapidly by the time the RB-47H was being delivered starting in 1955. The J47 engines, the ones used on the B-47 aircraft, were prone to compressor stalls if the throttles were advanced too quickly from a low power setting to a high power setting. A compressor stall would result in a dramatic reduction in the expected power from the affected engine. An aborted landing and a go around, by its very nature, requires rapid increases in power applied quickly so the procedure can be done safely. Any reduction in available power at that time was a critical factor. This would be particularly true if the affected engine were one of the outboard engines. It would create an asymmetrical thrust differential which could seriously challenge the pilot's ability to control the aircraft. This could be a very dangerous situation. The Boeing engineers added an approach chute (a smaller chute) to address this problem. The chute was to be deployed prior to approaching the runway. It was used on most approaches. It created drag so that engine power on approach could be kept at a higher level. Less throttle advancement would be needed on a go around. In the event of a go around the approach chute would be jettisoned.

The final problem was the result of the combination of the positive angle of attack as the aircraft sat on the ground and the tandem location of the main gear. The attitude at touch down needed to be similar to the attitude while it sat on the ground. The positive angle of attack, however, made the aircraft more difficult to land. At touch down the aircraft was in the takeoff attitude (positive angle of attack) when it was trying to land. The airspeed at the point of touch down was, therefore, more critical than in many of its predecessors or successors. The B-47 had been described to me by many of the pilots I have flown with as a good aircraft, but required good pilot techniques. When the speed and/or the landing attitude were not optimal, the aircraft had a tendency to bounce (It wanted to keep flying because it was in a flying attitude). Bouncing with the tandem type main landing gear tended to be in the form of porpoising. Porpoising in this case means that one main gear (most often the forward) would strike the runway first and bounce. The nose of the aircraft would then rise while the tail did not. When the rear main gear struck the runway it would also bounce. The front and rear gear are now bouncing up and down but in opposite directions. Once started the condition gets worse as the aircraft slows. The solution, of course, is to apply the power and go around for another try. An alternate technique, often used by pilots, was to deploy the brake chute at the top of the bounce to keep the aircraft from continuing to bounce. When the brake chute deployed it would cause a sudden and dramatic increase in drag. This resulted in a rapid decrease in airspeed which would stop the bounce. This technique generally resulted in hard landings and if the timing was bad could be very dangerous. Instructor pilots frowned on the use of this technique.

Operation

The B-47 and its replacement, the B-52, still required long takeoff and landing runs. The Strategic Air Command (SAC) addressed this problem by building longer runways at each of the bases where it operated. The runways at SAC bases were between 11,200 and 15,000 feet in length. The runways at most Air Forces Bases had been between 6,000 and 10,000 feet in length. The length of the runway should, ideally, allow an aircraft to accelerate to near take off speed, abort the takeoff and stop the aircraft on the existing runway. The B-47 could not do this even on the longer runways that SAC had provided. We often used between 8,000 and 9,000 feet of runway to break ground. Many of SACs alert aircraft started their take off rolls weighing over 200,000 pounds. They would require additional thrust using a system entitled "Assisted Take Off" (ATO). The ATO system consisted of a series of rocket bottles, housed in racks attached to both sides of the aircraft. They would be fired after the takeoff run was started. The most frequent solution to the problem, however, was to perform an acceleration check early enough in the takeoff roll to allow the aircraft to be stopped on the existing runway if the aircraft was not accelerating as expected. The check was performed at a point known as the decision point (we called it the "S-1" point). This increased the margin of safety for the crews. Once past the decision point the aircraft was committed to take off no matter what situation developed. The procedure was used as follows. The non-flying pilot would use a stop watch and when the prescribed time had elapsed he would call "S-1". The speed was checked and if it was normal the pilot flying the aircraft would say "Committed". The takeoff run began by advancing the throttles to full power with the brakes set. The brakes were released and the aircraft began to roll. The pilot flying the aircraft would say "Water" and the water/alcohol injection switches would be activated. When takeoff speed was reached one of the pilots would call "S-2". The aircraft would take off and climb out. The water/alcohol lasted about 120 seconds, long enough to get the aircraft airborne. When the water/alcohol ran out the change could be felt.

The B-47 carried all of its engines attached to pylons on the wings. The outboard engines were well out on the wing. If one of the outboard engines failed during the takeoff run a serious asymmetrical thrust differential problem developed. This could challenge the pilot's ability to maintain control of the aircraft. The problem was much greater at lower air speeds. It was most critical at lift off. The aircraft would tend to roll into the failed engine. The pilot would control this roll with the rudders. Several of the 55th's pilots informed me that they would have to apply full opposite rudder within three seconds of lift off or they would not be able to stop the roll and the aircraft would likely crash. This meant the pilot had to recognize the problem quickly. Recognition of a loss of an engine was more difficult in the B-47. The first indication of the loss of an engine's thrust would be from the engine instruments in the cockpit. In most of today's jet aircraft the most sensitive instrument (and the first to indicate a problem) is the Engine Pressure Ratio or EPR gauge. When an engine losses thrust the EPR gauge gives an almost instantaneous indication. The B-47 did not have EPR gauges. The next most sensitive instrument is the Exhaust Gas Temperature gauge. It measures the temperature of the exhaust gases in the rear of the engine. At 700 plus degrees this happens fairly quickly but not immediately. This fact, coupled with the short response time required, made the job much more difficult for the B-47 pilot.

The B-47 had a limited range, one of several factors which accounted for its early retirement and replacement with the B-52 aircraft. The B-52 had a much longer range and carried a much larger bomb load. Both aircraft were equipped for mid-air refueling so this range could be extended. The B-47 was a cramped and uncomfortable aircraft for its crew. The long flights, that were common in the B-52, would be very difficult in the smaller aircraft. SAC addressed this problem with its <u>Reflex</u> program. The alert forces in the B-47 were forward deployed to bases in Europe to shorten the flights.

Appendix C   Acknowledgments

There are numerous references throughout the book to United States government and Air Force policies, concepts and terms. I have not included any specific acknowledgements regarding them. Many were integral components of the body of working knowledge that was part of the job for those engaged in the reconnaissance business. Others were covered in detail within the <u>Professional Military Education</u> (PME) courses that all career Air Force Officers are required to complete. For Air Force Officers the PME series includes three courses. The first is entitled Squadron Officers School (SOS). It is taken by officers in the rank of First Lieutenant or by junior Captains. The second is entitled Air Command and Staff College (ACSC). It is taken by senior Captains and Majors. The third is entitled Air War College. It is normally taken by Lt. Colonels and full Colonels. Completing Air Command and Staff College is normally required for promotion to Lt. Colonel. A few officers are selected to complete these courses in a residence school. The vast majority, however, must complete them by correspondence, or in Air Force terms, as Directed Study. The Directed Study format includes numerous proctored exams. I completed Air Command and Staff College in 1981. The expected length of time for course completion was from two to three years. The course was substantially revised shortly after I completed it. I no longer have access to the course materials. I took extensive notes as I took the course in preparation for the exams. I still had these notes. I reviewed these notes as I prepared to write this book. It is from these notes that most of the material I've included in this book, as regards Government and Air Force concepts and policies, is drawn.

I was not certified as a pilot in any of the reconnaissance aircraft discussed in the book. I am a licensed pilot and understand basic flight principles. The references concerning aircraft flying characteristics is based mainly on discussions I had with pilot members of the crews that I was a part of.

Most of the dates and details of specific events I've discussed were drawn from my own logs and notes. No additional Acknowleddgments are made for those. The accuracy the reader attributes to them, therefore, depends on their view of my credibility.

I have included below specific acknowledgments concerning information that I have drawn from books.

Chapter 6
(Note 1) Winston Churchill coined the phrase "Iron Curtain" during a 1946 speech. He was trying to characterize the growing Communist threat: A wall of obsessive secrecy and pervasive Tyranny.
By Any Means Necessary By William E. Burrows, Page 50

(Note 2) Powers U-2 Aircraft was shot down by a Surface-To-Air missile over Sverdlovsk in Russia.
By Any Means Necessary By William E. Burrows, Page 242 Thru 244

(Note 3) In 1953 the Air Force began to convert some B-47 aircraft to RB-47 to replace the older propeller drive aircraft such as RB-50 in reece units.
By Any Means Necessary By William E. Burrows, Page 155

(Note 4) Delivery of the first RB-47H to the 55th SRW was in August of 1955. The last was delivered in January of 1957. The 55th was the only unit to receive this model. A total of 35 aircraft were delivered.
Boeing's B-47 Stratojet By Alwyn T. Lloyd. Page 115

(Note 5) The first EB-47E TT (Tell-Two) was delivered to the 55th SRW in December of 1958. The program began shortly there after. The missions were flown out of Incirlik AFB near Adana, Turkey. Flights to monitor launches from KasputinYar were flown over the Black Sea. Flights to monitor launches from Tyuratam were flown over northeastern Iran.
Boeing's B-47 Stratojet By Alwyn T. Lloyd. Page 114

Acknowledgments

(Note 6) The early B-47 aircraft were equipped with twin 50 caliber machine guns which used the B-4 fire control system.. Later versions (including the "E" and "H" model) were equipped with two 20 mm cannons and used the A-5 fire control system.
By Any Means Necessary By William E. Burrows Page 154
Boeing's B-47 Stratojet By Alwyn T. Lloyd. Page 92

(Note 7) Quotation concerning Reecce crews in the Burrows book.
By Any Means Necessary By William E. Burrows, Page 192

(Note 8) The families of reconnaissance crew members who lost their lives felt that they were lied to concerning the circumstances of their loved ones demise. They were not told much about what happened to their father/husband
By Any Means Necessary By William E. Burrows, Page 40

(Note 9) Powers U-2 Aircraft was shot down by a Surface-To-Air missile over Sverdlovsk in Russia.
By Any Means Necessary By William E. Burrows, Page 242 Thru 244

(Note 10) President Eisenhower had suspended reconnaissance flights after Powers was shot down. Two months later he had approved restarting reconnaissance flights but required them to be much further off shore than had been the rule earlier. The RB-47 flight was the first after Powers was shot down.
By Any Means Necessary By William E. Burrows, Page 242 Thru 244

(Note 11) Major Palm turned left putting the Russian fighter in his 6 O'clock just before being attacked.
By Any Means Necessary By William E. Burrows Page 251
The Little Toy Dog By William L. White, Page 35.

Acknowledgments

(Note 12) Henry Cabot Lodge Displays the RB-47's Route at the United Nations.

The Little Toy Dog By William L. White, Illustration between Page 42 and 43.

Chapter 7

(Note 13) The author has a table listing known RB-47 losses to hostile action. In note 4 in the table he states the aircraft "Fought a running gun battle with MIGs and crashed on landing". This note pertains to the RB-47E (Tell-Two) at Incirlik on April 3, 1965.

Boeing's B-47 Stratojet By Alwyn T. Lloyd. Page 181

(Note 14) Robb Hoover confirmed the first SA-2 site deployed to North Viet Nam in October of 1964.

By Any Means Necessary By William E. Burrows, Pages 195 and 196

Chapter 9

(Note 15) The author has a table showing the weights of the various models and configurations of the B-47. The design gross weight of the RB-47H is listed at 125,000 pounds. The maximum landing weight is also listed at 125,000 pounds.

Boeing's B-47 Stratojet By Alwyn T. Lloyd. Page 246

Appendix D   My Service Record

Log Book Summaries

Total Air Force Flight Time:	3506 Hrs 35 Min
Flight Time By Aircraft:	
T-29:	249 Hrs 5 Min
C-54:	112 Hrs 15 Min
RB-47E/H:	968 Hrs 30 Min
RC-135M	1436 Hrs 55 Min
RC-135C	423 Hrs 20 Min
RC-135R	297 Hrs 25 Min
Mid-Air Refuelings	191
Operational Reconnaissance Sorties	195
Combat Missions in Viet Nam	84

Personal Decorations:

Distinguished Flying Cross
Air Medal W/ 8 Oak Leaf Clusters
Air Force Commendation Medal w/ Oak Leaf Cluster

Service Time

Active Duty Service:	September 1961 to March 1970
Reserve Duty Service	March 1970 to March 1986
Retired:	March 1, 1986

Made in the USA
San Bernardino, CA
19 August 2014